# YEATS AND POSTMODERNISM

RICHARD FALLIS, *Series Editor*

# YEATS AND POSTMODERNISM

Edited by
LEONARD ORR

SYRACUSE UNIVERSITY PRESS

First Edition 1991
91  92  93  94  95  96  97  98  99        6  5  4  3  2  1

The paper used in this publication meets the minimum requirements of American National Standard for Information Sciences–Permanence of Paper for Printed Library Materials, ANSI Z39.48-1984. ∞™

**Library of Congress Cataloging-in-Publication Data**

Yeats and postmodernism / edited by Leonard Orr. – 1st ed.
      p.     cm. – (Irish studies)
   Includes bibliographical references (p.    ) and index.
   ISBN 0-8156-2506-5 (alk. paper)
   1. Yeats, W. B. (William Butler), 1865–1939–Criticism and
interpretation.  2. Postmodernism (Literature)–Ireland.  I. Orr,
Leonard.  II. Series: Irish studies (Syracuse, N.Y.)
PR5907.Y43    1991
821'.8–dc20                                               90-10122
                                                          CIP

Manufactured in the United States of America

# CONTENTS

# ACKNOWLEDGMENTS

Richard Fallis, editor of the Irish Studies series at Syracuse, has been most helpful in the development of this book. He helped shape the contents of the volume, advised me about potential contributors, and made a number of suggestions and corrections in the first version of the manuscript. I am very grateful for all of his assistance and encouragement. Kathleen O'Gorman helped me revise the manscript and check references. I also wish to thank Cynthia Maude-Gembler, my editor at Syracuse University Press, for her advice and corrections at several stages in preparation of the volume.

# YEATS AND POSTMODERNISM

1

# INTRODUCTION
## Yeats and Poststructuralist Criticism
LEONARD ORR

GEORGE STEINER, in *After Babel*, notes that we are "in the main, 'word-blind' to Pre-Raphaelite and Decadent verse. This blindness results from a major change in habits of sensibility. Our contemporary sense of the poetic, our often unexamined presumptions about valid or spurious uses of figurative speech have developed from a conscious negation of *fin de siècle* ideals. . . . We have for a time disqualified ourselves from reading comprehensively."[1] The change in time, the accretion of qualities that have become attached to period and movement labels, lead to a homogenizing, unconscious blindness for whatever is outside of a received critical perspective and traditional framework.

While this may seem self-evident in the "word-blindness" that Steiner addresses in the writers of the 1880s and 1890s, the case holds as well with modernism and with Yeats and Eliot as our chief examples of modernist poets. For some reason, Yeats, in particular, has been trapped within the literary historical construct of "modernism," while Joyce (with *Finnegans Wake*) and Pound (with the *Cantos*) have somehow crossed successfully into "postmodernism." This makes for tidy literary history, for we can see Yeats struggling through symbolism, decadence, nationalism, and aestheticism; then, with great effort and partially through young Pound's tutelage, Yeats *becomes* modern. He edits the *Oxford Book of Modern Verse*, realigns Pater's prose into poetry, and announces the modern age. Pound, meanwhile, becomes modern on his own at an early age after *A Lume spento*, reads Fenollosa, and discovers modern art and music. He must struggle through imagism and

1

vorticism until making a breakthrough around Canto 4 into postmodernism. Joyce on his own passes painlessly through naturalism and modernism and, using various sections of *Ulysses* as a transition, glides gracefully into postmodernism during the years spent writing *Finnegans Wake*, after which mere modernism is *passé*; World War II starts, and everything after the war is contemporary or postmodernist.

Like Parson Weems on the life of George Washington, the history of modernism and its relationship with postmodernism has become legendary—academically folklorized because of its convenience and progressive movement. Within modernism we have many subgroups, divisions made either by school or chronology. David Perkins speaks of the "high modernist mode" in his history of poetry. Frank Kermode has developed the notions of palaeomodernism and neomodernism. In a recent work, Frederick Karl, who believes in a complete continuity between modernism and postmodernism, finds that "in the work of Thomas Pynchon, we can see conservative Modern in *V. . . .* ; then moderate Modern in *The Crying of Lot 49*; followed by radical Modern in *Gravity's Rainbow,* in which avant-garde elements dominate, although intermixed with conservative and contemporary aspects. Joyce's movement from *A Portrait* to *Ulysses* to *Finnegans Wake* illustrates the same point."[2]

If we scan the many attempts to define or explain modernism, we find a certain collocation of ideas in which the modernist Yeats is immured. *Webster's Third International* explains that modernism refers to "a self-conscious and deliberate break with the past and a search for new forms of expression in any of the arts." Early modernism is often characterized by its formalism and organicism; its search for escape from time, its stasis; its impersonality and use of personas; its concern with mental processes and perception rather than the machinations of plot and, therefore, its use of stream-of-consciousness and interior monologue and free, indirect style; its rejection of the Victorian, of realism, of romanticism, of the sentimental. World War I, we are so often told, shook everyone's faith and brought in apocalyptic imagery and violent change. In the arts this led to discontinuous forms and fragmentation; the breaking up of traditional narrative and characterization; the use of collage and montage; the spatialization of time through the juxtaposition of images; and the nostalgic attempt to recreate in art the order that was now lacking in the outside world through the allusion to myth or the borrowing of epic structures or recasting of classical literary works or the mythopoetic imposition of an arbitrary structure.[3] The scholars of the modernist/postmodernist controversy usually fix upon Yeats's Byzantium imagery to place him among the modernists. Yeats seeks stillness, artifice, eternity, wholeness, unity, "a vision of oneness or fusion," and transcendence through art, escape, and closure.[4]

As for postmodernism, it may not even exist. "Postmodernism," Karl writes, "may be an invention of critics."[5] Naomi Schor notes that "[a]ccording to one ritual genealogy, postmodernism is an extension of modernism, an exacerbation of its most radical impulses," while in the second understanding of the term, postmodernism "is marked by a less spectacular return of the repressed of modernism, a sense of re-covery of the usable past unencumbered by nostalgia."[6] According to Hal Foster,

> postmodernism is defined as a rupture. In this it is like modernism which, despite historicism, often speaks a rhetoric of discontinuity. Like mod-ernism too, postmodernism is posed against a past perceived as inert; it thus relies, in part, on the old imperative of the avant-garde and its language of crisis. . . . Proponents of postmodernism tend to be highly conscious of historical moment. In effect, they would displace modern-ism, which, pushed back into its own reduction, foreclosed more than deconstructed. Rather than reduction, what is needed is a revision of modernism: an opening of its supposed closure. . . . [Postmodernism] may be less a break with modernism than an advance in a dialectic in which modernism is re-formed.[7]

In effect, Yeats has been left as a modernist because he has been studied almost exclusively from within a modernist framework, using the criti-cal techniques developed under modernist and premodernist aesthetics: New Criticism, biographical criticism (and Freudian psychoanalytic criticism), textual criticism, source studies and explications of allusions, and positivist literary historical analyses.

These approaches support a static history in which Yeats plays an important, if predictable, part in the drama of modernism. We might say that this had been done very thoroughly and usefully in Yeats criticism, as the research guides of Richard Finneran and the bibliog-raphies of K. P. Jochum show.[8]

The postmodernizing of Yeats is a risky enterprise, in part because it is a remembering or reconstituting of forgotten history, the rough edges, inconsistencies, and the irrational that has already been smoothed over and explained by forgetful categorizing. It is a vast project because it requires the rethinking of modernism and its various subcategories. Naomi Schor points out, "Contrary to what the prefix *post-* would suggest, postmodernism in all its multiple manifestations . . . is not the name of a belated movement that follows modernism as Romanticism follows Neoclassicism, or as modernism itself follows Victorianism; rather, it is a moment *in* and *of* modernism."[9]

It is easy to forget that "postmodernism" is now a period-concept of the same duration as the period-concept of modernism—about fifty years. But the critical essays on postmodernism in the 1960s and 1970s now seem, surprisingly, part of a New Critical enterprise that was already *passé* by the mid 1960s. This early critical examination of post-modern literature was concerned largely with the examination of the literary devices and techniques that were different from devices and techniques found in a monumentalized version of modernism. Post-modernism was in this way reduced to the sum of its devices and techniques: reflexivity; an exaggeration of modernism's impersonality and fragmentation; works that resisted closure and resolution; black humor; foregrounding of literary devices; the use of multiple voices, kitsch, "camp," and items from popular culture; the use of multiple and intrusive narrators who called attention to the work's fictionality; the breaking of narrative frames or fields of reference; and so on. Postmodernism treated this way could be considered a debilitated modernism, or a parasitic imitation of modernism that lacked the innovation and daring epistemological impetus of the modernists (according to Jurgen Habermas's reading).[10] Critics often split into modernists versus postmodernists and engaged in advocacy and polemic. Specialists in postmodernism, notably Ihab Hassan, again and again created lists of modernist and postmodernist characteristics and works.

It is interesting to note what has happened to this work. For example, Hassan's most recent book on postmodernism, *The Postmodern Turn*, reprints and substantially updates the lists that form the basis of earlier essays. He is still printing lists of opposed characteristics, but he now realizes that his previous views on periodization and separation are incorrect, joining with the consensus that finds postmodernism a revision of modernism. But he also joins, as does Karl and, to a lesser extent, Calinescu, Habermas, and others, in making an equivalence between postmodernism and poststructuralism, and in using the vocabulary of Derrida, Foucault, and poststructuralist critics and philosophers to define the difference with modernism, where previously the differences were found in artistic techniques and forms. Thus, in Hassan's present list we find arranged in two columns not only modernism's "form (conjunctive/closed)" versus postmodernism's "Antiform (disjunctive, open)," purpose versus play, design versus chance, hierarchy versus anarchy, "mastery/Logos" versus exhaustion/silence, finished work versus fragment, and distance versus participation but also "creation/totalization" versus "decreation/deconstruction," presence versus absence, *lisible* versus *scriptible*, "genital/phallic" versus "polymorphous/androgynous," paranoia versus schizophrenia, origin/cause versus difference/differance/trace, metaphysics versus irony, and determinacy versus indeterminacy.[11]

Hassan's dichotomous list making, while an advance over his earlier presentations of postmodernism, is interesting mainly to the extent that it shows the new awareness of the role theorists play in creating such categories for discussion as modernism and postmodernism, the new flexibility and interpenetrability of these concepts, the endlessness of the qualities that can be given to each concept, and the new complexity of the argument. The most influential current theorist of this new complexity is Jean-François Lyotard. In *The Postmodern Condition*, Lyotard notes

> The postmodern world would be that which, in the modern, puts forward the unpresentable in presentation itself; that which denies itself the solace of good forms, the consensus of a taste which would make it possible to share collectively the nostalgia for the unattainable; that which searches for new presentations, not in order to enjoy them but in order to impart a stronger sense of the unpresentable. A postmodern artist or writer is in the position of a philosopher; the text he writes, the work he produces are not in principle governed by preestablished rules. . . . The artist and writer . . . are working without rules in order to formulate the rules of what *will have been done*. Hence the fact that work and text have the characters of an *event*; hence also, they always come too late for their author, or, what amounts to the same thing, their being put into work, their realization (*mise en oeuvre*) always begin

too soon. *Postmodern* would have to be understood according to the paradox of the future (*post*) anterior (*modo*).

It seems to me that the essay (Montaigne) is postmodern, while the fragment (*The Athaeneum*) is modern.[12]

This understanding of postmodernism coincides with attempts to apply poststructuralist critical methods to earlier texts, as a postmodernism *avant la lettre*. For example, Herman Rapaport explains in *Milton and Postmodernism* that "by situating [Milton's] texts within a postmodern context, one comes to appreciate the strong philosophical relevance Milton's post-Renaissance and pre-Enlightenment texts have for the history of philosophy as we know it today and particularly as it has been reinterpreted by French intellectuals like Georges Bataille, Gilles Deleuze, Julia Kristeva, Philippe Sollers, Roland Barthes, Michel Foucault, René Girard, and Jacques Derrida."[13] A similar impulse lies behind such works as Naomi Schor and Henry Majewski's collection *Flaubert and Postmodernism*, Chaviva Hosek and Patricia Parker's anthology *Lyric Poetry: Beyond New Criticism*, and Jonathan Goldberg's *Voice Terminal Echo: Postmodernism and English Renaissance Texts*.[14] Similarly, Fredric Jameson chooses to reread Wyndham Lewis in terms of "the contemporary poststructuralist aesthetic, which signals the dissolution of the modernist paradigm—with its valorization of myth and symbol, temporality, organic form and the concrete universal, the identity of the subject and the continuity of linguistic expression—and foretells the emergence of some new, properly postmodernist or schizophrenic conception of the cultural artifact—now strategically reformulated as 'text' or 'écriture,' and stressing discontinuity, allegory, the mechanical, the gap between signifier and signified, the lapse in meaning, the syncope in the experience of the subject."[15] In these works, the link with postmodernism is really through poststructuralist critical perspectives and perceptions rather than through the more traditional attempts to catalog postmodernist qualities belatedly uncovered in the literary text (in the way in which *Tristram Shandy* and *Bouvard and Pécuchet* were long ago discovered to be postmodernist texts). The shift is from the object of study to the tools and ideas that can be used to approach an old subject anew. This is the idea behind the present collection and the explanation of the title, *Yeats and Postmodernism*.

It is surprising that there has been so little sustained poststructuralist analysis of Yeats. Daniel O'Hara recently argued that Yeats is one of the central figures in the development of poststructuralist theory. O'Hara claims that the "major critical movements from the 1940s to the 1970s—New Criticism, archetypal and phenomenological criticism, and a variety of post-structuralist discourses (revisionary psychoanalytic criticism, dialectical hermeneutics, and deconstruction) all owe a considerable debt to Yeats. Whether as sublime master of the concrete universal, demonic adversary of genuine Romantic visionaries, or seductive forerunner of the vertiginous interplay of self-subverting tropes, Yeats has repeatedly appeared as a representative case in point."[16] But there is nothing in Yeats criticism at all comparable to the poststructuralist analyses of Henry James or James Joyce.[17] While James and Joyce have long attracted a variety of post–New Critical analyses, and while fiction has received much more attention from recent criticism than has poetry, Yeats has been used by theorists mainly in examples within a longer theoretical argument or preparatory to a study of another figure; very few works have been studied (the same handful of poems again and again, often just a few lines cited repeatedly), and book-length criticism is missing.

Contemporary linguistic and structuralist analyses have dealt with just a handful of poems, and the analyses are usually quite technical and elaborately schematized; these have dealt mainly with "Leda and the Swan," "Among School Children," and "Sorrow of Love."[18] Feminist criticism has not made much of an inroad on Yeatsians, although there are a few noteworthy attempts.[19] Reader-response criticism has been fairly reluctant to deal with Yeats, again working with "Among School Children."[20]

A promising start was made in hermeneutic and phenomenological analysis of Yeats by Daniel O'Hara, whose *Tragic Knowledge: Yeats's Autobiography and Hermeneutics* is the only book devoted to applying hermeneutics (based on Paul Ricoeur) to Yeats. There are frequent references to Yeats throughout Paul Bové's *Destructive Poetics* and William Spanos's *Repetitions*.[21] Spanos reads "Sailing to Byzantium" in such a way that Yeats is made irrevocably a modernist (the "impulse to transcend the historicity of the human condition in the 'allatonceness' . . . of the spatialized work of symbolist literary art is brought into remarkably sharp focus when, by way of a Heideggerian 'destruction,' one perceives the similarity between the poetics of W. B. Yeats's 'Sailing to

Byzantium' and Stephen Dedalus' aesthetics of stasis in *A Portrait of the Artist as a Young Man*").[22] O'Hara and Bové perceive Yeats as a master ironist who subverts modernism itself. Bové, who also uses "Sailing to Byzantium" as the major text in his discussion of Yeats, argues that

> The persona has throughout the poem been "caught" in the temporal world which prompts the desired fiction of "Byzantium." The dualistic strategy around which the structure of the poem is built is itself a specific pose of the ironic consciousness. When this stance is "reduced" or "deconstructed," the metaphysical "interest" of the persona appears as the motive for his comforting projection of a lost, but recoverable, artificial paradise. In other words, what on first reading appears to be a movement out of the world and time into art and eternity, is shown by the circular form of the poem to be only an impossible myth, a fiction generated by a being in time who seeks the comfort of an Ideal dream and who hopes to find the Absolute freedom of infinite perception in an image of history. . . . Beckett, Ionesco, Sartre, the late Yeats, and many postmodern poets employ Kierkegaard's technique of mastered irony to destroy the potentially sterilizing pervasive irony of Modernism by revealing in their own work the false and atemporal assumptions behind the modern "Tradition."[23]

Almost all of the American deconstructive critics have felt compelled to analyze some works by Yeats: Harold Bloom, of course, in *Yeats*, Geoffrey Hartman in *Criticism in the Wilderness*, Paul de Man in *Allegories of Reading*, and J. Hillis Miller in *The Linguistic Moment*. Because of the stature of these critics as theorists, rather than as Yeatsians, their work has occasioned more argument and debate than that of the few critics who have applied reader-response or feminism.

Daniel O'Hara has criticized Bloom by noting that Yeats, in Bloom's reading, "ironically becomes the antithetical fulfillment of [the naive prophetic humanism of Blake and Shelley] with his embrace of a Gnostic Sophia. . . . Yet by decade's end Bloom had himself become an academic revision of what he beheld in Yeats: a 'professor' of humane letters espousing what according to Bloom in *Yeats* is the modern form of Gnosticism: historical determinism."[24]

Paul de Man and Geoffrey Hartman use "Among School Children" and "Leda and the Swan," respectively, to demonstrate the irretrievably indecidable, indeterminable nature of poetry. De Man suggests that it is possible to read the last line of "Among School Children" "literally rather than figuratively, as asking with some urgency the question . . . how can we possibly make the distinctions that would shelter us from the error of identifying what cannot be identified? . . . The figural reading, which assumes the question to be rhetorical, is perhaps naive, whereas the literal reading leads to greater complication of theme and statement."[25] Similarly, Hartman finds that "Leda and the Swan" "cannot be explained or grounded by the coordinates of ordinary perception, by stable space-time categories . . . I don't think I exaggerate the image/phantasm indeterminacy. . . . [Hartman raises numerous questions and enigmas posed by the poem and concludes:] These questions add up to a *hermeneutic perplexity*" and uncertainty upon uncertainty.[26] Later, Hartman argues that "Genuine rhetorical questions are antirhetorical. Their 'open-endedness, a refusal to speak the unspeakable, solve the unsolvable, resolve the unresolvable,' discloses a freedom of thought that was in doubt." He gives as an example of such indeterminacy and refusal of closure Yeats's "The Second Coming" and claims that to keep a poem in mind "is to keep it there, not to resolve it into available meanings. This suspensive discourse is criticism. The reader's 'willing suspension of disbelief' is really a suspension of accommodating and allegorical meanings, the sort that would comfort a seduced yet disbelieving mind. . . . The seduction of understanding through a fiction should provoke something more active than bemusement or suspended disbelief: it should provoke me to break, however provisionally, the very frame of meaning I bring to the text."[27]

J. Hillis Miller's recent reading of Yeats is curiously traditional and narrow; he concentrates on emblematic strategies, the topography or geometric/formal analogues, and traditional rhetorical figures in "Nineteen Hundred and Nineteen." Miller also surrounds himself with his fellow theorists, ranging from Derrida and de Man to Freud and Walter Benjamin. But his essay is mainly an affirmation of de Man's *Allegories of Reading*. "The meaning of the Yeatsian emblem can be identified not in relation to what the emblem signifies, in a sign-thing structure . . . but in relation to other emblems, whether in the same poem or in other texts in the tradition, in a sign-sign relation. This relation is characterized by the temporal gap between the two emblems and to some common essence or archetype. Distance and unlikeness separate emblem from emblem. Across that gulf the interpreter must leap."[28]

Miller's chapter on Yeats concludes with the sentence, "Each is destroyed and renewed by being made into a sign that stands for that which there is no standing and no standing for."

Otherwise, we have very few examples of deconstructive criticism of Yeats: a section of a dissertation by Richard H. Hart, Lawrence Lipking's widely known parodic deconstructive reading of "Sailing to Byzantium," and scattered comments in recent works that claim that Yeats's works deconstruct themselves.[29] For example, Patrick J. Keane's apologetic "Critical Epilogue," at the end of the seventh chapter of his recent book *Yeats's Interactions with Tradition*, agonizes over exactly how deconstructive he is or is not, which deconstructors he feels closest to, and how modest is his own contribution to deconstruction. Keane also surrounds himself with contemporary theorists (Culler, de Man, Hillis Miller, Iser, Fish, Derrida, Ingarden, and Bloom are all summoned up in the three-page epilogue), blurring the differences.[30]

When we see the richness of possible poststructuralist approaches and ideas, nicely displayed in such collections as Joseph Natoli's *Tracing Literary Theory*, and the variety, quantity, and polysemantic nature of Yeat's work, poetry, prose, and plays, then it is all the more surprising that so little has been done. The criticism surveyed here deals with a handful of the poems and, in one case only, the autobiographies and, in one other work, the drama.

The essays in this volume begin the process of postmodernizing Yeats. Ronald Schleifer's essay considers the defining gestures of postmodern rhetoric found in Yeats, utilizing the work of Lyotard, Jameson, O'Hara, and Derrida. William Bonney analyzes Yeats's historical tropes (using the theories of Hayden White and Morse Peckham) in *A Vision* and a number of poems. Kieran Quinlan examines Yeats and the Irish Revival and current Irish opinions of Yeats and the Revival in light of the New Historicism. William Johnsen presents an ideological analysis of "Leda and the Swan" based on feminism, Marxism, and the work of René Girard. Kathleen O'Gorman's essay is a speech-act analysis of two of Yeats's plays, while Steven Putzel uses reception theory to reconstruct Yeats's understanding of his audience for his theater, both real and ideal. Kitti Carriker provides a new look at Yeats's poem "The Dolls" by reading it through Freud's notion of the Uncanny and Julia Kristeva's recent work on abjection. Cheryl Herr's essay provides a conversation or a juxtaposition of the major concepts of Foucault's work, especially the notion of the *episteme* from *The Order of Things*, and Yeats's *Vision*. Finally, R. B. Kershner, using Bakhtin and medical/ psychological studies of dyslexia, considers the written versus the oral and the inner dialogization of Yeats's writing.

I hope that this work will provide some ideas for longer and alternative poststructuralist approaches to Yeats. It is clear that many of these essays hinge on history, and Yeats's use and analysis of history, and here Walter Benjamin's theories may be especially fruitful. Poststructuralist historical and political analysis of Yeats is still at an early stage, although W. J. McCormack's *Ascendancy and Tradition* provides an exciting rereading and point of departure.³¹ I do not know of any Lacanian analyses of Yeats, although that seems like an obvious need, and Yeats's work and career would seem to provide a base for a cultural semiotics analysis. We lack sophisticated Marxist, feminist, and reader-response criticism of Yeats.

The essays in this volume are meant to be provocative but not hermetic, explorative and suggestive instead of definitive and closed.

## NOTES

1. George Steiner, *After Babel: Aspects of Language and Translation* (London: Oxford Univ. Press, 1975), 14–15.

2. Frederick R. Karl, *Modern and Modernism: The Sovereignty of the Artist 1885–1925* (New York: Atheneum, 1985), 14.

3. See the bibliographies on modernism in Matei Calinescu, *Five Faces of Modernity: Modernism, Avant-Garde, Decadence, Kitsch, Postmodernism* (Durham, N.C.: Duke Univ. Press, 1987); Maurice Beebe, "Introduction: What Modernism Was," *Journal of Modern Literature* 3, no. 5 (1974): 1065–84 [special issue, "From Modernism to Post-Modernism"]; Alistair Davis, *An Annotated Critical Bibliography of Modernism* (Totowa, N.J.: Barnes and Noble, 1982); and in the very large and useful collection edited by Malcolm Bradbury and James McFarlane, *Modernism 1890–1930* (New York: Penguin Books, 1976). Works that define or map literary modernism include Monique Chefdor, Ricardo Quinones, and Albert Wachtel, eds., *Modernism: Challenges and Perspectives* (Urbana: Univ. of Illinois Press, 1986); Richard Ellmann and Charles Fiedelson, Jr., eds., *The Modern Tradition: Backgrounds of Modern Literature* (New York: Oxford Univ. Press, 1965); Peter Faulkner, *Modernism* (London: Methuen, 1977); Joseph Chiari, *The Aesthetics of Modernism* (London: Vision Press, 1970); Robert Kiely, ed., *Modernism Reconsidered* (Cambridge, Mass.: Harvard Univ. Press, 1983); Michael H. Levenson, *A Genealogy of Modernism: A Study of English Literary Doctrine, 1908–1922* (New York: Cambridge Univ. Press, 1984); see also James Longenbach, *Stone Cottage: Pound,*

*Yeats, and Modernism* (New York: Oxford Univ. Press, 1988); Richard Bernstein, ed., *Habermas on Modernity* (Cambridge, Mass.: MIT Press, 1985); David Lodge, *The Modes of Modern Writing: Metaphor, Metonymy and the Typology of Modern Literature* (Ithaca: Cornell Univ. Press, 1977); David Perkins, *A History of Modern Poetry: From the 1890s to the High Modernist Mode* (Cambridge, Mass.: Harvard Univ. Press, 1976); Carlos Baker, *The Echoing Green: Romanticism, Modernism, and the Phenomena of Transference in Poetry* (Princeton: Princeton Univ. Press, 1984); Monroe K. Spears, *Dionysus and the City: Modernism in Twentieth-Century Poetry* (New York: Oxford Univ. Press, 1970); Edward Lobb, *T. S. Eliot and the Romantic Critical Tradition* (Boston: Routledge & Kegan Paul, 1981); George Bornstein, *Transformations of Romanticism in Yeats, Eliot, and Stevens* (Chicago: Univ. of Chicago Press, 1976); Ricardo Quinones, *Mapping Literary Modernism: Time and Development* (Princeton: Princeton Univ. Press, 1985); Paul Douglass, "'Such as the Life Is, Such is the Form': Organicism Among the Moderns," in *Approaches to Organic Form: Permutations in Science and Culture*, ed. Frederick Burwick (Dordrecht and Boston: D. Reidel, 1987), 253–73; and Paul Douglass, "The Gold Coin: Bergsonian Intuition and Modernist Aesthetics," *Thought* 58 (1983): 234–50.

    4. E.g., Alan Wilde, *Horizons of Assent: Modernism, Postmodernism, and the Ironic Imagination* (Baltimore: Johns Hopkins Univ. Press, 1981), 10, 30, 33, 38.

    5. Karl, *Modern and Modernism*, 401.

    6. Schor, "Introduction," in *Flaubert and Postmodernism*, ed. Naomi Schor and Henry F. Majewski (Lincoln: Univ. of Nebraska Press, 1984), xi.

    7. Hal Foster, "Re: Post," in *Art after Modernism: Rethinking Representation*, ed. Brian Wallis (New York: New Museum of Contemporary Art, 1984), 200.

    8. See Finneran's bibliographic essays on Yeats criticism in Finneran, ed., *Anglo-Irish Literature: A Review of Research* (New York: MLA, 1976) and *Recent Research on Anglo-Irish Writers* (New York: MLA, 1983); K. P. S. Jochum, *W. B. Yeats: A Classified Bibliography* (Urbana: Univ. of Illinois Press, 1978); and Jochum's annual bibliographies in *Yeats: An Annual of Critical and Textual Studies.*

    9. Schor, "Introduction," x–xi.

    10. See Bernstein, ed., *Habermas on Modernity* (n. 3); Habermas, "Modernity versus Postmodernity," *New German Critique* 22 (1981): 3–14; and Martin Jay, "Habermas and Modernism," *Praxis International* 4.1 (1984): 1–14.

    11. Ihab Hassan, *The Postmodern Turn: Essays in Postmodern Theory and Culture* (Columbus: Ohio State Univ. Press, 1987), 91–92.

    12. Jean-François Lyotard, *The Postmodern Condition: A Report on Knowledge*, trans. G. Bennington and B. Massumi (Minneapolis: Univ. of Minnesota Press, 1984), 81; see also Lyotard's *Le postmoderne expliqué aux enfants: correspondance, 1982–1985* (Paris: Galilée, 1986). On postmodernism, see the bibliography in Calinescu and Hassan (nn. 3 and 11); Lawrence F. McCaffrey, ed., *Postmodern Fiction: A Bio-Bibliographical Guide* (Westport, Conn.: Greenwood Press, 1986); Brian McHale, *Postmodernist Fiction* (New York: Methuen, 1987); Christa and Peter Burger, eds., *Postmoderne: Alltag, Allegorie und Avantgarde* (Frankfurt am Main: Suhrkamp, 1987); Herbert Blau, *The Eye of Prey: Subversions of the Postmodern* (Bloomington: Indiana Univ. Press, 1987); Leonard

Orr, ed., *De-Structing the Novel: Essays in Applied Postmodern Hermeneutics* (Troy, N.Y.: Whitston, 1982); Dietmar Kamper and Willem van Reijen, eds., *Die Unvollendete Vernunft: Moderne versus Postmoderne* (Frankfurt am Main: Suhrkamp, 1987); John Fekete, ed., *Life after Postmodernism: Essays on Value and Culture* (New York: St. Martin's Press, 1987); Jonathan Arac, ed., *Postmodernism and Politics* (Minneapolis: Univ. of Minnesota Press, 1986); Hal Foster, ed., *The Anti-Aesthetic: Essays on Postmodern Culture* (Port Townsend, Wash.: Bay Press, 1983); Ihab Hassan and Sally Hassan, eds., *Innovation/ Renovation: New Perspectives on the Humanities* (Madison: Univ. of Wisconsin Press, 1983); Albrecht Wellmer, *Zur Dialektik von Moderne und Postmoderne: Vernunftkritik nach Adorno* (Frankfurt am Main: Suhrkamp, 1985); Stefano Tani, *The Doomed Detective: The Contribution of the Detective Novel to Postmodern American and Italian Fiction* (Carbondale: Southern Illinois Univ. Press, 1984); Charles Newman, *The Post-Modern Aura: The Act of Fiction in an Age of Inflation* (Evanston, Ill.: Northwestern Univ. Press, 1985); Stanley Trachtenberg, ed., *The Postmodern Moment: A Handbook of Contemporary Innovation in the Arts* (Westport, Conn.: Greenwood Press, 1985); Peter Koslowski et al., *Moderne oder Postmoderne? zur Signatur des gegenwartigen Zeitalters* (Weinheim: Acta Humaniora, 1986); Andreas Huyssen, *After the Great Divide: Modernism, Mass Culture, Postmodernism* (Bloomington: Indiana Univ. Press, 1986); Burghart Schmidt, *Postmoderne—Strategien des Vergessens: ein kritischer Bericht* (Darmstadt: Luchterhand, 1986); Brian Wallis, ed., *Art after Modernism: Rethinking Representation* (New York: New Museum of Contemporary Art, 1984); Wolfgang Welsch, *Unsere postmoderne Moderne* (Darmstadt: Acta Humaniora, 1987); Charles Jencks, *Post-Modernism: The New Classicism in Art and Architecture* (New York: Rizzoli, 1987).

13. Herman Rapaport, *Milton and the Postmodern* (Lincoln: Univ. of Nebraska Press, 1983), 1.

14. On Schor and Majewski, see n. 6, above; also, Chaviva Hosek and Patricia Parker, eds., *Lyric Poetry: Beyond New Criticism* (Ithaca: Cornell Univ. Press, 1985); Jonathan Goldberg, *Voice Terminal Echo: Postmodernism and English Renaissance Texts* (London and New York: Methuen, 1986).

15. Fredric Jameson, *Fables of Aggression: Wyndham Lewis, the Modernist as Fascist* (Berkeley: Univ. of California Press, 1979), 20.

16. Daniel O'Hara, "Yeats in Theory," in *Post-Structuralist Readings of English Poetry*, ed. Richard Machin and Christopher Norris (Cambridge: Cambridge Univ. Press, 1987), 349–68.

17. I am thinking of such works as John Carlos Rowe, *The Theoretical Dimensions of Henry James* (Madison: Univ. of Wisconsin Press, 1984); Donna Przybylowicz, *Desire and Repression: The Dialectic of Self and Other in the Late Works of Henry James* (University: Univ. of Alabama Press, 1986); John Paul Riquelme, *Teller and Tale in Joyce's Fiction: Oscillating Perspectives* (Baltimore: Johns Hopkins Univ. Press, 1983); Cheryl Herr, *Joyce's Anatomy of Culture* (Urbana: Univ. of Illinois Press, 1986); Derek Attridge and Daniel Ferrer, eds., *Post-Structuralist Joyce* (Cambridge: Cambridge Univ. Press, 1984); and Patrick McGee, *Paperspace: Style as Ideology in Joyce's Ulysses* (Lincoln: Univ. of Nebraska Press, 1988).

18. See Roman Jakobson and Stephen Rudy, "Yeats' 'Sorrow of Love' Through the Years" and Jakobson, "On Poetic Intentions and Linguistic Devices in Poetry," both reprinted in Jakobson, *Verbal Art, Verbal Sign, Verbal Time* (Oxford: Blackwell, 1985); Kathe Davis Finney, "Crazy Jane Talks with Jonathan Culler: Using Structuralism to Teach Lyric Poetry," *CEA Critic* 43.3 (1981): 29–36; R. A. York, *The Poem as Utterance* (London: Methuen, 1986) (109–27 on Yeats); Christopher Butler, "Metaphor in the Text" and "'Leda and the Swan': Three Approaches," in *Interpretation, Deconstruction, and Ideology: An Introduction to Some Current Issues in Literary Theory*, ed. Christopher Butler (Oxford: Clarendon, 1984), 8–18, 36–45; and Anthony L. Johnson, "Sign, Structure, and Self-Reference in W. B. Yeats's 'Sailing to Byzantium'," in *Literary Theories in Praxis*, ed. Shirley F. Staton (Philadelphia: Univ. of Pennsylvania Press, 1987), 135–54.

19. See Gayatri Chakravorty Spivak, "Finding Feminist Readings: Dante–Yeats," in *American Criticism in the Poststructuralist Age*, ed. Ira Konigsberg (Ann Arbor: Univ. of Michigan Press, 1981), 42–65; Cassandra Laity, "From Fatal Woman to New Woman: Yeats's Changing Image of Woman in His Art and Aesthetic," *DAI* 45 (1985): 3646A, and "W. B. Yeats and Florence Farr: The Influence of the 'New Woman' Actress on Yeats's Changing Images of Women," *Modern Drama* 28.4 (1985): 620–37; Declan Kiberd, *Men and Feminism in Modern Literature* (London: Macmillan, 1985) (103–35 on Yeats).

20. I note only Maqsood Hamid Mir, "The Phenomenological Response Theory: A Model for Synthesizing Reader Response and Literary Text in Teaching College English," *DAI* 44 (1984), 3390A–91A (which uses, predictably, "Among School Children").

21. Daniel O'Hara, *Tragic Knowledge: Yeats's Autobiography and Hermeneutics* (New York: Columbia Univ. Press, 1981); Paul Bové, *Destructive Poetics: Heidegger and Modern American Poetry* (New York: Columbia Univ. Press, 1980); William Spanos, *Repetitions: The Postmodern Occasion in Literature and Culture* (Baton Rouge: Louisiana State Univ. Press, 1987).

22. Spanos, *Repetitions*, 33. Spanos's reading of "Sailing to Byzantium" appears on 33–38 but informs his entire book; see 90–91, 232–33.

23. Bové, *Destructive Poetics*, 121–22, 129–30.

24. Daniel O'Hara, "The Genius of Irony: Nietzsche in Bloom," in *The Yale Critics: Deconstruction in America*, ed. Jonathan Arac, Wlad Godzich, and Wallace Martin (Minneapolis: Univ. of Minnesota Press, 1983), 124; see similar comments on the conversion experience of Bloom in his Yeats book in Jonathan Arac, *Critical Genealogies: Historical Situations for Postmodern Literary Studies* (New York: Columbia Univ. Press, 1987), 12–22; Bové, *Destructive Poetics*, 25.

25. Paul de Man, *Allegories of Reading: Figural Language in Rousseau, Nietzsche, Rilke and Proust* (New Haven: Yale Univ. Press, 1979), 11.

26. Geoffrey Hartman, *Criticism in the Wilderness: The Study of Literature Today* (New Haven: Yale Univ. Press, 1980), 24–25.

27. Ibid., 273, 274. On de Man's reading of Yeats, see Jonathan Arac, *Critical Genealogies*, 246–47; Christopher Norris, "Some Versions of Rhetoric: Empson and de Man," in *Rhetoric and Form: Deconstruction at Yale*, ed. Robert Con Davis and Ronald Schliefer (Norman: Univ. of Oklahoma Press, 1985), 195–96, and Norris's remarks

on de Man and Jakobson in *Deconstruction: Theory and Practice* (London and New York: Methuen, 1982), 99–108, which uses "Leda and the Swan" in his examples; Craig Owens, "The Allegorical Impulse: Toward a Theory of Postmodernism," in *Art After Modernism*, ed. Brian Wallis (note 7), 203–35. On Hartman's understanding of Yeats, see Jonathan Arac, "Afterword," in *The Yale Critics*, 194.

28. J. Hillis Miller, *The Linguistic Moment: From Wordsworth to Stevens* (Princeton: Princeton Univ. Press, 1985), 342–43.

29. Richard Hood Hart, "The Lyric as Fictive Rhetoric: Skeptical Deconstructions of Poems in the Major British Tradition," *DAI* 45 (1984): 849A; Lawrence Lipking, "The Practice of Theory," *Profession 83* (1983): 21–28.

30. Patrick J. Keane, *Yeats's Interactions with Tradition* (Columbia: Univ. of Missouri Press, 1987). I should note that I was struck by this section of Keane's book because it was a superfluous defense in the middle of a fine study.

31. W. J. McCormack, *Ascendancy and Tradition in Anglo-Irish Literary History from 1789 to 1939* (Oxford: Clarendon, 1985) (several chapters are devoted to Yeats). I thought that McCormack's book was a real breakthrough in Yeats criticism and that it should be more widely known. See also Terry Eagleton, "Politics and Sexuality in W. B. Yeats," *Crane Bag* 9.2 (1985): 138–42.

2

# YEATS'S POSTMODERN RHETORIC

RONALD SCHLEIFER

AN EXAMINATION OF A COMPLEX, double conception of rhetoric in Yeats is neither universal nor accidental, but it arises at a particular historical moment within the limits of particular discursive possibilities. It arises within the rhetoric of modernism, yet points to the related phenomenon of postmodernism. In the famous definition of the "mythical method," T. S. Eliot describes and exemplifies the complexity of the modernist rhetoric that I am examining. "In using the myth," Eliot writes, "in manipulating a continuous parallel between contemporaneity and antiquity, Mr. Joyce is pursuing a method which others must pursue after him. . . . It is simply a way of controlling, of ordering, of giving a shape and a significance to the immense panorama of futility and anarchy which is contemporary history. It is a method already adumbrated by Mr. Yeats, and of the need for which I believe Mr. Yeats to have been the first contemporary to be conscious. . . . It is, I seriously believe, a step toward making the modern world possible for art."[1] What concerns me here is less Eliot's understanding of Joyce's achievement than his description of the "panorama" of contemporary life and its articulation in language. For I contend that the mythical parallel described by Eliot is, in fact, what he explicitly denies that it is in his review of Ulysses—simply a kind of scaffolding that Joyce uses, then discards, after contemporary history, with its futility and anarchy, rises up and is represented in language.

In this, Eliot repeats a recurrent gesture of modernist rhetoric: he delimits a phenomenon that is not capable of being reduced to "order"—that is not even susceptible to linguistic order—and he asserts

16

that, nevertheless, it is "parallel" to the classical order of myth that somehow underlies its "surface" disorder. Robert Langbaum offers the standard narrative account of this when he suggests that the "'mythical method,' as Eliot calls it, allows the writer to be naturalistic, to portray modern chaos, while suggesting through psychological naturalism a continuing buried life. . . . The mythical method gives a doubleness of language to parallel our own doubleness (doubleness between the apparent and buried) of consciousness and selfhood."[2] The problem with such an account, as Langbaum himself suggests, is that it *naturalizes* the terror and disgust inherent in Eliot's response to contemporary history.[3] But more than this, it naturalizes the important antinaturalistic impulse in modernist language. In fact, as Langbaum argues, modernism may replace the naturalism and realism of late nineteenth-century literature with its own "psychological naturalism"; but a more interesting way of examining modernism—especially in light of the postmodern phenomenon that follows it—is to see its continuity with the antinaturalism of the symbolist movement of the 1890s. Daniel O'Hara recently called this antinaturalist, antiromantic impulse in Yeats the "demonic sublime"; and tracing Yeats's treatment in criticism since the end of World War II, O'Hara sees the culmination of Yeats's profound influence on criticism in Paul de Man's distinction between natural "image" and esoteric "emblem" in Yeats.[4] Most important, then, the antinaturalism of the symbolist movement is antirepresentational: it treats language, as Clive Scott argues, no longer "as a natural outcrop of the person but as a material with its own laws and its own peculiar forms of life."[5] Such treatment, as I note elsewhere, focuses on the syntactics of literature, the signifier rather than the signified, syntax rather than semantics.[6]

In other words, the apocalyptic antirepresentation of modernism "marks" what Jacques Derrida describes in Mallarmé's work as the articulation or circumscription of the "ideality" of nothingness. Here idea and intellection are *without* content or the representation of determined content: spirit transcends any content, any material determination, any taint of representation in an operation which is

> not a unified entity but the manifold play of a scene that, illustrating nothing—neither word nor deed—beyond itself, illustrates nothing. Nothing but the many-faceted multiplicity of a lustre which itself is

nothing beyond its own fragmented light. Nothing but the idea which is nothing. The ideality of the idea is here for Mallarmé the still metaphysical name that is still necessary in order to mark nonbeing, the nonreal, the nonpresent. . . . This "materialism of the idea" is nothing other than the staging, the theater, the visibility of nothing or of the self. It is a dramatization which *illustrates nothing,* which illustrates *the nothing,* lights up a space, re-marks a spacing as a nothing, a blank; white as a yet unwritten page, blank as a difference between two lines.[7]

It is the antirepresentational impulse in modernism, its symbolist focus on the play of signifiers and the concomitant positing of "the nothing" behind this play that, I think, most closely connects modernism with postmodernism.

The great difference between modernism in its symbolist moment and postmodernism is the difference between the "metaphysical name" described by Derrida and the "staging" of that name. In fact, in this passage Derrida describes the antirepresentational metaphysics of modernism—its turning away from the immense panorama of futility and anarchy of the contemporary world by turning to *another* world that Yeats called in 1893 the "subtlety, obscurity, and intricate utterance . . . of our moods and feelings [which] are too fine, too subjective, too impalpable to find any clear expression in action or in speech tending towards action."[8] This turning away, as Derrida says elsewhere, "is a departure from the world toward a place which is neither a *non-place* nor an *other* world. . . . This universe articulates only that which is in excess of everything, the essential nothing on whose basis everything can appear and be produced within language. . . . Only *pure absence*— not the absence of this or that, but the absence of everything in which all presence is announced—can *inspire,* in other words, can *work.*"[9] Such work is the "metaphysical" work of symbolism: it includes Eliot's (and Conrad's and Yeats's and even Lawrence's) visceral abhorrence of the material plenitude of the world (the futility and anarchy of the Congo or Ireland's filthy modern tide or apeneck Sweeney's animal movements) and a concomitant, antirepresentational aesthetic that implies the possibility of inscribing and discerning ideality beneath and behind the ruined fragments of experience.

But if Derrida describes the metaphysical "name" of symbolism and its "turn" toward some other "place," he also describes the fully immanent "operation" that creates that metaphysics as a "theatrical" effect—the immanent relationship between naming and turning.[10] In these terms, the difference between postmodernism and modernism is the difference between the articulation or "staging" of *nothing* in discourse and the hypostatization—the metaphysical naming—of *the nothing* as a kind of transcendental "object" of linguistic appropriation. For the postmodern, the articulation of "nothing," in one way or another, is hardly a crisis; it hardly imagines, as Yeats said, that "where there is nothing, there is God." For the postmodern, the crisis of representation that symbolism addresses and the further crisis of materialism— the "body of that death" described by Mallarmé (in Symons's translation)[11]—in relation to the spirit and language is old hat, hardly news, simply something else. It has none of the social and political programmatics—what Fredric Jameson calls "the protopolitical vocation and terrorist stance"[12]—of the older modernism.

That crisis was most starkly expressed (not self-consciously "staged") in the symbolist movement in literature, of which Arthur Symons said that Yeats was the chief representative in English (*Symbolist Movement*, xix). It was so because the crisis of modernism is best understood as predicated on a conception of the *inadequacy* of language to experience— the inadequacy, that is, of any "natural" signifier to the transcendental signified of an hypostatized *nothing* (what Yeats variously called the "immortal moods," "the Divine Essence," or simply "perfection,")[13] that symbolism attempts to delineate. Its method, however, is the *elaboration* of the signifier, the development of intricate syntactic strategies to circumscribe and thus *negatively* represent the unrepresentable, the unspeakable.[14] But remove the transcendental signified from this project—the "perfected emotions" that Yeats speaks of early in his career—and we are left only with the "theatrical" play of signifiers, a radical version of the "pastiche" that Jameson sees as characterizing the postmodern. "Pastiche," he writes, "is, like parody, the imitation of a peculiar mask, speech in a dead language: but it is a neutral practice of such mimicry . . . devoid of laughter and of any conviction that alongside the abnormal tongue you have momentarily borrowed, some healthy linguistic normality still exists."[15] Postmodern pastiche speaks a "dead language," while the "modernist" symbolist gesture responded to the futility and anarchy of the contemporary world with its *antithetical* language of parody, disdain, and vision. Its rhetoric was predicated on the "mythical" "depths" of antinatural vision and intuition: in de Man's description of Yeats's articulation of "emblems" discovered *within* natural "images," this poetic discourse "substitutes 'names and meanings' for the thing itself and, in gnostic fashion, searches for Being not in the divinely created thing, but in language as the vessel of divine intellect" ("Image and Emblem," 170). Remove such "depths," such transcendental signifieds as "divine intellect"—make "the nothing" simply "nothing"—and the linguistic strategies of modernist representations seem remarkably postmodern, remarkably close, not to the "celebration" of futility and anarchy that postmodernism sometimes seems to be, but to their quiet acceptance that the postmodern always also—always already—is.

Of course, the transcendental signified, the "metaphysical name," cannot be "removed." It can only be shown not to have been there in the first place. Such a showing is what Derrida means by the "staging" and "dramatization" of the antirepresentational "play of a scene that . . . illustrates nothing." The mode of the "staging" of modernist discourse leads to the larger question of rhetoric, and more specifically to "postmodern" rhetoric.

Hugh Kenner examined the rhetorical power of modern poetry—especially the symbolist rhetoric described by Derrida—in terms of the strategies developed by modernists to set words "free" from the historical occasions of their enunciation. Kenner argues that symbolism creates its meanings and effects by "imitating" or "counterfeiting" the way in which the passage of time erases the occasion of enunciation, the "vehicles" bearing its metaphoric "tenor." The example that Kenner narrates is from *Cymbeline*: "Golden lads and girls all must / As chimney-sweepers, come to dust." After describing the "magic" that "irradiates the stanza" so that "we, the heirs of Mallarmé and Valéry and Eliot, do not simply pass over 'golden' but find it richly Shakespearean," he notes that in Shakespeare's Warwickshire, "golden boys" is the name for dandelions, and they are called "chimney-sweepers" when they go to seed. The modernist or symbolist strategy, then—its postmodern rhetorical "staging"—is to turn *linguistically* to the other world, the "*nonplace*" described by Derrida. "We may want to say," Kenner argues, "that Shakespeare wrote about happenings in the world, the world that contains mortal men and sunlight and dandelions, and that a post-Symbolist reading converts his work into something that happens in the language, where "golden" will interact with "dust" and "wages" and "lads" and "girls" and "chimney-sweepers," and where "dust" rhymes with "must," mortality with necessity. Thus the song seems to us especially fine when we can no longer say what the phrase "golden lads" was meant to name."[16] By means of this narrative, Kenner can *situate* the linguistic representation or suggestion of a "depth" of transcendental significance too fine and impalpable to seem to have material embodiment within an historical context of enunciation.

In this way, the question of representation in language – the question of rhetoric – hangs over modern studies of literature and modernism in general in terms of the occasion of enunciation. Moreover, it does so in Eliot's terms of mythical "depth" as opposed to linguistic and experiential "surfaces." Such a conception – a "metaphysical naming" – of "depth" allows the world and its materialism – Conrad's imperialism, the religious politics of Ireland, the sheer multiplicity of the America from which Eliot fled – to fade away and reveal beneath the "body of that death" transcendental value, what Yeats describes in "Michael Robartes Remembers Forgotten Beauty" as "the loveliness / That has long faded from the world." But it does so only by repressing its own rhetoricity.

In other words, the difference between depth and surface that I am suggesting characterizes the difference between modernism and postmodernism in terms of rhetoric. This difference is based upon two seemingly incompatible senses of language and rhetoric. Language presents what O'Hara calls the symbolic and "unselfconscious linguistic formations" of "the great narrative myths of the culture,"[17] and rhetoric studies linguistic strategies to articulate the preexisting significance that it unself-consciously describes – the immaterial transcendental signifieds that inhabit Yeats's vision. But language also creates or "stages" the "effects" of meaning themselves, the felt, "given," sense of meanings beyond the complete control of its users, or what O'Hara calls the "semantic innovation" of metaphor in "self-reflective" discourse (*Tragic Knowledge*, 170). In this context, rhetoric studies the staging of meaning as a linguistic effect created by the scaffolding configurations of language; created, that is, by its play of signifiers.

This opposition is of great urgency because it suggests two ways of reading. We can choose to understand both literature and our world in terms of myth and symbol, in terms of the causation, as Eliot says, of a controlling order analyzed, quite literally, in "depth," where "depth" itself does not call for rhetorical analysis—the analysis of what Derrida has recently called "the rhetoricity of rhetoric."[18] Or, as I will suggest, we can stay on the surface of things in a kind of "postmodernism" to discover scaffolded topographies and configurations of textual play in situating our understanding—including understanding the "effect of depth" itself to which language gives rise—in terms of a postmodern rhetoric of modernism. For what is "scaffolded" in modernist literature after all is the particular discourse of modern rhetoric, the panorama that Eliot describes in his original title for *The Waste Land*: "he do the police in different voices." That is, the discourse of literary modernism at least partially articulates the so-called "anarchy" of history, not in terms of human intentions, "buried" or "parallel" orders of shape and significance, harmonies of voice and base—in other words, not in terms of the emotions of monumental secret and originative causes behind things—but in terms of palpable, rhetorical effects residing on the accidental surfaces of discourse.

In any case, this is where postmodernism—in criticism as well as in literature, and in the *problem* of this hierarchical distinction between parasitical and superficial criticism and profound and original "literature"—draws our attention: to the *surface* of things, to what Richard Rorty calls "textualism" rather than "idealism"—the pragmatics of asking how things work and what *effects* they have, rather than what they mean. "Pragmatism," Rorty writes, "is the philosophical counterpart of literary modernism, a kind of literature which prides itself on its autonomy and novelty rather than its truthfulness to experience or its discovery of pre-existing significance. Strong textualism," he concludes, "draws the moral of modernist literature and thus creates genuinely modernist criticism."[19] In another essay, Rorty contrasts pragmatism to an earlier tradition that "thinks of truth as a vertical relationship between representations and what is represented." Pragmatism, on the other hand, "thinks of truth horizontally. . . . This tradition does not ask how representations are related to nonrepresentations, but how representations can be seen as hanging together;"[20] that is, as *effectively* and pragmatically functioning rhetorically.

It is in this sense of the pragmatics of the momentary, repetitious configurations of meaning that Jameson defines postmodern rhetoric. Postmodernism, he notes, contains two important features. "First," he says, "the falling away of the protopolitical vocation and the terrorist stance of the older modernism and, second, the eclipse of all of the affect (depth, anxiety, terror, the emotions of the monumental) that marked high modernism and its replacement by what Coleridge would have called fancy or Schiller aesthetic play, a commitment to surface and to the *superficial* in all the senses of the word."[21] Such a conception of superficial "pragmatism," although Rorty does not say it, character- izes "postmodernism" beyond Jameson's description. In postmodern- ism, Jean-François Lyotard notes that the narrative function is "dispersed in clouds of narrative language elements—narrative, but also denota- tive, prescriptive, descriptive, and so on," a dispersal that Lyotard goes on to describe as "a pragmatics of language particles" or "valencies" in- tersecting; that is, "hanging together." Arthur Kroker and David Cook define the pragmatics of the "postmodern scene" more hyperbolically, figuring the postmodern scene as a "disembodied eye" that "is nothing less than a pure sign system: it cannot be embedded in a chain of fi- nalities because the floating eye as a sign-system signifies the cancella- tion of vertical being." In a different idiom, Charles Newman charac- terizes the pragmatism of postmodernism as an "*inflation of discourse,* manifesting itself in literature through the illusion that technique can remove itself from history by attacking a concept of objective reality which has already faded from the world, and in criticism by the de- velopment of secondary languages which presumably 'demystify' real- ity, but actually tend to further obscure it."[22]

What these descriptions share is a definition of understanding in which cause gives way to effect as the mode of explanation; how phenomena work, how they are *configured* (that is, how they hang to- gether), rather than their secret cause, is the nature of explanation. Like symbolism, this rhetoric focuses on the signifier rather than on the signified, but it does so not in the service of the recovery of the signified somewhere else—what Yeats called "the abundance and depth of Nature" (*E&I*, 87), but which is, as de Man demonstrated, the locus of "terror and annihilation, apocalyptic rather than eschatological" ("Image and Emblem," 177)—but rather in the service of simply that "play" on the surface.

This is apparent in another "modernist" writer contemporary with Eliot, Joyce, and Yeats who describes and exemplifies the pragmatic, "postmodern" play of the surface in modernist discourse—Ferdinand de Saussure. In the last chapter of *The Course in General Linguistics*, Saussure argues against the causal explanation of descriptive linguistics in favor of a kind of Darwinian chaos and accident, the purely accidental nature of any particular language form. "No characteristic" of language, he writes, "has a right to permanent existence; it persists only through sheer luck."[23] "Mere phonetic modifications," he adds, "which are due to blind evolution, result in alternations. The mind seizes upon the alternations, attaches grammatical values to them, and spreads them, using the analogical models which chance phonetic developments provide" (231). The mind seizes phonetic accidents retrospectively, not as causes but as superficial phenomena to be put to some use, to be made to hang together "superficially" and to function linguistically.

While such a pragmatics characterizes postmodernism, the moment of literary modernism is characterized by the intersection of these two different concepts of explanation and significance, the intersection of naming and staging, or, in de Man's later terms describing "Among School Children," the intersection of grammatical and rhetorical meaning.[24] Eliot's anxious need to find a grounding method in the chaos of Joyce's vision and that of his own, like Yeats's need to articulate a visionary, transcendental resolution of experience not only in the apocalyptic, "symbolist" poetry of the 1890s but even in a high modernist poem such as "Among School Children," seems to encompass the tension between the old concept of metaphysical meaning and the new concept of pragmatic function. Perhaps it is the enabling tension of modernist practice. But the transformation from cause to effect, from causal to functional explanation, or, in Saussure's terms, the transformation from a mode of understanding based upon the diachronic discovery of the origin to one based upon a synchronic apprehension of relationships between and among phenomenal data, is at the heart of what I call the postmodern rhetoric of modernism.

This is most clear in Yeats's "high" modernism, and again, Eliot is instructive. In 1940, with characteristic generosity, Eliot came to praise Yeats after his death and described in his work another version of the mythical method, a kind of "impersonality" of the lyric poet "who," Eliot writes, "out of intense and personal experience, is able to express a general truth; retaining all the particularity of his experience, to make of it a general symbol."[25] "In becoming more Irish," he says of Yeats, "he became at the same time universal" (301). This is high praise indeed; and by the end of Eliot's essay, he himself is mythologizing Yeats, marking him as "one of those few whose history is the history of their own time, who are part of the consciousness of an age which cannot be understood without them" (308).

Now, certainly, Yeats participates in this kind of "mythological method," what Auden calls more modestly the transformation of the occasional poem into "a serious reflective poem of at once personal and public interest."[26] But the "method" of this mythology is horizontal rather than vertical, despite all of Yeats's talk of "the deeps of the mind," of the Shakespearean ideal of "depth only," of vision and trance. In "Among School Children," for example, Yeats certainly "universalizes" his experience in much the same way that Eliot universalizes his wife's neurotic discourse in "A Game of Chess." But like Vivien's language–"Speak to me. Why do you never speak. Speak."–Yeats's situation in the classroom questioning is altogether accidental, provided by the chance developments of the Irish Free State. Moreover, below the scaffolding of his myths and vision, is the sheer phenomenal power of the poetry hanging together, discovering coherence in what he calls "the Path of the Chameleon," the bewildering incoherence of his particular experience. Thus, more important than the aesthetic questions at the end of the poem is the order of love the mind finally seizes upon (its shape and significance), which Yeats stages throughout his poem, configuring the accidents of his experience–the nuns, mothers, and lovers imagined in the classroom–into the transcendental discourse of Plato, Aristotle, and Pythagoras. In this, Yeats, like Leopold Bloom before him, articulates a kind of female discourse of nun, mother, lover in what he imagines to be a "universal" male philosophic voice. He devises an "antithetical" language in which the accidents of a schoolroom filled with girls and women can transcend that situation to give rise to "representative" human values figured in male philosophers and artists. But more generally, he makes the surface of his experience, like the surface discolorations of the lapis lazuli about which he writes, create his rhetorical effects–the effects of (transcendental) meaning.

Take, for instance, what most critics understand as the center of the poem, the apostrophe at its end:

> O Presences
> That passion, piety or affection knows
> And that all heavenly glory symbolize–
> O self-born mockers of man's enterprise.

The passion, piety, or affection that knows the object of the apostrophe, "Presences," corresponds to the occasions of desire described in the poem—the lover's passion, the nun's piety, and the mother's affection. But it is even more interesting that the apostrophe itself is a representative example of—a rhetorical strategy in—the antirepresentational mythologizing force of modernist discourse. Apostrophe, Jonathan Culler argued, offers "a poetic presence through an image of voice, . . . the pure O of undifferentiated voicing."[27] As such, apostrophe is radically antinatural; it is against narrative, time, and history. As Derrida said, it cannot be assimilated to the accusative case of speech or to language in general: it is "not a category, a *case* of speech, but, rather the bursting forth, the very raising up of speech."[28] In these terms, it is, in A. J. Greimas's structuralist analysis, a "surface" linguistic phenomenon approaching—signifying—the "deep meaning" of the "primal cry" of undifferentiated language.[29]

That is, apostrophe substitutes what Culler describes as "a temporality of discourse for a referential temporality." "In lyrics of this kind," he says, "a temporal problem is posed: something once present has been lost or attenuated; this loss can be narrated but the temporal sequence is irreversible, like time itself. Apostrophes displace this irreversible structure by removing the opposition between presence and absence from empirical time and locating it in a discursive time" ("Apostrophe," 150). The temporal problem of "Among School Children," of course, is the problem of temporality itself, the poet's aging, and what Yeats calls in his diary note for the poem, "the old thought that life prepares for what never happens."[30] Instead of absences, its apostrophe posits and addresses—it *names*—Presences that give shape and significance to history. In "Among School Children" apostrophe transforms images begetting fresh images, on and on, and on, in the furious complexity of postmodernism, into transcendental presence. It does so, as Culler says, by creating not "a predicable relation between a signifier and a signified, a form and its meaning, but the uncalculable force of an event" ("Apostrophe," 152). Such an "event" is the "occurrence" of a symbol or a myth, situated, as O'Hara describes symbolism, "on the border between the realms of language, dreams, and the sacred" (*Tragic Knowledge*, 170). Just as Yeats figures the disappointment and anger at approaching death in terms of birth in the almost archetypal gesture of modernism of stanza v—a gesture of asserting "vital" depths below the meaningless surface of experience figured in the "representation" of a child as a "shape" upon its mother's lap—so apostrophe delimits transcendental, unpresentable Presences as the object of situated address.

It does so in an "antithetical" discourse: death is articulated by describing birth in a language that makes life itself—"that must sleep, shriek, struggle to escape"—a vast chaos whose only virtue is as a naturalistic storehouse of images that can be transformed into symbolist emblems of the unarticulable. Such an apostrophic discourse is remarkably violent: it includes the object of address only by violating it in ways that Yeats's rhetorical question violates the affection of mothers and mothering:

> What youthful mother, a shape upon her lap
> Honey of generation had betrayed, . . .
> Would think her son, did she but see that shape
> With sixty or more winters on its head,
> A compensation for the pang of his birth,
> Or the uncertainty of his setting forth?

The violence here is borne by conceiving "compensations" for affection only in terms of a logic of cause and effect—the same logic that governs the paradoxes of the final stanza and Yeats's symbolist project more generally. The bitter furies of complexity that children (and lovers and other images) occasion might well be answered by an image of skipping on waves rather than fighting them, or a conception of the sea as buoyant rather than "dolphin-torn" and "gong-tormented." They might as well be answered by reading postmodern stagings in Yeats's modernist discourse.

Still, like Langbaum's reading of Eliot and Yeats, most of the critics of "Among School Children" describe the ending of the poem in terms of symbol and depth rather than in terms of surface and buoyancy: Cleanth Brooks speaks of "the vision of totality of being and unity of being" in the last stanza of the poem; Richard Ellmann suggests that the poem at least hints at "an escape from mortality"; and Frank Kermode describes the final image of the poem as "the work of a mind which is itself a system of symbolic correspondences, self-exciting, difficult because the particularities are not shared by the reader." More recently, George Lensing asserted that the poem's ending creates "a powerful truce with time"; Douglas Archibald notes that the Presences at the end become "the poem's only conceivable audience"; and David Young suggests, in his own narrative interpretation, that "the 'sixty year old smiling public man,' haunted by memories and imaginings, evolves into the defiant, exultant speaker of the poem's close."[31] These understandings of the poem share Culler's sense of the nature and function of apostrophe, its ability to control and order and shape experience verbally, creating discursive mastery over the bitter furies of complex temporality by positing a depth beneath the surface of time and history. Even de Man, in his controversial use of "Among School Children" to assert that the opposition between grammatical questioning and rhetorical questioning—an analysis which, were it brought to the questioning of youthful mother, would betray an analytic energy that disregards the human cost of Yeats's vision—even de Man suggests that the apostrophe at the poem's end is a transcendental, universalizing touchstone of understanding.

These interpretations point to what Lyotard calls the "sublimity" of modernism—its attempt "to present the fact that the unpresentable exists. To make visible that there is something which can be conceived and which can neither be seen nor made visible."[32] This, I think, describes Yeats's own sense of "depth," his sense that "Shakespeare's people make all things serve their passion . . . : birds, beasts, men, women, landscape, society are but symbols, and metaphors, nothing is studied in itself, the mind is a dark well, no surface, depth only."[33]

But here, Yeats is also describing the pragmatics of his own symbolism, the fact that poetry, as he understands it, *finds* its symbols at hand in the same way that language, in Saussure's description, seizes upon the accidents of phonetic development and attaches meaning to them. The poem, as already noted, began, as Yeats himself wrote to Olivia Shakespear, as a "curse upon old age,"[34] an articulation of the *impossibility* of the transcendental, universalizing apostrophe with which it ends (or even de Man's thematizing of that impossibility): its curse simply articulated a broken heart. Of course, such a recourse to "origin"—to a "cause"—is precisely what I am arguing that postmodern rhetoric eschews, but it is instructive in Yeats's case. As Lyotard says, the postmodern is "that which, in the modern, puts forward the unpresentable in presentation itself; . . . that which searches for new presentations, not in order to enjoy them but in order to impart a stronger sense of the unpresentable" ("What is Postmodernism?" 81). Yeats's apostrophe attempts to transform the images of experience into a symbol of unpresentable Presences. In this attempt, however, he presents the unpresentable in presentation itself; namely, the arbitrary nature of his signs. The poem presents the accidents of experiences—mothers and birth, nuns and children, aging lovers—as occasions for an apostrophic speech about unpresentable, blossoming labor.

The postmodern in Yeats's modernism is the radical contingency of the images that he hangs together in his poetry. The examples of apostrophe offered by Culler, besides that of the ending of "Among School Children" (Blake, Shelley, Rilke), are contrasted with narrative and historical description. "If one brings together in a poem a boy, some birds, a few blessed creatures, and some mountains, meadows, hills and groves," Culler writes, "one tends to place them in a narrative where one thing leads to another; the events which form ask to be temporally located. . . . But if one puts into a poem *thou shepherd boy, ye blessed creatures, ye birds,* they are immediately associated with what might be called a timeless present but is better seen as a temporality of writing" ("Apostrophe," 149). "Among School Children" does both: it offers the historically located description of the "images" that nuns, mothers, and remembered lovers worship—all of which, as Kermode says, are very difficult because they are accidental, famous, so to speak, for fifteen minutes, unpresentable "particularities not shared by the reader" (*Romantic Image*, 83). The poem also offers the apostrophe to the transcendental and "timeless" "Presences" somehow buried "beneath" these accidents of history, implied by these accidents as a primal cry implies some inarticulate "deep" meaning, because otherwise—postmodernly—all that would be left would be material accidents subject to the meaningless changes of time.

In this way, modern and postmodern, the poem narrates its own "mythological method" of transforming historical occasion to symbolic event. The specific method of this apostrophic mythologizing, however, is the local violence of transforming the subjects of desire from female to male, so that in stanza vi the figure of Plato—itself assumed from the "accidental" simile in the second stanza of Plato's parable—becomes the figure of piety, Aristotle the figure for the mother, and Pythagoras the figure for the passionate lover. Moreover, Plato, Aristotle, and Pythagoras are linked signifiers in a linguistic chain. In other words, Yeats seizes upon the accidents of his experience, imposes the hierarchical order of sexual difference (marked in the "universalization" of the neutral male terms), and transforms the chaotic metonymies of female life—mother, child, nun, lover—which mix spiritual and material existence indiscriminately, into the transcendental synecdochic order of male philosophic discourse. "Image" becomes "Presence" as female becomes male, and with this transformation, the metonymy of "nuns and mothers" becomes the activity of symbolization, "Presences," symbolizing the unpresentable, "all heavenly glory." Such glory, like the transformation of schoolgirls of the poem sewing and reminding Yeats of Maud, to the "son" of stanza v, creates a male preserve as its "universalizing," "mythical method": it makes the world possible for art by making experience male experience, even as Maud's "present image floats into the mind" as formed, not by the accidents of the experience that she chose for herself and had thrust upon her, but by quattrocento finger. It makes it possible by articulating the accidental materialism of metonymy into the ideal order of synecdoche and, even more, the hierarchical metaphoric order of material female signifiers functioning as "forgotten" vehicles for transcendental "neutral" (i.e. male) signifieds.

Here, then, is an apostrophe of modernism not unlike Eliot's mandarin definition of the mythical method. The apostrophe itself, as Culler argues, "makes its point by troping not on the meaning of a word but on the circuit or situation of communication itself" ("Apostrophe," 135). Apostrophe, he continues, proceeds by "deflection"; that is, it moves horizontally, even though, as he says, critics turn aside from apostrophes with embarrassment and attempt "to repress them or rather to transform apostrophe into description" ("Apostrophe," 13). Like Yeats, modernist critics repress rhetoric and transform the stagings of apostrophe into metaphysical namings. Greimas, as I have mentioned, describes this process in technical semiotic terms—which are themselves postmodern terms—as the nature of poetry; namely, "the shortening of the distance between the signifier and the signified . . . to reachieve the 'primal cry,'" which is, he argues, an "illusory signification of a 'deep meaning,' hidden and inherent in the plane of expression" ("La linguistique structurale," 279). Modernism traffics in deep meanings, while postmodernism locates meaning itself—including "deep" meanings—on the contingent, configured surface of experience and discourse. This is why, I believe, recent literary criticism—heirs to the "structuralism" of

Saussure and his followers (including Greimas and the various stripes of "poststructuralist" criticism, many of which are cited in this essay in an attempt to define postmodernism)—only achieves Rorty's "genuine modernist criticism" in its focus on the postmodern moment of modernism and on the effective play of discursive surfaces rather than on the search for adequate "causes."

"History is necessity," Yeats wrote in a late diary entry, "until it takes fire in someone's head and becomes virtue or freedom."[35] Such fire, however, is a discursive effect residing on the surface of things. In just the way "Among School Children" seizes upon the language of experience to create a discursive *effect* suggesting a "truce with time," "an escape from mortality," or a vision of unity, so modernism makes a virtue of necessity and creates at least the illusion of coherence within futility and anarchy. The futility and anarchy of modernism, however, are measured against the depths of mind and meaning and against what is lost, just as the pain and uncertainty of child-rearing are measured against images and promises of "what never happens."

With a twist of the wrist, however, modernism eschews depths for surfaces and thinks of truth rhetorically, playfully, and phenomenally; with a postmodern gesture, the panorama of contemporary history becomes "fun." As Nietzsche says in *The Gay Science*, "all people who have depth find happiness in being for once like flying fish, playing on the peaks of waves; what they consider best in things is that they have surface: their skin-coveredness."[36] Yeats never quite conceived of the sea as a surface, preferring always to imagine what its depths threw forth. Yet his shells and gods and dolphins, like the children and nuns and philosophers of "Among School Children," take their place within a topology of figures and an edifice of surfaces constituting modernism. What I have done in situating these figures within the poem—and within the modernist enterprise—is to read the surface rhetorically, as not only Saussure but also his postmodern (poststructuralist) readers have taught us, as a configuration, a way of making, not finding, sense in the world and making it, perhaps, possible for art.

NOTES

1. T. S. Eliot, "*Ulysses*, Order, and Myth," in *Selected Essays*, ed. Frank Kermode (New York: Harcourt, 1975), 177–78.

2. Robert Langbaum, *The Mysteries of Identity* (New York: Oxford Univ. Press, 1977), 89–90.

3. For an examination of Langbaum's "naturalizing" reading of modernism, which more extensively contrasts the "positive impulse" that he sees in Eliot, Yeats, Lawrence, and others with the "terror" and "despair" explicitly described by Yeats in his poetic project, see my review dealing with *The Mysteries of Identity* in *MLN* 93 (1978): 1052–59.

4. Daniel O'Hara, "Yeats in Theory," in *Post-Structuralist Readings of English Poetry*, ed. Richard Machin and Christopher Norris (Cambridge: Cambridge Univ. Press, 1987), 349–68. O'Hara traces the "sublime" in Yeats, a "vision of power" (350) becoming "wholly demonic, a desperate 'evasion of dying'" (358), as a model and impetus of twentieth-century literary theory. Yet his final description of this Yeatsian sublime seems to be a description of postmodern sensibility: "the sublime," he concludes, "discloses the essential nature of all literary ideas—the fundamental groundlessness that makes every effort to theorize on their basis in the manner of academic philosophy a ridiculous enterprise at worst and at best a diverting work of literary art. . . . An elaborate literary artifice produces an apocalyptically ironic vision destructive of all device as its own irrational self-representation as rhetoric. What else could result from this comically hollow affirmation of an annihilating prospect of descent to first principles but such a 'purely' literary conception of the sublime?" (p. 259). See also Paul de Man, "Image and Emblem in Yeats," in *The Rhetoric of Romanticism* (New York: Columbia Univ. Press, 1984), 145–238; this source is cited in the text as "Image and Emblem."

5. Clive Scott, "Symbolism Decadence and Impressionism," in *Modernism: 1890–1930*, ed. Malcolm Bradbury and James McFarland (Harmondsworth, Middlesex: Penguin Books, 1976), 212.

6. Ronald Schleifer, "The Pathway of *The Rose*: Yeats, the Lyric, and the Syntax of Symbolism," *Genre* 18 (1985): 375–96.

7. Jacques Derrida, *Dissemination*, trans. Barbara Johnson (Chicago: Univ. of Chicago Press, 1981), 208.

8. W. B. Yeats, "Nationality and Literature," in *Uncollected Prose, Vol. I*, ed. John Frayne (New York: Columbia Univ. Press, 1970), 271.

9. Jacques Derrida, *Writing and Difference*, trans. Alan Bass (Chicago: Univ. of Chicago Press, 1978), 8.

10. For a penetrating discussion of the "theatrical" element in modernism, see Stephen Melville, *Philosophy Beside Itself* (Minneapolis: Univ. of Minnesota Press, 1986), esp. chap. 1.

11. Cited by Symons in *The Symbolist Movement in Literature* (New York: Dutton Books, 1958), 70.

12. Fredric Jameson, "Foreword," in Jean François Lyotard, *The Postmodern Condition*, trans. Geoff Bennington and Brian Massumi (Minneapolis: Univ. of Minnesota Press, 1984), xviii.

13. W. B. Yeats, *Essays and Introductions* (New York: Collier Books, 1968), 148. This source is quoted throughout the text as *E&I*.

14. See Ronald Schleifer, "The Pathway of *The Rose*," esp. 383–94.

15. Fredric Jameson, "Postmodernism, or The Cultural Logic of Late Capitalism," *New Left Review* 146 (July–Aug. 1984): 65.

16. Hugh Kenner, *The Pound Era* (Berkeley: Univ. of California Press, 1971), 122, 123. See also Hugh Kenner, *The Counterfeiters* (New York: Dutton Books, 1973).

17. Daniel O'Hara, *Tragic Knowledge: Yeat's "Autobiography" and Hermeneutics* (New York: Columbia Univ. Press, 1981), 170. This source is cited in the text as *Tragic Knowledge*.

18. Jacques Derrida, *Memoirs for Paul de Man*, trans. Cecile Lindsay, Jonathan Culler, and Eduardo Cadava (New York: Columbia Univ. Press, 1986), 109.

19. Richard Rorty, "Nineteenth-Century Idealism and Twentieth-Century Textualism," in *Consequences of Pragmatism* (Minneapolis: Univ. of Minnesota Press, 1982), 153.

20. Richard Rorty, "Philosophy as a Kind of Writing: An Essay on Derrida," *Consequences of Pragmatism*, 92.

21. Fredric Jameson, "Foreword" *The Postmodern Condition*, xviii.

22. Jean-François Lyotard, *The Postmodern Condition*, xxiv; Arthur Kroker and David Cook, *The Postmodern Scene* (New York: St. Martin's Press, 1986), 79; Charles Newman, *The Postmodern Aura* (Evanston, Ill.: Northwestern Univ. Press, 1985), 10.

23. Ferdinand de Saussure, *Course in General Linguistics*, trans. Wade Baskin (New York: McGraw Hill, 1959), 229.

24. Paul de Man, "Semiology and Rhetoric," in *Allegories of Reading* (New Haven: Yale Univ. Press, 1979), 11–12.

25. T. S. Eliot, "Yeats," in *On Poetry and Poets* (New York: Noonday Press, 1961), 299.

26. W. H. Auden, "Yeats as an Example," in *The Permanence of Yeats*, ed. James Hall and Martin Steinmann (New York: Collier Books, 1950), 313.

27. Jonathan Culler, "Apostrophe," in *The Pursuit of Signs* (Ithaca: Cornell Univ. Press, 1981), 142. This source is cited in the text as "Apostrophe."

28. *Writing and Difference*, 103.

29. A. J. Greimas, "La linguistique structurale et la poétique," in *Du Sens* (Paris: Seuil, 1970), 279 (cited in the text as "La Linguistique structurale"). (my translation). For an account of Greimas's structural analysis of poetry, see my *A. J. Greimas and the Nature of Meaning* (Lincoln: Univ. of Nebraska Press, 1987), 151–54.

30. Cited in Thomas Parkinson, *Yeats: The Later Poetry* (Berkeley: Univ. of California Press, 1964), 93.

31. Cleanth Brooks, *The Well Wrought Urn* (New York: Harvest Books, 1947), 185; Richard Ellmann, *The Identity of Yeats* (New York: Oxford Univ. Press, 1954), 229; Frank Kermode, *Romantic Image* (New York: St. Martin's Press, 1957), 83 (cited in the text as *Romantic Image*); George Lensing, "'Among School Children': Questions as Conclusions," *College Literature* 13 (1986): 7; Douglas Archibald, *Yeats* (Syracuse, N.Y.: Syra-

cuse Univ. Press, 1983), 222; David Young, *Troubled Mirror: A Study of Yeats's "The Tower"* (Iowa City: Univ. of Iowa Press, 1987), 91.

32. Jean-François Lyotard, "What Is Postmodernism?" in *The Postmodern Condition*, trans. Regis Durand, 78.

33. *The Autobiography of W. B. Yeats* (New York: Collier Books, 1965), 194.

34. *The Letters of W. B. Yeats*, ed. Alan Wade (New York: Macmillan, 1955), 719.

35. W. B. Yeats, *Explorations* (New York: Macmillan, 1962), 336.

36. Friedrich Nietzsche, *The Gay Science*, trans. Walter Kaufmann (New York: Vintage Books, 1974), 217.

# 3

# HE "LIKED THE WAY HIS FINGER SMELT"
Yeats and the Tropics of History

WILLIAM BONNEY

W. B. YEATS has much to say about history. He strives much of his life to collect details about the past from sources both occult and scholarly and to assemble these details into a conceptual structure that might salvage them and him from randomness and futility because he claims to perceive "things doubled—doubled in history, world history, personal history."[1] Thus, for example, he can sweepingly define the very nature of existence and affirm that there are "two living countries, one visible and one invisible," even as he variously states that "All external events . . . are . . . an externalization of character," that "all knowledge is biography," and that history itself is but "the history of the mind."[2] In this respect, Yeats's historiography is an extension of attitudes characteristic of the early romantic period as expressed by writers like Wordsworth, who in works like *The Prelude* used contemplation of the past as a way to pursue ontological unity, to become "conscious of myself / And of some other Being" (bk. 2, ll. 32–33) and thereby "enshrine the spirit of the past / For future restoration" (bk. 11, ll. 342–43).

Of course, such perceptions of the ultimately subjective essence of the historical process and of human access to vestiges of this process effectively prevent men like Wordsworth and Yeats from being acknowledged as historians by the practitioners of historiography who dominate contemporary centers of academic power, and who typically assume that historical narratives are verbal structures that are adequate simultaneously to the task of uncovering supposedly pre-existent facts and stories and of representing them in such a way so as to create a final correspondence between these verbal structures and some prior but recoverable empirical reality. Wordsworth feared such epistemological pretensions and went so far as to portray the wielders of them rhetorically as satanic persons who by circumscribing the past dare to delimit the future, "who with a broad highway have overbridged / The froward chaos of futurity" (bk. 5, ll. 371–72).

But vatic pronouncements are of scant predictive value with regard to effecting a recovery of items for museum showcases, and subjective and self-consciously figurative discussions of temporal process have typically languished in a category deprecatingly called "imaginative" and consequently opposed to traditional and presumably factual historical narratives. Contemporary theory has changed all this and created an intellectual context for skeptical assertions like those made long ago by Charles Lamb: "The mighty future is as nothing, being everything! the past is everything, being nothing!"[3] That is, the very concept "history" has become problematic because the word refers both to an object of knowledge and to an explanatory analysis of this object. Moreover, the object does not exist empirically because past events cannot themselves be studied—only enigmatic remains of them endure in the form of semantically open artifacts, written records, and current social practices, and such inaccessible data can be represented only verbally and fictively.[4]

Appropriately, the very concept of an "historical fact" as an event that "really took place" has been challenged by Claude Lévi-Strauss, who asks "but where did anything take place?" "Each episode . . . resolves itself into a multitude of individual psychic moments. Each of these moments is a translation of unconscious development, and these resolve themselves into cerebral, hormonal or nervous phenomena, which themselves have reference to the physical or chemical order. Consequently, historical facts are no more *given* than any other. It is the historian, or the agent of history, who constitutes them by abstraction and . . . under the threat of an infinite regress."[5] This criticism of the naïve concept of an "event" echoes Nietzsche's assertion that the physiology of perception and the creation of metaphor are identical—a declaration made a century ago when Nietzsche observed: "A nerve-stimulus, first transcribed into an image! First metaphor! The image again copied into a sound! Second metaphor! And each time [the creator of an utterance] leaps completely out of one sphere right into the midst of an entirely different one."[6] After this epistemologically dubious perceptual process occurs and Nietzschesque initial metaphors are established within the human mind, the quest for comprehension begins with a further tropological maneuver—the identification of what is familiar with what is not, an indefensible assumption, "this is that." Indeed, even the basic unit of logic, the syllogism, is a consequence of sciential discontinuity that is spanned by troping: "The move from the major premise (All men are mortal) to the *choice* of the datum to serve as the minor (Socrates is a man) is itself a tropological move, a 'swerve' from the universal to the particular which logic cannot preside over, since it is logic itself that is being served by the move."[7] Considerations such as this lead Michel Foucault to conclude that all semiosis is finally just catachresis, just misuse, since there are no natural means of binding a signifier to any signified.[8] More generally, theories of discourse that illuminate the tropological essence of thought and communication suggest that an existential continuum blurs error into accuracy and invalidates the credulous use of absolutisms with regard to distinguishing fictive from factual.

Nowhere have such theories had more impact in contemporary thought than among professional historians, many of whom, largely as a result of the work of Hayden White, now acknowledge that "historical interpretation, like a poetic fiction, can be said to appeal to its reader as a plausible representation of the world by virtue of its implicit appeal to those 'pre-genetic plot-structures' . . . that define the modalities of a given culture's literary endowment."[9] White suggests that to qualify as "historical," an event must be "susceptible to at least two different narrations of its occurrence."[10] Historical narratives, therefore, are "verbal fictions, the contents of which are as much *invented* as *found*," essentially "extended metaphors" that fashion the events that they report according to "some form . . . familiar in . . . literary culture," admixtures of "established and referred facts," at once "a representation that is an interpretation and an interpretation that passes for an explanation of the whole process mirrored in the narrative," always manifested as the aftermath of "a contest between contending poetic figurations of what the past *might* consist of."[11] Thus, White declares that "we should no longer naively expect that statements about a given epoch or complex of events in the past 'correspond' to some preexistent body of 'raw facts.' For we should recognize that what constitutes the facts themselves is the problem that the historian, like the artist, has tried to solve in the choice of the metaphor by which he orders his world."[12]

The frequency with which White compares the writing of history to the fabrication of aesthetic structures is a consequence of his rigorous efforts to dissect historical narratives in an attempt to reveal the linguistic means whereby these narratives substitute another sign system for a supposedly extralinguistic referent that they pretend, with detached precision, merely to describe. White expertly combines his professional knowledge of historiography with modern analyses of the dynamics of language in a way that makes his theoretical work particularly illuminating when it is applied to texts contrived by artists who, like Yeats, repeatedly discuss both historical details and the all-encompassing temporal process that generates them.

In his book, *Metahistory: The Historical Imagination in Nineteenth-Century Europe*, White presents the following analysis of the act of historicizing:

> Before the historian can bring to bear upon the data of the historical field the conceptual apparatus he will use to represent and explain it, he must first *prefigure* the field—that is to say, constitute it as an object of mental perception. This poetic act is indistinguishable from the linguistic act in which the field is made ready for interpretation as a domain of a particular kind. That is to say, before a given domain can be interpreted, it must first be construed as a ground inhabited by discernible figures. The figures, in turn, must be conceived to be classifiable as distinctive orders, classes, genera, and species of phenomena. Moreover, they must be conceived to bear certain kinds of relationships to one another, the transformations of which will constitute the "problems" to be solved by the "explanations" provided on the levels of emplotment and argument in the narrative.[13]

In other words, White assumes that the historian's task is to "construct a linguistic protocol, complete with lexical, grammatical, syntactical, and semantic dimensions, by which to characterize the field and its elements *in his own terms* . . . and thus to prepare them for the explanation and representation he will subsequently offer to them in his narrative." Most pertinent to the problem of defining rhetorically a given poet's version of the historical process is White's contention that this "preconceptual linguistic protocol will . . . be—by virtue of its essen-

tially *prefigurative* nature—characterizable in terms of the dominant
tropological mode in which it is cast." Thus, "the theory of tropes provides . . . a basis for classifying the deep structural forms of historical
imagination in a given period." White defines the trope that dominates
nineteenth-century historicism as irony, and goes on to suggest that
this is a result of an "ambivalence concerning all the principal problems of . . . historiographical representation," owing to the fact that by
the end of the Enlightenment, men such as Gibbon, Hume, and Kant
had "dissolved the distinction between history and fiction on which
earlier thinkers . . . had based their historiographical enterprises."[14]

There is little need to rehearse the frequency with which critics
of Yeats assert that irony is characteristic both of his theoretical discussions of the oscillatory annulments of the historical process and of his
poetic portrayals of various narrators experiencing the consequences
of this process. Harold Bloom's comments are typical. He states that
"Yeats is too skilled an ironist to allow any poem the burden of [a] simple and drastic . . . dualism." Although Bloom feels that there is such
a constituent as "the irony of the Yeatsian dialectic," it is a "complex
irony" generated by "the poet" who "never expects to find anything but
endless cycle, the spinning of the Great Wheel by the Gnostic composite god of history, deity of a meaningless death . . . and an absurd
life."[15] Such a conception of irony is an invention of nineteenth-century
writers such as Friedrich Schlegel, who conceives of "the Observable
Irony of nature with man as victim" and therefore asserts, "It is equally
fatal for the mind to have a system and to have none."[16] This sort of
irony Schlegel terms the "amazement of the thinking spirit at itself,"
the "only entirely voluntary and nevertheless completely conscious dis-
simulation" that "incites a feeling of the insoluble conflict of the absolute and the relative, of the impossibility and the necessity of total
communication."[17] Unrelated to traditional *eironeia*, Schlegel's irony
suggests that "history is nothing more than the result of a temporality
which stems from the need of the individual to define 'what I was' in
order to rationalize 'what I am,'"[18] a temporality that in the nineteenth
century causes "philosophy . . . to reside in the gap between history and
History, between events and the Origin,"[19] and that Yeats similarly con-
strues as "a mathematical line drawn between hope and memory."[20]
Indeed, Yeats's adoption of an essentially Schlegelian irony is manifested repeatedly and can be illustrated by the way in which he cancels

all hope for authentically cumulative progress by means of references to an implicitly futile mortality: although "all realization is through opposites," and "the human mind" can contain "all that is significant in human history," to "die into the truth is still to die."[21]

It is noteworthy that when Yeats discusses history in the abstract, his interpretive remarks and rhetoric at times echo those of Jacob Burckhardt. Yeats observes approvingly that contemporary "men, for the first time since the seventeenth century, see the world as an object of contemplation, not as something to be remade," just as Burckhardt affirms "contemplation" to be "the right and duty of the historian; it is . . . our freedom in the very awareness of universal bondage."[22] Moreover, soon after having read Spengler's *Decline of the West*, Yeats enthusiastically announces that "there is no difference in our interpretation of history (an interpretation that had never occurred to anybody before) that is not accounted for by his great and my slight erudition."[23] All this is suggestive because Yeats's understanding apparently parallels that of Hayden White, who claims that Burckhardt's "view . . . was precisely the same as Spengler's, though arrived at by different means," and that both historians impose interpretively (thus constitutively) the trope of irony upon temporal process. According to White, "the effect of any genuinely Ironic conception of history [is a] de-reifying of language," an "attempt to lay bare the complexities obscured by premature or imperfect linguistic usage," a "creative denaming in the interests of moral ambiguity" that makes an *alazon* (victim of irony) of all men due to "a fatal asymmetry between the processes of reality and *any* verbal characterization of those processes."[24]

Yeats frequently indicates that he is aware of both the inevitably linguistic essence of human perception and of the consequently unstable and contradictory qualities thereby introduced into consciousness. History cannot transcend verbiage because "the world only exists to be a tale [for] coming generations," a tale that is largely incoherent, it seems, for even in the conceptual utopia of Byzantium, according to Yeats, "language had been the instrument of controversy."[25] Linguistic structures generate myth and thought, which, in turn, foster human culture. But Yeats declares, "All civilisation is held together by artificially created illusions"; thought is merely "trash and tinsel"; and myth is without empirical substantiation, consisting only of "statements our nature is compelled to make and employ as a truth though there cannot be sufficient evidence" and is therefore worthy of annulment because "a myth that cannot be . . . consumed becomes a spectre." Overall, however, "There is no improvement: only a series of sudden fires, each . . . as necessary as the one before it."[26]

Within this context, Yeats deprecatingly judges his own ontic syntheses to be just a "phantasmagoria in which I endeavour to explain my philosophy of life and death" (CP, 453). Even *A Vision* is merely "my lunar parable," "my dream," although he laments nevertheless the "destructiveness" of the semantic perversions that he witnesses in Ireland, and of the "mechanical logic and commonplace eloquence which give power to the most empty mind . . . crushing as with an iron roller all that is organic" and negating thereby vital mythic unity, as being "a most un-Celtic thing."[27] Yeats's acultural historical transformations are necessarily violations of linguistic coherence and are signalled, figuratively, by cacophony, "the irrational cry . . . the scream of Juno's peacock,"[28] and, literally, by absurdities such as those that occurred in 1916 when the commandant-general and president of the provisional government, Patrick Pearse, surrendered in the post office, the repository of failed words and thus the monument of futile causes.

Yeats perceives temporal process as being definitively ironic, and, moreover, by means of this rhetorical figure, he manifests skepticism about the adequacy of his own perceptions and definitions. As Hayden White describes historiography composed from this perspective, the "trope of Irony . . . provides a linguistic paradigm of a mode of thought which is radically self-critical with respect not only to a given characterization of the world of experience but also to the very effort to capture adequately the truth of things in language." This kind of irony is "metatropological, for it is deployed in the self-conscious awareness of the possible misuse of figurative language" and "points to the potential foolishness of all linguistic characterizations of reality."[29] This is the sort of irony that renders history incomprehensible and that Schlegel diagnoses in his essay "On Incomprehensibility" as being controllable only by "an irony that might be able to swallow up all these big and little ironies and leave no trace of them at all."[30] Large and small ironies for Yeats are results of the humanly unavoidable but intellectually indefensible "assertion of the eternity of what nature declares ephemeral."[31] These ironies can be contained only within poetic structures that mimic the historical process by generating a profoundly unstable tropology that, for instance, portrays a transcendent locale (in "News for the Delphic Oracle") that paradoxically only celebrates flux and generation and creates a figurative utopia like Byzantium, only later paradoxically to eliminate it completely from an historical panorama summarized by Yeats in this way: "Civilization rose to its high tide mark in Greece, fell, rose again in the Renaissance but not to the same level."[32]

The repetition of the word "paradoxically" in the previous sentence is meant to stress the way in which Yeats's figures of speech and thought, like words that have a double antithetical prefix (such as "para") call into existence seemingly opposed, paired concepts that nevertheless are not strictly self-negating semantically. As Yeats remarks, "I imagine everywhere the opposites" that are "no mere alternation between nothing and something . . . but true opposites, each living the other's death, dying the other's life."[33] Yeats's paradoxes are parasitic in the original positive sense of a parallel guest at dinner: the word "parasite" is derived from the Greek *parasitos*, denoting someone who shares another's grain (*para*, signifying proximity, and *sitos*, meaning grain).[34] Although Yeats uses the word "opposites," it is inadequate to denote his concept of temporality, every moment of which finally is blightingly unique, for "no disaster is like another,"[35] even though fugitive similarities may encourage phrases like "now as at all times" (*CP*, 124).

The extreme subtlety of Yeats's unstable tropes of thought eludes semantic frontal assault and is best approached indirectly. Note how Yeats himself contrives to undo even one of his favorite phrases: at one time he observes "all things dying each other's life, living each other's death," while at another time he detects "each 'living the other's life, dying the other's death'."[36] Such rhetorical shifts, suggesting but not confirming simple inversion, constitute what for Yeats is the basis of the pervasively ironic sort of historiography that, as Hayden White puts it, "delights in exposing the paradoxes contained in every attempt to capture experience in language" and "tends to dispose the fruits of consciousness in aphorisms, apothegms, gnomic utterances which turn back upon themselves and dissolve their own apparent truth and adequacy."[37] Or, to express it in terms of the intellectual anarchy that Yeats ponders at the close of *A Vision*, "How work out . . . the gradual coming and increase of the counter movement, the *antithetical* multiform influx."[38]

Narrative such as this, laced with the trope of irony, subverts stable patterns of response, being "consonant with the interest of . . . historians who perceive behind . . . the welter of events . . . an ongoing structure of relationships or an eternal return of the Same in the Different."[39] For Yeats, "the Same" seems to be a nearly repetitive temporal process that ensures only that "there is no improvement," no matter how much specific turmoil may be generated by "the Different," as "every historical phase has its victims, poisoned rats."[40] Tranquility at the level of the individual may be accomplished by voluntarily acting out the metaphor of predation that is definitive of temporality. A self-consumptive unity can be sought by offering oneself "to his own soul as Buddha offered himself to the famished tiger," since "life exists merely through willing and joyous or unwilling and mournful sacrifice of life," and "all life has the same root."[41]

Try as he may, Yeats finds it impossible to reconcile the "joyous" and the "mournful." He can intellectualize and structure the historical process into an exquisite and inevitable geometry that explains and even justifies specific change, its constituents nested "one inside another, each complete in itself, like those perforated Chinese ivory balls" and graphically reduced like the "diagrams in Law's *Boehme*, where one lifts a flap of paper to discover both the human entrails and the starry heavens." But finally, this perception is merely a series of similitudes, "stylistic arrangements of experience comparable to the cubes in the drawing of Wyndham Lewis," a "flap of paper" indeed. Yeats knows that his patterned cosmic comforts are probably nonexistent, "for . . . things return, but not wholly, for no two faces are alike."[42] This knowledge displaces joy with mourning, darkens universal comedy with personal pain and regret, and leads both to an assertion that "we begin to live when we have conceived life as a tragedy" and to a declaration that "I find my peace by pitting my whole nature against something."[43]

Yeats's essentially ironic destablization of language in much of his work is partly a consequence of a radical clash between two quite different perceptions of the historical process. When Yeats contemplates great temporal sequences, he can fabricate aesthetic analogies that permit him an intellectual accommodation to the certain prospect of personal and cultural annihilation. As a result, he can conceive of macrocosmic flux largely as a comedy, offering, like the literary genre, the festive potential for "occasional reconciliations of the forces at play in the social and natural worlds." But Yeats seldom seems to be emotionally at ease with his gyres and circles, nor with the cyclic patterns of time that they inscribe and describe, for the very trajectories that figure forth superhuman principles of order also denote tragic futility to an individual, and in tragedy "there are no festive occasions, except false or illusory ones."[44] Thus, Yeats is disoriented and dismayed by specific events of contemporary history, in spite of his repeated affirmations of general and inclusive celestial tidiness. For instance, he defines the Easter 1916 uprising as the "Dublin tragedy" and laments, "I am very despondent about the future. At the moment I feel that all the work of years has been overturned."[45] That is, Yeats's radically varying comic and tragic expositions of temporality derive from different perspectives taken toward strife. A tragic perspective is generated by an agent who contemplates the conclusion of an action that was performed with a definite design and within the context of a world that collides with and frustrates his desire and annuls his effort, whereas a comic viewpoint is fabricated by an agent who regards such a collision from a resolvent position located in time beyond the experience of annulment that embroils and probably consumes the tragic actor.

The intellectual and emotional stress resulting from the clash of these perspectives is manifested by Yeats as tropological inconsistency. He cannot decide, in effect, whether as temporal emergents "we may . . . push ourselves up, being ourselves the tide," or whether "these things are fated" and "we may be pushed up."[46] At most, he seems to conceptualize existential ferment merely as an exploding, fecund linearity as his "intellect" struggles to "synthesize in vain, drawing with its compass-point a line that shall but represent the outline of a bursting pod." Indeed, Yeats even summarizes such struggles: "I have sat in my chair turning a symbol over in my mind, exploring all its details, defining and again defining its elements, testing my convictions and those of others by its unity, attempting to substitute particulars for an abstraction like that of algebra. . . . But nothing comes—though this moment was to reward me for all my toil."[47]

A useful, if perhaps simplistic, way to highlight Yeats's ultimately unrewarding skirmishes with tropes is to note the relatively crisp vocabulary that he characteristically uses in the titles of poems that elucidate the private lives of narrators who often are the means whereby the author's most intimate and compelling anxieties and (usually compromised) aspirations are dramatized and contemplated. These titles often consist of distinct common nouns or place names, "the minute particulars of mankind" (CP, 168), and suggest that Yeats's personal experience of life emplotted as a tragedy at least provides him with a focus for his rhetorical figures, however intense his sardonic despair may be at the lachrymose spectacle of the erosion of all that he loves and is. Such titles can be contrasted with the equivocal, even conceptually paralyzing, titles of poems in which Yeats seeks to articulate (and thereby reveal) comprehensive but evanescent processes of historical change. The vaguery of designations such as "Easter, 1916," "Meditations in Time of Civil War," or "Nineteen Hundred and Nineteen" is symptomatic of the radically fluctuating tropologies that both define these works internally and display Yeats's own intellectual turmoil as he tries to emplot, as agents of ultimately comic transmutations, the macrocosmic forces that ensure his seemingly tragic destruction. This issue can be approached by contrasting the manner in which human existence is figuratively expressed in the quite private acknowledgment of "tragic buskin," in the poem "Coole Park and Ballylee, 1931" (CP, 239–40), with the tropological obfuscation of the same concept, "the living stream" (CP, 179), and in poems such as "Easter, 1916" and "Meditations in Time of Civil War"—works that endeavor to talk about "life" within the framework of the universal comedy of inevitable and disconcerting cultural change.

In "Coole Park and Ballylee, 1931," Yeats's narrator is tensely situated in a physically and psychologically detached location within the confines of the ancient tower at Ballylee. Below him he sees rushing water that leads his meditation geographically on a declining flow to the environs of Coole Park and figuratively on a descent to the unpleasant subjects of individual and cultural decrepitude. His tension is a negative consequence of his initial choice of metaphor for the human psyche: when the traditional Neoplatonic watery figure for the soul steeped in the imperfect realm of generation is connected to the structural facts of the surrounding landscape, a linear concept condenses that carries the soul through a series of horizontal and vertical vicissitudes to a lake, and onward to an implicitly terminal and annihilatory "drop into a hole." The narrator's despondent reaction to his own metaphor causes him in the second stanza to regard the winter season and the leafless trees that border the lake as externalizations of his gloom: "For Nature's pulled her tragic buskin on / And all the rant's a mirror of my mood." The word "for" signifies causality, at once defining the explaining the chill and unadorned landscape as being the result of an hypostatized feminine "nature" having adopted a "tragic" costume and thereby having reflected his melancholy. This judgmental response to the wintery landscape is related in the present tense. It thus exists as part of the narrator's current state of awareness and contrasts with the remainder of stanza two, which consists of a description of a moment in the past when he stood hidden amidst a "copse" of (presumably leafed) "beeches" and was surprised by the sound of a flock of swans ascending in "sudden thunder" from the lake.

This recollection transforms the narrator's mood. The white color of the swans and their ascending motion directly counter the hue and trajectory of the figurative soul-stream of stanza one, "darkening through 'dark'" to "drop / Run underground," briefly "rise," only finally to "drop into a hole." In response to this memory, he quickly abandons the figure of the stream in order to create a new trope for the soul—the swans' "stormy white" that "seems a concentration of the sky" and that "like the soul . . . sails into the sight / And in the morning's gone, no man knows why." This innovation replaces the depressing, horizontal, linear inevitability of the dark, passive, and merely elemental watercourse with the white swans' flight—an aesthetic analogy that possesses eidetic color and a living will that permit it conceptually to transcend the terminal descent of the darkling current and connote an experience of beauty sufficiently extreme and "pure" both to correct postlapsarian deficiency and deformity (being "so lovely that it sets to right / What knowledge or its lack had set awry") and reduce formerly dangerous blackness to a mere child's mistaken perception and a contrary-to-fact verb ("a child might think / It can be murdered with a spot of ink").

The narrator clearly experiences a certain solace as a result of his modified trope. Although words connotative of horizontality, decline, and death are still present in his meditation, they now seem to have little emotional impact: the "sound of a stick" signaling Lady Gregory's halting steps echoes the prior mention of a foundering forest, "dry sticks under a wintry sun" and the swans' white only "might" be "murdered" by child's play. The simile joining the concepts "soul" and "swan" seems to overwhelm the earlier metaphoric assertion that "water" *is* the "generated soul," which assertion was qualified severely even as it was made by being cast in the tentative form of a rhetorical question. The soul's watercourse, running out of darkness into dark, survives to penetrate the artistic subjects that define the middle of the poem (stanzas three and four) only in the form of an indirect reference to a line by Lady Gregory describing the stream that connects Yeats's property with her estate: "Its transit is as has been said of human life 'from a mystery through a mystery to a mystery.'"[48] This line, thoroughly revised, becomes a way of stating the negative qualities that are not to be found in the "great rooms" of Coole, "where none" amidst the aesthetic continuities of redemptive "old marble heads, old pictures," ever "out of folly into folly came."

But that was years ago, and a past tense in this happy context is painful to acknowledge. For in this poem it repeals with finality both inclusive absolutisms like "every" or "none" or first-person plural verbs ("we were the last romantics"), as well as the authentic aristocracy that was defined by an acuity of perception that made possible entire categories of human experience, such as "content" and "joy" and "ambition satisfied." Indeed, as "Coole Park and Ballylee, 1931" draws to a close, the narrator is forced to connect the pronoun "we" with the uncongenial physical and intellectual concept of nomadic, horizontal randomness (antithesis of landed traditions and upward continuities), admitting that in the odious present "we shift about . . . / Like some poor Arab tribesman and his tent," and thus sadly lack beneficent absolutes ("whatever most can bless") and redemptive aesthetic qualities ("traditional sanctity and loveliness").

This absence is figured forth in the poem by means of the word "but," establishing a conceptual discontinuity and illustrating a hard consequence of the fact that, truly, "all is changed." In regretful recognition of this fact, the narrator once more revises his figures. He now isolates the concepts of aesthetics and vertical movement (flight) completely from the unacceptable metamorphosis of the phenomenal world and identifies them safely with a winged phantom, Pegasus, the mythic emblem of artistic inspiration and talent, while leaving the former host of these concepts (the flock of swans) to dwindle into a singular noun and languish perilously without volition, dominated by dim horizontal flow, as "that high horse," now "riderless," disdainfully wings above the mundane diminishment located "where the swan drifts upon a darkening flood." Although earlier in the poem the narrator seems to have innovated the vehicle for a simile (the beauty of the swans' whiteness and vertical ascent) that promises partially to emancipate him from depressing contemplation of mere mortality, this simile, with its dominant aesthetic component, eventually leads him to reflect upon precisely those exquisitely crafted, aristocratic qualities in human civilization that he treasures and that are rapidly vanishing, thus making a confrontation with an overwhelming mortality even more emphatic. As demonstrated, this problem proves to be insurmountable, illuminating an essential constituent of this poem: a dramatization of the ultimate futility of efforts to elude tropologically a blighting consciousness of fatal flux. That is, the tragic emplotment of temporality on the microcosmic level generates a certain anguish, which in "Coole Park and Ballylee, 1931" Yeats articulates as a series of displacements: one rhetorical figure follows another during the narrator's efforts to communicate as he tries ineffectually to avoid conscious encounters with the very tragedy implicit in the preconceptual demarcation of his topic that is effected by the first of these figures. The narrator's initial identification of the human soul with the plummeting, abyssal current is a metaphor created by means of the verb "to be." His later abandonment of this figure in order to concoct an evasive elaboration leads him to fashion a simile: "That stormy white / . . . like the soul." Thus, his efforts to elude depressing implications of mortality are negated by the way in which he begins his utterance because a similitude typically indicates a relatively superficial, only partial joining of different ideas, whereas a metaphor denotes a fundamental merging at the level of essences. Just as the narrator's simile cannot undo the metaphor that at once initiates the poem and defines important aspects of his personality, so his precipitous concluding allusion to a winged mythological beast, "that high horse," Pegasus, is also powerless to annul this initiation, for it is in effect the mere citation of a metaphoric vehicle devoid of a tenor, as if such a strategically disabled trope might airily escape all mundane frailties.

Although in "Coole Park and Ballylee, 1931" the narrator uses a variety of tropes during his utterance Yeats exercises purposeful manipulative control over these variations and uses them to exemplify one man's melancholy reaction to the compelling, if vexing, facts of decline and death. A certain degree of tropological destabilization is evident, but its parameters develop sequentially and function as a means of rather precise characterization: reactions to a conception of existence as clad in "tragic buskin" are manifested as the narrator's quest for adequate figures of speech. Quite different tropological instabilities are typically present in poems that address macrocosmic historical issues.

Consider the metaphor of "the living stream," which appears in "Easter, 1916" (CP, 177–80), a figure that seems at first almost to duplicate that of the soul's torrent in "Coole Park and Ballylee, 1931" because both works use the idea of life-as-a-stream to profile the anxiety engendered by the terrors of time within the mind of a thoughtful and troubled, if feckless, narrator. However, in "Easter, 1916," the speaker seeks to accomplish a compensatory, perhaps even redemptive, orientation toward public slaughter and futility of collective effort within the framework of an all-encompassing, profoundly comic temporality, and the linguistic consequences of this effort make apparent the sort of dubious and catachrestic space that Yeats seems to inhabit mentally whenever he tries to forge such an orientation.

The narrator's task in "Easter, 1916" is straightforward. He wants to come to terms intellectually with the deaths by execution of fifteen leaders of the Irish Volunteers of the Irish Republican Brotherhood, and to do so he apparently must satisfy himself that the executions have lasting, perhaps transcendent, significance. His strategy superficially recalls that of the speaker in "Coole Park and Ballylee, 1931": he struggles to supplant the vocabulary of purposeless mortal catastrophe with the oracular rhetoric of aesthetic perpetuity, to replace a metaphor denoting terminal linearity ("the living stream") with a comforting simile suggesting poetic commemoration and domestic nurture ("name / As a mother names her child"). But the effort degenerates into a schizophrenic stutter of conflicting rhetorical questions, intermingling first and third person singular and plural points of view as figurative language grows insurgent and opaque.

The narrator begins his statement by describing judgmentally his recent life of superficial social interaction with its degenerate verbiage, its "meaningless words"—symptoms of an inauthentic, trivial comedy "where motley is worn," consisting of a "mocking tale or gibe / To please a companion / Around the fire at the club." He proceeds to enumerate the similarly unappealing earlier lives of several of the victims, reiterating his evaluative responses and affirming that his "song" is about men and women who (like he in his more modest way) have just abandoned "the casual comedy." He then makes it clear that his own recent enlightenment is due to the way in which the violent deaths of these people "transformed utterly" his understanding of the significance of their existences.

However, the basis of the narrator's judgments is not yet well defined, and in fact seems to lack consistency, for he condemns both his own earlier placid indulgence in trivial and secure social convention as well as the victims' brash and audacious, if shrill and distorted, lives. In an effort to provide such a definition, he offers the metaphoric specification of authenticity that occupies the third stanza, the intellectual crux of the poem. Here, all phenomena moving through time are compared to the flow of a linear watercourse, and a constant, visible transmutation is identified as the index of authentic existence. This transmutation establishes a principle that unifies all things, both organic and inorganic, because, for example, the "birds that range / From cloud to tumbling cloud, / Minute by minute they change," even as the "shadow of cloud on the stream / Changes minute by minute."

Whatever resists change is compared to "a stone / To trouble the living stream." Of course, a rock is as subject to temporal transformations as are animals and cloud shadows. But for the purposes of this trope, the fact that the changes in the rock are not at all conspicuous seems to be the basis for the narrator's use of a lapidary metaphor to signify an unacceptable resistance of mutability that is futile anyway because statically obsessed "hearts with one purpose" are only apparently exempt; they only "seem / Enchanted to a stone." Parallels of vocabulary and syntax virtually prove that in the narrator's mind rapid and salient change equals legitimate life: "Minute by minute they change" determines that "minute by minute they live." Furthermore, the repeated use of the word "change" elsewhere in the poem indicates the reason for the narrator's awed approbation of the recent victims. Sudden death makes starkly visible the normally subtle, yet definitive, cosmic principle of mutability. Through shocking precipitance, an event takes on transpersonal significance and becomes an aesthetically poised beacon, revelatory and paradigmatic. Finally, as if to lend a quality of absolute validity to this idea, the speaker eradicates all evidence of personal narrative perspective from the third stanza, using no pronouns that might suggest the operation of a fallible perceiver's opinion and thus qualify the import of this metaphoric definition of existential legitimacy.

But the poem does in fact feature a perceiver. And he fallibly fashions a metaphor valorizing raw mutability ("the living stream"), even as he uses an analogy connotative of aesthetic timelessness ("beauty") to designate the events and moments whereby this principle of change is disclosed. This potentially incoherent perspective is at best difficult to sustain, as is denoted by the immediate detonation of the poem into a series of four rhetorical questions. These disjunctive interrogations, in turn, frame a brief, spasmodic attempt by the narrator to confront the corrosive fact of death in a way that might be consistent with his repeated suggestion that fatal temporality can be emplotted as a profoundly comic process. He asserts that those who survive the political executions should now play a "part" that annuls any "part" played earlier in the "casual comedy," solemnly commemorate the dead verbally ("utterly," indeed?), and "murmur name upon name, / As a mother names her child / When sleep at last has come / On limbs that had run wild."

The development of the narrator's tropes in "Easter, 1916" strikingly resembles the speaker's creation of a sequence of rhetorical figures in "Coole Park and Ballylee, 1931." In both poems, a contemplative toil is dramatized with conceptual alternatives as a persona tries to reconcile destructive temporality with a desire for continuity. And in both works, a metaphor is used to express the fact of lethal flux, while a simile is employed to articulate a more appealing conceit that might correctively and comfortingly displace the hostility of the initial metaphor. But the resemblance stops here. In "Coole Park and Ballylee, 1931," the speaker's fabrication of tropes is pursued with control and determination and is accomplished consciously, even discussed openly—e.g., "Another emblem there!" (CP, 239)—as he works to assimilate a personal and "tragic" (CP, 239) sense of time. In "Easter, 1916," the narrator grapples in vain with the recalcitrant facts of mass executions and futile effort as he tries to formulate a conciliatory sense of history. His tropes become incoherent, manifesting the frustration and disorientation that the discontinuities of his rhetorical questions and reflexive negations acknowledge. Note how the similitude of a doting mother muttering the name of her somnolent child, by means of which the narrator defines analogically the redemptive aesthetic function of commemorative verse, is immediately followed by a subversive doubt as to the adequacy of this simile: "To murmur . . . / As a mother names her child / When sleep at last has come / On limbs that had run

wild. / What is it but nightfall?" As if this were not sufficiently disruptive, the narrator then answers his own question and denies the trope
that he has just produced: "No, no, not night but death." Still, death,
though disconcerting, may nevertheless be incorporated within an ultimately purposeful, resolvent, profoundly comic structure of history —
a perspective that has been present in much of the poem all along.
However, the next line directly challenges even this assumption, asking, "Was it needless death after all?"

Hereafter, confusion increases, peaking when the narrator asks,
"And what if excess of love / Bewildered them till they died?" For when
he utters his "what if?" query, he in effect suggests that the narrowly
extremist lives of the victims, which in stanza two he condemns specifically by means of the evaluative context that he articulates figuratively
in stanza three, are not to be condemned at all. This seemingly incon-
sequential question, in fact, subverts the judgmental logic of the entire
poem as stated in the third stanza, where, by means of the trope of
life-as-a-stream, the flow of rapid change is authenticated and petrific
obsession, having "one purpose alone," is denigrated. Small wonder,
then, that the narrator proceeds to drop this issue altogether. After
having denied the very foundation of his soliloquy, he leaps irration-
ally to the subject of his role as composer of memorializing "verse" and
affirms that the simple gesture of creating such verse is sufficient to
cancel the sort of questions that he himself just raised. And had his
questions not rendered the content of his verse discontinuous, even
incoherent, perhaps his willful affirmation might suffice. But his poem
is internally self-negating and can scarcely compensate by means of
the simple fact of its existence for the conceptual disarray that defines
the narrator's final perspective toward both historical process and the
significance of individual and cultural dissolution within the context
of that process. Conceived in a certain way, the events of this deadly
Eastertide perhaps may indeed give birth teleologically to a terrific
"beauty," although, owing to the cumulative tropological and logical
collapse of the statement wherein this assertion is made, the legitimacy
of the delivery is discredited.

In marked contrast to the proper nouns naming precise geographi-
cal locations, and to the controlled, private, "tragic" narration of "Coole
Park and Ballylee, 1931," the vagueness of a title like "Easter, 1916" only
anticipates the cognitive murk of the poem itself, with its travail to

engender by aesthetic means a compensatory teleology. It is possible to comment theoretically upon Yeats's poems that are contrived as responses to indefinite, inclusive years (or moments) in public history. Although the rhetorical figure, "the living stream," that dominates stanza three of "Easter, 1916" can loosely be called metaphor, it more precisely should be termed metonymy (or "name change"), and, accordingly, its function can be specified in this way: various observations are made by the narrator of phenomena whose physical attributes are impermanent (from cloud shadows that move to people who are shot and die); the narrator then abstracts from these observations the general concept "change," treating the specific instances of impermanence as if they were manifestations of a universal principle of mutability lurking behind these instances and functioning as their noumenal cause. This tropological move can be strongly criticized as being the merely linguistic source of all manner of illusory, transcendent agents. Nietzsche expresses such criticism:

> popular superstition [for example] divorces the lightning from its brilliance, viewing the latter as an activity whose subject is the lightning. . . . But no such agent exists; there is no "being" behind the doing, acting, becoming; the "doer" has simply been added t ɔ the deed by the imagination—the doing is everything. The common man actually doubles the doing by making the lightning flash; he states the same event once as cause and then again as effect. The natural scientists are no better when they say that "energy *moves*," "energy *causes*." For all its detachment and freedom from emotion, our science is still the dupe of linguistic habits; it has never yet got rid of those changelings called "subjects."[49]

One way to approach the paralogisms and discontinuities in Yeats's poems that portray a perplexed narrator (who contemplates public events and strives to create and sustain a vision of compensatory order in historical flux) is to understand that, as Hayden White suggests, a metonymic representation of temporality is not a suitable figure whereby to express teleological intimations: "metonymizing of the world, . . . preliminary encoding . . . in terms of merely contiguous relationships," guarantees "the removal of . . . teleology from phenomena which every *modern* science seeks to effect."[50]

The disorienting stress that Yeats causes his narrators to experience in such occasional poems as "Easter, 1916" is a destructively inten-sified dimension of the opposition that he himself encounters whenever he recalls his own disjunctive definitions of existence—e.g., "life exists . . . through willing and joyous or unwilling and mournful sacrifice of life"[51]—since what may be "joyous" and purposeful at the collective, macrocosmic level tends to be "mournful" and drearily metonymic on the personal, microcosmic plane. Yeats can cope inclusively, if not re-solvently, with this clash by composing a variety of separate works that project various, even mutually negating, responses to human experi-ence. But the occasional poems often feature a narrator who, confined to the uninviting exclusiveness of a single utterance, only succeeds in generating a maze of recalcitrant, even irreconcilable, concepts and rhetorical figures. It is just such a maze that White explores theoreti-cally with the observation that "dialectical tension" in historiography "usually arises from an effort to wed a mode of emplotment [in·this case, teleological or profoundly comic] with a mode of argument [in this case, mechanistic or metonymic] . . . inconsonant with it."[52] More-over, this sort of tension may indeed be unavoidable, "because history has no stipulatable subject matter uniquely its own; it is always writ-ten as part of a contest between contending poetic figurations of what the past *might* consist of."[53] And a typical consequence of a metonymic figuration of temporality is the kind of inclusive and destabilizing irony that characterizes Yeats's work, for, as White notes, such "irony is the linguistic strategy underlying and sanctioning skepticism as an explana-tory tactic . . . and either agnosticism or cynicism as a moral posture,"[54] and whoever "approaches history as a field of cause-effect [or metonymic] relationships is driven, by the logic of the linguistic operation itself, to the comprehension of that field in Ironic terms."[55]

Still, further elaboration is called for. To conceive of circumstances as "tragic," as does the narrator in "Coole Park and Ballylee, 1931," is to conceive of the spectacle of personal experiences and of one's own life as possessing closure, and to indulge in the luxury of a fantasy of termination, a "drop into a hole" (CP, 239). But one can also mediate in time of civil war, so to speak—define and contemplate a configura-tion of events as being part of an ongoing process of ruthless mutabil-ity that is bewildering in its details but, when understood generally and with detachment, is productive of "abstract joy" (CP, 204). In the latter instance, events are made to function as devices of transition, not as signs of termination, and can be emplotted in a way that conflicts with a tragic sensibility. The characterological and tropological instabilities that appear in Yeats's poems portraying various meditations in this or that time are a result of the fluctuating purposes served by the events as parts of the narrowly serial, broadly cyclical emplotments of history implicit in these works. Hayden White addresses this issue directly:

> it is a fiction of the historian that the various states of affairs which he constitutes as the beginning, the middle, and the end of a course of development are all "actual" or "real" and that he has merely recorded "what happened" in the transition from the inaugural to the terminal phase. But both the beginning state of affairs and the ending one are inevitably poetic constructions, and as such, dependent upon the modality of the figurative language used to give them the aspect of coherence. This implies that all narrative is not simply a recording of "what happened" in the transition from one state of affairs to another, but a progressive *redescription* of sets of events in such a way as to dismantle a structure encoded in one verbal mode in the beginning so as to justify a recoding of it in another mode at the end. This is what the "middle" of all narratives consists of.[56]

Yeats's poems that articulate meditations-in-progress about temporal transmutations-in-progress are virtual dilations of the "middle," of that liminal dimension of language and experience that is augured by conjunction, by what Aristotle condemns as a *phone asemos* and that Jacques Derrida calls "everything that operates *between* significant members" and therefore "has no sense because it does not refer to an independent unit, a substance or a being." Such intervals "can no longer be included within philosophical (binary) opposition, but . . . inhabit philosophical opposition, resisting and disorganizing it, *without ever* constituting a third term, without ever leaving room for a solution in the form of speculative dialectics."[57]

If, in fact, "the multiplication of levels of signification" suggests the existence of "a discourse in crisis"—in this case the "analytico-referential" discourse that emerged during the seventeenth century and that still is a threadbare cincture of twentieth-century semantics—then Yeats's apparently deliberate subversions of characterological and tropological coherences in his meditations-in-progress-on-process quite possibly reflect the crises that become acute in Western epistemology at the time of Yeats's writing. During these years, Werner Heisenberg and Neils Bohr explore the "philosophical and scientific consequences of the input of the experimental instrument of knowledge into the observation, experiment, and knowledge it made possible"; such research bears "marks of a discourse at its limits."[58] More specifically, Gaston Bachelard asserts that intellectual development in the early twentieth century—e.g., quantum mechanics and the associated principles of uncertainty and complementarity—makes conventional philosophical disquisition obsolete and requires a radically different form of logic that is itself emancipated from the precepts of the excluded middle and noncontradiction that constitute the substrata of Aristotelian thought. Bachelard recommends the development of "dialectical surrationalism," a tripartite structure that would create a formal provision for the fugitive revelations of the "middle," the conjunction, the Derridean "third term," by supplementing the traditional binary absolutes "false" and "true" with an equally legitimate class of "absurd."[59]

Aristotle insists that absurdity, the *alogon*, be avoided in discourse. Yet the word "discourse" is itself derived etymologically from the concept "to run back and forth" and thus evokes that untrustworthy conjunctive interval that disturbs post-Baconian analytico-referential modes of communication.[60] And there are few more dramatic examples of "running back and forth" in modern literature than Yeats's historical meditations, for, in spite of deceptively informative titles that supposedly identify the time and topic of each process of rumination, there usually exists little or no internal evidence whereby a reader might confirm such an identification; and the destabilized points of view and rhetorical figures effectively frustrate the applications of traditional logic whereby any incisive conception might be formed either of the meditator or of the figures that constitute and emplot the subjects of his scrutiny. Just as titles such as "Easter, 1916," "Meditations in Time of Civil War," or "Nineteen Hundred and Nineteen" offer at the outset a promise of specific detail that is immediately betrayed once the poems begin, so the neat numerical ordering of the interiors of the latter two poems implies that some kind of structural clarity and rigidity exists that determine the sequential development of the narrators' utterances, when actually few, if any, conventional devices signaling continuity can be found. Even the permissive unifying principle of analogy is eroded by the sheer randomness and heterogeneity of the topical proceedings of such poems, so that the term "anasemic" has been used to denote the manner in which these statements evolve according to "an ana-analogy of elements that do not really belong together in the same space."[61]

Perhaps, indeed, "some unfamiliar kind of discursive class" is emerging here and is challenging such conventions as the "discrete denotated objects of knowledge, analytical knowledge . . . , discursive transparency, objective grasp," and even 'the subject',"[62] since, as Morse Peckham notes, the "aim of Romantic and modern historiography has been to dissolve the regnant constructs not merely of the past but far more important the ideologies which these constructs exemplified."[63] Yeats's own appeal to concepts such as tradition and the device of a first-person narrator are every bit as misleading as his poetic imposition externally of dated titles and internally of ordinal numbers, for even as he discusses these concepts, he obfuscates them: "I must choose a traditional stanza, even what I alter must seem traditional. . . . Talk to me of originality and I will turn on you with rage. I am a crowd, I am a lonely man, I am nothing."[64]

And an "embrace of nothing" (CP, 203) is what the tenuous cohesions of "Meditations in Time of Civil War" seem to dramatize, as once again a narrator wrestles with his own recalcitrant figurations of the concept "life" within an utterance whose content anticipates wholesale ruination even as it attempts to show that a proper grasp of the indifferent processes that induce cultural and individual annihilation can be a (presumably compensatory) source of "abstract joy" (CP, 204).

In closing, consider, for the sake of brevity, only a part of section I of this very complex poem. A speaker contemplates in quite general terms a version of civilization that he assumes is vanishing. But he is not even able to affirm with consistency or confidence that such a culture ever in fact existed, and he therefore begins his statement with the now-familiar schizoid stammer about definitive terms that is the signature of a Yeatsian historiographic meditator. His initiating concept, describing a certain kind of civilization, may indeed be "mere dreams," although this sudden qualification is itself immediately annulled by an appeal to a mythic author (Homer), the certitude of whose ancient mental contents the narrator assumes he can confirm and then proceed to use in order to eradicate the doubts that he has just expressed regarding the validity of his own conceptual overture: "Mere dreams, mere dreams! Yet Homer had not sung / Had he not found it certain beyond dreams." As in his other poems of this sort, Yeats causes his narrator to concoct a strategy whereby he seeks to encyst his depressing thoughts of obliteration within a resolvent context composed of aesthetic analogies that connote poise and value in defiance of temporal flux. Thus, he invokes both Homeric certainties and "ancestral houses" rigorously embellished with "levelled lawns," "gravelled ways," "escutcheoned doors," and "polished floors," as though an argument might be constructed from a mere list. Moreover, the items mentioned in the list constitute at last just a series of rhetorical questions because their nominations are bracketed by no less than four repetitions of the anxious phrase "what if?" A daunting syntactic problem looms as a result of this magnified self-doubt: it is difficult to determine whether or not these aesthetic attainments, figuring forth comforting continuity, are as thoroughly impugned by the framing rhetoric of dubiety as was the narrator's initial description of abundant cultural "life." And this conceptual stalemate threatens to preclude any discursive progress. However, its effect can be reduced by noting that, uniquely, the allusion to what Homer "found . . . certain beyond dreams" does not in fact appear inside a compromising grammatical structure. Although the "now" of the poem, the time at which the speaker formulates his utterance, offers a spectacle suggesting that even inclusive principles of historical continuity are interrupted, the statement that cites this spectacle depends upon a contrary-to-fact verb, and therefore (perhaps) "now it" (only) "seems as if" cosmic discontinuities hold sway.

In any case, characterological discontinuities surely reign supreme. This observation by Morse Peckham illuminates them: "Even when the . . . personality shows a high degree of discontinuity in the course of a work, the decisions about what discontinuities to present are ideologically controlled."[65] As indicated earlier, a controlling idea in much of Yeats's writing is a post-Schlegelian irony, defined by Hayden White as a "metatropological" device "deployed in the self-conscious awareness of the possible misuse of figurative language,"[66] and derived from a basically metonymic portrayal of temporality that is harried by the understanding that alternative and contradictory linguistic protocols can be employed with equal legitimacy to constitute an object of discourse, which object might be figured forth in terms of a tragedy of linear termination or a comedy of cyclical renewal. Within this context, note how at the outset of his meditations in time of civil war, the harried narrator fruitlessly manipulates the tropological gist of his concept "life." Like the persona of "Easter, 1916," he generates an essentially metonymic and evaluative figuration of existence: he assumes that the phenomena of aristocratic (i.e., the most esteemed) vitality are manifestations of a noumenal agent of causality, which he calls "life," and which apparently has its own remote origins, for the analogy he employs to express this agent in tangible terms is that of a lavish fountain. (Yeats's derivation of this analogy from Coleridge's "Kubla Khan" seems obvious.) Thus, on an exemplary aristocratic estate, the accoutrements of "flowering lawns" and "planted hills" are instances of the bountiful way hereabouts "life overflows . . . / And rains down life until the basin spills, / And mounts more dizzy high the more it rains." But if indeed an eternal and aqueous principle of causation exists, its timelessness is severely compromised when it is described by means of a rhetorical device that necessarily includes the notion of a linear trajectory. The causal (even mechanistic) sequence implied by metonymic relationships is inconsistent with the synchronic poise of this watery principle's refusal to "stoop to a mechanical / . . . shape." In "Kubla Khan," Coleridge uses the figure of terminal oblivion, a "sunless sea," to resolve such problems at least partially. In the present case, though, the semantic clashes in this passage persist and are embodied in the surpassing inanity of the narrator's defining assertion that "life overflows . . . / And rains down life." They dictate both that a static, concave vessel ("the basin"), which normally does not possess vectored qualities, here must flow ("spills"), and that a placid marine object (the "sea-shell") be "flung" from an inland body of water that does not contain such objects, from "out . . . the obscure dark of the rich streams." Difficulties like these probably are important, signalling the "profound disruption of the logic of narrative by narratives staging their rhetorical power, displaying causality as a trope, [which] entails the disqualification of basic terms like *event* and *structure*, or *form* and *substance*, to evoke the disjunction at work."[67]

It is possible, then, that texts such as Yeats's meditations-in-time require techniques of reading that are only now being developed. It is a challenge to the fundamental structures of human perception to apply language and binary logic as tools of analysis and comprehension to modes of discourse that are designed to subvert just these tools.

Whatever the reasons, it seems that poems like "Easter, 1916" and "Meditations in Time of Civil War" do not even try to make conventionally coherent statements. Perhaps Yeats is demonstrating, by means of his narrators' semiotic drifting, the very limits of conceptualization that must as yet elude direct description, and he thereby illustrates Peckham's acute conjecture that recent literature is "marked by exemplifications for which there [is] no existent explanation."[68] Like his narrators, Yeats, of course, spends much of his own life contending with irreconcilable tropes of thought. He at last seems to be suggesting that decisions to conceive of temporal flux as "mournful" or "joyous," tragic or comic, are never final or concordant, and thus are only to be made ironically, as analogues of the fishy sort of historiography that Saint Joseph innovated when he at once fathered the Age of Pisces and, inhabiting an unspeakable interval, discovered "he liked the way his finger smelt" (CP, 329). And it is likely that the semantics of Yeats's (perhaps transcendent, surely generative) piscatorial conjunctions will be inconceivably aromatic for some time to come.

## NOTES

1. W. B. Yeats, *Letters on Poetry to Dorothy Wellesley* (London and New York: Oxford Univ. Press, 1940), 149.

2. W. B. Yeats, *The Collected Plays of W. B. Yeats* (London: Macmillan, 1953), 301; Yeats, *The Autobiography of William Butler Yeats* (New York: Macmillan, 1953), 292; Yeats, *Explorations* (New York: Macmillan, 1962), 397; W. B. Yeats, *The Letters of W. B. Yeats*, ed. Allan Wade (London: R. Hart-Davis, 1954), 887.

3. Charles Lamb, *The Works of Charles and Mary Lamb*, ed. E. V. Lucas (New York: Putnam, 1903–5), 2:9.

4. Cf. Hayden White, *The Tropics of Discourse* (Baltimore: Johns Hopkins Univ. Press, 1978), 101–20.

5. Claude Lévi-Strauss, *The Savage Mind* (Chicago: Univ. of Chicago Press, 1966), 257.

6. Friedrich Nietzsche, *The Complete Works of Friedrich Nietzsche*, ed. Oscar Levy (New York: Russell and Russell, 1964), 2:178.

7. White, *Tropics*, 3.

8. Hayden White, *The Content of the Form* (Baltimore: Johns Hopkins Univ. Press, 1987), 115.

9. White, *Tropics*, 58.

10. White, *The Content of the Form*, 20.

11. White, *Tropics*, 51, 82, 91, 98.

12. Ibid., 47.

13. Hayden White, *Metahistory: The Historical Imagination in Nineteenth-Century Europe* (Baltimore: Johns Hopkins Univ. Press, 1973), 30.

14. Ibid., 30, 31, 48.

15. Harold Bloom, *Yeats* (New York: Oxford Univ. Press, 1970), 66, 206, 254.

16. See D. C. Muecke, *Irony and the Ironic* (New York: Methuen, 1970), 23–24.

17. Friedrich Schlegel, *Dialogue on Poetry and Literary Aphorisms*, trans. E. Behler and R. Struc (Philadelphia: Univ. of Pennsylvania Press, 1968), 31.

18. Eugenio Donato, "Of Structuralism and Literature," in *The Structuralist Controversy*, ed. Richard Macksey (Baltimore: Johns Hopkins Univ. Press, 1970), 169.

19. Michel Foucault, *The Order of Things: An Archaeology of the Human Sciences* (New York: Pantheon, 1970), 219.

20. See Thomas R. Whitaker, *Swan and Shadow: Yeats's Dialogue with History* (Chapel Hill: Univ. of North Carolina Press, 1964), 27.

21. W. B. Yeats, *If I Were Four and Twenty* (Dublin: Cuala Press, 1940), 8; W. B. Yeats, *Essays and Introductions* (New York: Macmillan, 1961), 440; W. B. Yeats, *A Vision* (London: Macmillan, 1937), 271.

22. See Whitaker, 94.

23. Ursula Bridge, ed., *W. B. Yeats and T. Sturge Moore: Their Correspondence 1901–1937* (London: Routledge and Kegan Paul, 1953), 105.

24. White, *Metahistory*, 227, 232, 263.

25. Yeats, *Mythologies* (New York: Macmillan, 1959), 301; Yeats, *A Vision*, 279.

26. Yeats, *Collected Plays*, 210; W. B. Yeats, *The Collected Poems of W. B. Yeats* (New York: Macmillan, 1966), 284 (hereafter cited as *CP*); Yeats, *Explorations*, 392; Bridge, 154.

27. A. Norman Jeffares, *A Commentary on the Collected Poems of W. B. Yeats* (Stanford: Stanford Univ. Press, 1968), 159, 228.

28. Yeats, *A Vision*, 268.

29. White, *Metahistory*, 37.

30. Friedrich Schlegel, *Friedrich Schlegel's 'Lucinde' and Fragments*, trans. P. Firchow (Minneapolis: Univ. of Minnesota Press), 267.

31. W. B. Yeats, *Pages from a Diary Written in Nineteen Hundred and Thirty* (Dublin: Cuala Press, 1944), 8.

32. W. B. Yeats, *On the Boiler* (Dublin: Cuala Press, 1939), 37.

33. Jeffares, 215–16.

34. See J. Hillis Miller, "The Critic as Host," in *Deconstruction and Criticism*, ed. Harold Bloom (New York: Seabury Press, 1979), 219–20.

35. W. B. Yeats, *Per Amica Silentia Lunae*, cited in Bloom, 182.

36. Jeffares, 243; Yeats, *Explorations*, 395.

37. White, *Metahistory*, 233.

38. Yeats, *A Vision*, 302.

39. White, *Metahistory*, 233.

40. Bridge, 154; Wade, 819.

41. Yeats, *Autobiography*, 328; E. J. Ellis and W. B. Yeats, eds., *The Works of William Blake* (London: B. Quaritch, 1893), 1:273; W. B. Yeats, *Plays and Controversies* (London: Macmillan, 1923), 161.

42. Yeats, *Explorations*, 434; Yeats, *A Vision*, 24–25; Yeats, *Essays and Introductions*, 288.

43. Yeats, *Autobiography*, 116; letter to Ethel Mannin, cited in Whitaker, 266.

44. White, *Metahistory*, 9.

45. Wade, 613.

46. Yeats, *On the Boiler*, 29.

47. Cited in Whitaker, 97, 113.

48. See Jeffares, 154.

49. Cited in White, *Metahistory*, 335.

50. White, *Tropics*, 131–32.

51. Ellis and Yeats, 1:243.

52. White, *Metahistory*, 29.

53. White, *Tropics*, 98.

54. Ibid., 73–74.

55. White, *Metahistory*, 67.

56. White, *Tropics*, 98.

57. Jacques Derrida, "White Mythology: Metaphor in the Text of Philosophy," *NLH* 6 (1974): 41; Jacques Derrida, *Positions*, cited in Gregory Ulmer, *Applied Grammatology* (Baltimore: Johns Hopkins Univ. Press, 1985), 28. Derrida's work needs to be put into the informative and disturbing context recently provided by John M. Ellis in *Against Deconstruction* (Princeton: Princeton Univ. Press, 1989).

58. Timothy J. Reiss, *The Discourse of Modernism* (Ithaca: Cornell Univ. Press, 1982), 357, 366.

59. See Ulmer, 26–27.

60. See White, *Content of the Form*, 105.

61. See J. Hillis Miller, *The Linguistic Moment* (Princeton: Princeton Univ. Press, 1985), 337.

62. Reiss, 382.

63. Morse Peckham, *Romanticism and Ideology* (Greenwood, Fla.: Penkevill, 1985), 60.

64. Yeats, *Essays and Introductions*, 522.

65. Peckham, 60.

66. White, *Metahistory*, 37.

67. Cynthia Chase, *Decomposing Figures: Rhetorical Readings in the Romantic Tradition* (Baltimore: Johns Hopkins Univ. Press, 1986), 8.

68. Peckham, 254.

## 4

## UNDER NORTHERN LIGHTS

Re-visioning Yeats and the Revival

KIERAN QUINLAN

UNLIKE JAMES JOYCE, whose ever-widening linguistic gyrations have long since inspired contending interpretations of his works and have even led to a gradual destabilizing of our sense of the English language itself, Yeats, to date—apart perhaps from his preoccupations with the occult— has attracted relatively more orthodox and homogeneous schools of research and criticism. Joyce's tower, far from resisting the many hordes of French-influenced scholarly invaders, has subversively welcomed them with sirenlike signifiers, while Yeats's more remote Norman fortress has seemed set on evoking the admiration of foreigners while at the same time keeping them at a respectful distance from a self-fortified and for- tifying Irishry. Put another way, Yeats's style does not so automatically or so patently deconstruct itself as does that of Joyce.

In recent years, however, some loosening of the Yeatsian edifice has occurred in certain of its aspects, particularly in his own country— from within the fortress itself, so to speak. During his lifetime, Yeats was sometimes beaten down by Ireland's history. Patrick Pearse referred to him in 1899 as, "a mere English poet of the third or fourth rank and as such he is harmless. But when he attempts to run an 'Irish' Lit- erary Theatre it is time for him to be crushed." Yeats has been resub- jected to that beating by yet another generation of Irish writers who once again have much more than an academic interest in his influ- ence.[1] Because this phenomenon in its present form is of necessity an Irish one, I want to concentrate here on Yeats as seen by a set of writ-

64

ers and scholars from that country who are most closely identified with this revaluative process; that is, the Field Day group of Seamus Heaney, Seamus Deane, and others that was formed in Derry in the early 1980s.[2] And because, furthermore, all of these writers/scholars are involved, with varying degrees of theoretical sophistication, in a deeply politicized, loosely New Historicist approach to Yeats (Tom Flanagan has described Deane as negotiating "between Foucault and, as it were, the village pump"), I shall begin by outlining the assumptions that such an attitude implies and also give some attention to a few of the considerable difficulties that have been associated with it—difficulties that are well reflected in the criticisms of these authors that have been made by Irish observers such as Donoghue and Conor Cruise O'Brien.[3] It is fairly clear that, whatever the outcome, we are, as Donoghue stressed in his 1986 Clark lecture on Yeats at UCLA, "at the end of a period in which the theory of literature was construed in philosophical terms. Our setting is now much more overtly political. Issues are named as ideological as soon as they are recognized as issues at all."[4]

The New Historicist school of critical theory is, of course, by no means well defined. However, while the movement is extremely heterogeneous in its functioning, drawing eclectically on the work of Bakhtin, Foucault, Althusser, Lacan, Said, and many others not perhaps readily identified with it, at the moment it seems strongest in the area of English Renaissance studies. Stephen Greenblatt, a Shakespearean scholar at Berkeley, is the person most often associated with this school of thought, although, again, a current series of books under the heading "The New Historicism: Studies in Cultural Poetics," of which he is the general editor, covers a range of authors as widely diverse as Herodotus, medieval mystics, Shakespeare, James Clarence Mangan, and the American Naturalists. Greenblatt has contrasted the new with the old historicism in the following manner:

> the new historicism [is] set apart from the dominant historical scholarship of the past and the formalist criticism that partially displaced this scholarship in the decades after World War Two. The earlier historicism tends to be monological; that is, it is concerned with discovering a single political vision, usually identical to that said to be held by the entire literate class or indeed the entire population. . . . The new historicism erodes the firm ground of both criticism and literature. It tends to ask

questions about its own methodological assumptions and those of others. . . . Moreover, recent criticism has been less concerned to establish
the organic unity of literary works and more open to such works as fields
of force, places of dissension and shifting interests, occasions for the
jostling of orthodox and subversive impulses.[5]

Greenblatt's summary is useful; but it will also be instructive to take
a brief look at Jean E. Howard's "New Historicism in Renaissance
Studies," where matters are explained in greater detail.[6]

In what way, then, is the New Historicism really new? In what
way does it differ from the positivistic histories that preceded it? According to Howard, the old view of history, as found in Tillyard's *Eliza-
bethan World Picture* for example, assumes that "history is knowable;
that literature mirrors or at least by indirection reflects historical reality; and that historians and critics can see the facts of history objec-
tively" (Howard, 18). Contemporary theory, on the other hand, questions
such assumptions. A certain understanding of Saussurean linguistics,
for instance, would—at least as presented by Howard—challenge the
premise that language functions referentially at all, so that in this case
the traditional idea that literature simply reflects reality would become
untenable. Indeed, Howard poses the question at one point that "if
one accepts certain tendencies in poststructuralist thought," then is
the possibility of an historical criticism even conceivable? (18–19).

More significant, however, is reader-response theory as developed
by Norman Holland, Stanley Fish, Hans Robert Jauss, and others. This
theory shows that the interpreter can never escape his or her own historical situatedness. Thus, "it seems necessary to abandon the myth
of objectivity and to acknowledge that all historical knowledge is produced from a partial and positioned vantage point." This being the
case, "instead of evoking a monolithic and repressive 'history,' one must
acknowledge the existence of 'histories' produced by subjects variously
positioned within the present social formation and motivated by quite
different senses of the *present* needs and *present* problems which it is
hoped will be clarified or reconfigured through the study of the past"
(Howard, 22–23). Though such an approach has an initial liberating
effect, one might want to question whether it does not, in fact, tend
to validate historical readings that are narrowly self-serving and intellectually restrictive. It is also claimed that history and literature do not

just stand together side by side or as shifting foreground (literature) against stable background (history), for both, as Hayden White has pointed out on a number of occasions, are equally the narrative constructions of situated critics (Howard, 23).

Again, the New Historicists stress that literature is operative *in* society and not just a passive commentary on it:

> Rather than erasing the problem of textuality, one must enlarge it in order to see that *both* social and literary texts are opaque, self-divided, and porous, that is, open to the mutual intertextual influences of one another. This move means according literature real power. Rather than passively reflecting an external reality, literature is an agent in constructing a culture's sense of reality. It is part of a much larger symbolic order through which the world at a particular historical moment is conceptualized and through which a culture imagines its relationship to the actual conditions of its existence. In short, instead of a hierarchical relationship in which literature figures as the parasitic reflector of historical fact, one imagines a complex textualized universe in which literature participates in historical processes and in the political management of reality (Howard, 25).

Thus, while literature may indeed be but one discourse among the many by which the culture represents reality to itself, by that very fact it is not without significant influence.

A literature powerful in this way possesses, of course, a certain ideological content. So, although Louis Althusser's revised Marxist theory argues for "the *relative* autonomy" of literature and other cultural institutions from the material base, it also shows that ideology is present everywhere. It cannot be absent from literature; therefore, literature, contrary to what the Russian formalists have suggested, is not a "special and unique form of writing with its own inherent and universal properties, one of which is the way it acquires internal distance from the ideological material which traverses it" (Howard, 29). Furthermore, borrowing from Bakhtin, Howard goes on to present the possibility that literary texts are not "organically unified wholes," but that novelized discourse "is polyvalent, riddled with 'unofficial' voices contesting, subverting, and parodying dominant discourses." The task of a New Historical criticism in this case "is to find a way to talk about and discriminate among the *different* ways in which literature is traversed by—and produces—the ideologies of its time" (Howard, 30).

Finally, as Howard notes, the New Historicists are antiessential-ist, rejecting a traditional humanism in favor of the idea that man does not possess a "transhistorical human essence" but rather is the product of the social and historical forces of his era. She offers examples from Nancy Chodorow on how "mothering" is not innate but socially con-structed, and from Foucault on "the relatively late emergence of the concept of 'man' as a self-sufficient, autonomous being possessed of in-teriority and self-presence" (Howard, 20). While the precise meaning of these assertions may not be clear—or at least may require more de-tailed philosophical argument—the general opposition to essentialist thinking on the part of participants in this movement is noteworthy.

The program that Howard has set forth here is probably not ca-pable of total satisfactory fulfillment. She is compelled to comment that even Greenblatt is not always faithful to his own aims, privileging as he does certain cultural discourses from among the myriad available to him without giving sufficient justification for his choices, or lapsing into an unreflective essentialism. To recover *all* the voices of the past, though desirable, is simply not feasible. Therefore, the best that can be hoped for under the circumstances is a broader area of receptivity than that which has heretofore prevailed, one that is constantly aware of its own vulnerability and need for supplementation; likewise, as many commentators have pointed out, essentialist thinking is—even when there is a commitment to doing so—almost impossible to avoid completely.[7]

When examining the extent to which the program presented by Howard is operative among the Field Day writers, one is struck first by the differences in fundamental motivation between scholars work-ing in the United States and scholars working in Ireland. Thus, almost at the very beginning of her essay, Howard makes the very honest con-fession that one of the reasons for the popularity of the new move-ment is that academics have grown weary of "teaching texts as ethereal entities floating above the urgencies and contradictions of history and of seeking in such texts the disinterested expression of a unified truth rather than some articulation of the discontinuities underlying any con-struction of reality."[8] The Irish situation on this score, however, is radi-cally different: the rethinking of Yeats's contribution has little to do with the practical demands of the classroom as such and arises instead much more from the actual political urgencies of the day in the world outside. The tragedy that has been occurring in Northern Ireland for almost twenty years has made the Irish writer and the Irish critic acutely aware of certain tensions in their inherited culture that previously had gone unnoticed or that had been glossed over as legitimate requirements of a literature that was conceived of in formalist terms and in the creation of which Yeats's role as national mythologizer was significant. The "reading of the Irish as martyrs to abstraction—a reading sponsored most notoriously in the poetry of Yeats—is the greatest single obstacle to a full understanding of the situation in Ireland today," observes Declan Kiberd, another scholar associated with the Field Day group.[9] Or, as Edna Longley stated in Belfast in 1985, there is (outside Ireland) "a tendency to perceive Ireland and Irish literature through the fading aura of yesteryear Dublin, in preference to the chilly lens of contemporary Belfast"; the implication is that in Ireland itself, that particular perception is no longer available to the critical mind.[10] Above all, the Irish critics are not primarily concerned with what Howard has identified as the temptation of mere "'new readings' suited to the twenty-five-page article and the sixty-minute class": for them the Yeats "problem" is far more crucial than that.[11]

Again, perhaps because the political consequences are more immediate in Ireland, the generally Marxist orientation of the New Historicism is less evident—or takes a rather different form—there than it is in the American academic arena. It should be mentioned, however, that the Irish critics, although they acknowledge the importance of the material base of the culture, have also been accused of failing to give it more than perfunctory treatment. In other words, they remain very much "traditional intellectuals" as defined by Foucault, preoccupied with questions of national identity rather than questions that deal with the economic order of things.[12] As such, of course, they are with the New Historicists in having little difficulty in seeing literature as "traversed by . . . the ideologies of its time."

The Field Day group, then, presents its program in the following terms:

> In brief, all the directors felt that the political crisis in the North and its reverberations in the Republic had made the necessity of a reappraisal of Ireland's political and cultural situation explicit and urgent. All of

the directors are northerners. They believed that Field Day could and should contribute to the solution of the present crisis by producing analyses of the established opinions, myths and sterotypes which had become both a symptom and a cause of the current situation. The collapse of constitutional and political arrangements and the recrudescence of the violence which they had been designed to repress or contain, made this a more urgent requirement in the North than in the Republic, even though the improbability of either surviving in its present form seemed clear in 1980 and is clearer still in 1985.[13]

The first myths to be examined were those, as indicated earlier, that were so powerfully developed by Yeats at the beginning of the century, for both he and the leaders of the subsequent Irish revolution had "between them, mobilized energies on behalf of a carefully selective image of Ireland's past," an image that has undergone ominous revival in the present crisis in Northern Ireland.[14]

Before dealing specifically with Heaney and Deane's revisioning of Yeats and the Revival, I reemphasize the point that both of these poets and critics are quite self-conscious and self-declared Northerners of Catholic background, and that the crisis in that province has an urgency for them greater than it has for those whose experience had been entirely within the confines of Southern Ireland. Thus, for them the circumstances in which Yeats formed his notion of what was peculiarly "Celtic" has all the immediacy that the similar—and more extensive—development of the idea of the "Orient" has for a writer like Edward Said, who is of Palestinian origin. Indeed, we know that Yeats's conception of the Celtic was partly influenced by Renan and Arnold and that it had some of the same implications as those connected with the development of the western view of the Orient. The latter, as Said has shown, has its origins in the alliance between French and British colonial expansionism and genuine, but nationalistic, academic research in the nineteenth century. Likewise, according to Deane, "The cultural response to the idea of the Irish as a Celtic people and the political response to the form the Irish problem took in the nineteenth century are closely intertwined."[15]

Moreover, just as Said is concerned that "one aspect of the electronic, postmodern world is that there has been a reinforcement of the stereotypes by which the Orient is viewed," Deane is worried that some people in Ireland will become involved in an alienating mystique, "the spiritual heroics of a Yeats or a Pearse, to believe in the incarnation of the nation in the individual. To reject it is to make a fetish of exile, alienation and dislocation in the manner of Joyce or Beckett. Between these hot and cold rhetorics there is little room for choice. Yet the polarisation they identify is an inescapable and understandable feature of the social and political realities we inhabit. . . . They inhabit the highly recognizable world of modern colonialism." For Deane, as for Said, such colonial stereotyping must come to an end: "Everything, including our politics and our literature, has to be rewritten – i.e. re-read."[16]

While Heaney's rereading of Yeats in a 1979 essay, "A Tale of Two Islands: Reflections on the Irish Literary Revival," and elsewhere can be seen initially as an attempt at a kind of Bloomian clearing of imaginative space for his own poetic work, his purposes are really much wider than that.[17] He is concerned that "much that had been known and loved in Ireland was half-frustrated in its expression by the mighty beauties of the art of the Irish Literary Revival," beauties that Yeats had imposed on his followers rather than received from them. The task, then, is not merely to demythologize the repressive and monolithic Yeatsian inheritance by pointing out its inconsistencies and inadequacies, but also – and even more so – to give confident affirmation to the alternative tradition of Carleton, Joyce, and Kavanagh by showing how this tradition is much more in touch with the realities of Irish life. Heaney is not perhaps a remythologizer (though he sounds like one at times) but rather a pursuer of what he calls "a near myth" because that is the only way in which he can structure the facts of his bourgeois Irish Catholic experience (Heaney, "Tale," 19).

Heaney's criticism of Yeats's understanding of the Irish tradition has, of course, numerous precedents. Indeed, it goes back almost to the very beginning of the Anglo-Irish poet's career. It is present again in Stephen Dedalus's reflections in *Portrait* and in *Ulysses*. In 1931, Daniel Corkery wrote of Yeats, AE, James Stephens, and others as not being indigenous interpreters of Irish culture, as – "to use the American phrase" – writers who did not belong.[18] Later, Patrick Kavanagh would dismiss the Irish literary revival as "a thorough-going English-bred lie."[19]

Finally, in a famous paper read before the annual meeting of the Modern Language Association in New York in 1966, Thomas Kinsella suggested that when Yeats looks back over the course of literature in Ireland,

> He values what he can in Gaelic literature, and uses it, as we know; but his living tradition is solely in English. . . . Its literature and its human beings are specialized and cut off, an Anglo-Irish annex to the history of Ireland. He yokes together Swift and Burke and Berkeley and Goldsmith for his writers. . . . It is English literature, not Irish, that lies behind them and their line—as he sees it—is ending in his own time. . . . I believe that Yeats's isolation is at least partly a matter of choice. He refuses to come to terms with the real shaping vitality of Ireland where he sees it exists; to take the tradition in any other way would have been to write for Daniel O'Connell's children, for De Valera and Paudeen at his greasy till; to recognize these as the heirs of Anglo-Ireland's glory, and of the fruits of the 1916 Rising (which—for its "gallantry"—Yeats is almost tempted to include in his Anglo-Irish system).[20]

Kinsella concludes that while Yeats had a greatness that *perhaps* was capable of integrating the different strains in Irish culture, he chose instead "to make this impossible by separating out a special Anglo-Irish culture from the main unwashed body." Joyce, on the other hand, in spite of his explicit isolation and rejection of things national, had a relationship to his country that was "direct and intimate" (Kinsella, 64).

Heaney's approach to Yeats is not only in the tradition of Kavanagh and Kinsella, but it has been further exacerbated by the continuing crisis in Northern Ireland that underlines the ambiguity of Yeats's political loyalties and his dormant unionism and nationalism. Thus, for example, in "To Ireland in the Coming Times," the poet declares the apparent purpose of his artistic endeavors:

> Know, that I would accounted be
> True brother of a company
> That sang, to sweeten Ireland's wrong,
> Ballad and story, *rann* and song.

Heaney's comment on this poem, in which Yeats goes on to request that he be counted with "Davis, Mangan, Ferguson," is that

Yeats's brisk tetrameters have somehow disinfected the political content of Davis and muffled the nationalist pulse of Mangan. For it was indeed the spirit of the Unionist, Sir Samuel Ferguson, who moved most influentially through the mind of the young poet, because it was in Ferguson's handling of legendary material that Yeats perceived, consciously or unconsciously, a way of maintaining fidelity to the political and cultural postures of his own class, the middle-class Protestant establishment. At the same time he staked a claim in the very roots of the nationalist Catholic ethos by annexing to himself those native myths and legends and treating them as a unifying rather than a divisive factor. In his *Autobiographies* he gives us an image of Ireland after the death of Parnell being like soft wax, ready to be pressed into a shape determined by the writers, and in articles, poems and speeches Yeats kept striking the shape he wished to conjure. From beginning to end, it is this arrogant but not improper declaration, this *fiat*, which makes him the powerful figure, artistically and culturally, that he is (Heaney, "Tales," 4–5).

Still, while what Yeats is said to have done was "not improper"—though the phrase does call its propriety into question—it frequently was inaccurate, the western peasants of both Yeats and Synge sacrificing the realities of their harsh lives to become "impeccably aesthetic" (Heaney, "Tale," 8).

Heaney brings out this last point well in a comment on Yeats's annexation of William Carleton into his network of forebears of the Celtic Twilight. In an attempt "to escape the tedious actualities and impoverishments of the century which Carleton lived and wrote," Yeats calls him "'the greatest novelist of Ireland by right of the most Celtic eyes that ever gazed from under the brow of storyteller.'" However, objects Heaney, "it is not the fabled Celtic quality which is significant about Carleton. Rather, it is the marks he bears in his sensibility and watermarks into his writing of experiences not archetypal but historical, not ennobling but disabling" ("Tale," 11–12). Carleton was forced to deny what he was and become a member of the established (Anglican) church in order to rise in the world, whereas a Synge or a Yeats had the freedom to choose his patterns of rejection. In other words, it is the real privation, intellectual and spiritual, of what Kavanagh refers to as "the normal barbaric life of the Irish country poor" that Yeats fails to comprehend in the luxurious "rag-and-bone shop" of his aristocratic heart.[21] Heaney's Carleton, on the other hand, wrote "without any sacral sense of the race he belonged to, a figure of controversy because of his apostasy but a witness to a realistic, politicized Ireland that the nineteenth-century poets and their revival heirs could not or would not voice."[22]

Heaney makes his most telling argument for Yeats's isolation when he compares Carleton's account of "The Lough Derg Pilgrim," published in 1828, with Yeats's late poem on the same subject ("The Pilgrim"). The latter comes from a period when Yeats is generally thought to be more earthy and accepting—even, according to some critics, more Irish and perhaps influenced by Joyce's example—than previously. For Heaney, however, although Carleton's narrative is distorted by the demands of his own religious apostasy, "what remains most potently in the mind is the substance of what is being condemned." Yeats's pilgrim is merely a "hard-riding country gentleman, more a case of indomitable Irishry than penitential action" ("Tale," 13):

> Round Lough Derg's holy island I went upon the stones,
> I prayed at all the Stations upon my marrow-bones,
> And there I found an old man, and though I prayed all day
> And that old man beside me, nothing would he say
> But fol de rol de rolly O.

It is, of course, Joyce who is conceived of as struggling with his impoverished, fragmented culture from within. In Stephen's diary at the end of *Portrait*, we find an account of the pretentious John Alphonsus Mulrennan's visit with an old man in a mountain cabin in the west of Ireland. Stephen records that he fears the old man's "redrimmed horny eyes"; it is with him that he feels he must struggle "till he or I lie dead," although Stephen adds immediately that he wishes the old man no harm. Heaney's comment is that "Stephen fears him because . . . that mountain cabin where he lodges is hung with the nets of nationality, religion, [and] family" from which the young artist is trying to escape. But Stephen will not destroy him because "the old man is as much a victim as the writer. His illiterate fidelities are the object of Stephen's scepticism, the substance of what Stephen rejects; and yet they are part of Stephen himself." Heaney then offers Yeats's view in contrast: "Yeats's stance . . . towards the old man [is] very different. [The old man] is for

[him] a portal, a gleam of half-extinguished thought. [Yeats] would give him artificial respiration[,] whereas Stephen's impulse is to strangle him" ("Tale," 17–18). In other words, Joyce is involved in a family quarrel, while Yeats is merely a sympathetic, but uncomprehending, bystander.

Finally, there is the relationship between Yeats and Kavanagh. In his 1977 essay "A Sense of Place," Heaney contrasts various responses to the same or to very similar Irish landscapes. He judges Kavanagh to have been more intimate with the culture shared by the majority of Irish people than Yeats was. And Kavanagh was such, according to Heaney, precisely because of his fidelity to the "unpromising, unspectacular countryside of Monaghan" and to its rural speech.[23] Kavanagh, the great opponent of the whole ethos of the Irish Revival, strove to convey both his affection for and hatred of the reality of the life that he actually lived for many years in rural Ireland: "There is nothing programmed about his diction, or about his world. 'Who owns them hungry hills?' says the ungrammatical cattle-jobber in the poem 'Shancoduff' but as he speaks we know that the poet is neither savouring nor disdaining 'them hills' as opposed to 'those hills.' The poet meets his people at eye-level, he hears them shouting through the hedge and not through the chinks in a loft floor, the way Synge heard his literary speech in Co. Wicklow" (Heaney, "Sense," 138). To praise Kavanagh in the way that Heaney does is, quite obviously, a kind of political statement, for its asserts the territorial and cultural rights of a whole mass of Irish people who, in the Chestertonian phrase, "have not spoken yet."

In contrast to Heaney, Seamus Deane seems intent on a total demythologizing of the Irish literary inheritance and is much more severe not only on Yeats and Synge, but also on Carleton, Joyce, and even Beckett. In fact, although on occasion he appears to be indulging in a vendetta with the Yeatsian tradition in particular, his more recent views of this author seem at times to accord him the right to compose an Ascendancy tradition motived by his needs in the late nineteenth and early twentieth centuries, even if that composition requires radical questioning from a new group motivated by "*present* needs" that conflict with the needs of Yeats. In all events, Yeats's assertion that an essential "Irishness" exists to which he himself belongs is, for Deane, not acceptable. Like Kinsella and Heaney, Deane judges Yeats as not being intimate with Irish history, culture, and tradition. At the same time, however, he is more questioning of that accumulation—more dubious than they that it has an identifiable character. Thus, in "A General Introduction for My Work," Yeats expresses his ambivalent attitude toward his inheritance:

> The "Irishry" have preserved their ancient "deposit" through wars which, during the sixteenth and seventeenth centuries, became wars of extermination; no people, Lecky said . . . have undergone greater persecution, nor did that persecution altogether cease up to our own day. No people hate as we do in whom that past is always alive; there are moments when hatred poisons my life and I accuse myself of effeminacy because I have not given it adequate expression. . . . Then I remind myself that though mine is the first English marriage I know of in the direct line, all my family names are English, and that I owe my soul to Shakespeare, to Spenser, and to Blake, perhaps to William Morris, and to the English language in which I think, speak and write, that everything I love has come to me through English; my hatred tortures me with love, my love with hate. . . . This is Irish hatred and solitude.[24]

The Irish reader of Catholic background, like Heaney and Deane, will simply not grant to Yeats that initial identification with a persecuted race, however well intentioned the impulse behind it might be. Perhaps it is the histrionic quality of the passage that makes such a reader at first suspicious about the quotidian sincerity of the emotion being expressed. It is clear, in any case, that Yeats immediately recognizes his debt to the English tradition that has given him everything that he loves. It is as though he began to examine his Irish heritage only to discover that in the final analysis he was colonial English; or, as Deane states the case in a comment on the above passage, "The pathology of literary unionism has never been better defined."[25]

Deane suggests, however, that it is simply not enough to show that the myths that Yeats created—be they of essential "Irishness," martyrdom, or ascendancy—are wrong. It is not enough, for example, to interpret a poem like "Ancestral Houses" as being "about the tragic nature of human existence itself":

> Some violent bitter man, some powerful man
> Called architect and artist in, that they,
> Bitter and violent men, might rear in stone
> The sweetness that all longed for night and day,
> The gentleness none there had ever known.

According to Deane, the implied historical content of the poem cannot be dismissed. Thus, "the assumption that this or any other literary work can arrive at a moment in which it takes leave of history or myth . . . and becomes meaningful only as an aspect of the 'human condition' . . . is, of course, a characteristic determination of humanist readings of literature which hold to the ideological conviction that literature, in its highest forms, is non-ideological" (Deane, "Heroic," 46). Ideology is everywhere, however, and even the revival itself can be seen as the appropriation of Irish culture by

> those who were losing their grip on Irish land. The effect of these rewritings was to transfer the blame for the drastic condition of the country from the Ascendancy to the Catholic middle classes or to their English counterparts. It was in essence a strategic retreat from political to cultural supremacy. From Lecky to Yeats and forward to F. S. L. Lyons we witness the conversion of Irish history into a tragic theatre in which the great Anglo-Irish protagonists . . . are destroyed in their heroic attempts to unite culture of intellect with the emotion of multitude, or, in political terms, constitutional politics with the forces of revolution (Deane, "Heroic," 48).

However, unlike Heaney, Deane does not see a solution in a simple exaltation of the alternative tradition of Carleton, Joyce, and Beckett, for they, too, have been distorted by preoccupations with "paralysis, inertia, the disabling effects of society upon the individual" ("Heroic," 50). Such "worn oppositions . . . used to be the parentheses in which the Irish experience was isolated" (58). What is needed now, as the preface to Ireland's Field Day calls for (in a passage that echoes Deane's essay), is: "the possibility of a more generous and hospitable notion of Ireland's cultural achievement . . . as the basis for a more ecumenical and eirenic approach to the deep and apparently implacable problems which confront the island today" (viii).

Conor Cruise O'Brien tends to see Deane and others like him simply as modern-day cultural nationalists whose anticolonial political rhetoric, "larded with Third Worldly quotations from the school of Franz Fanon, is really good old Catholic Irish nationalism in trendy gear."[26] Certainly that element is present, and when writers of Irish Catholic background—whether they be atheists, agnostics, or believers—are provoked or are under pressure, they take the opportunity to express some

of the rage that they have long felt about the character of the Irish
Revival. Denis Donoghue remarks, for example, that Deane allows nationality, tradition, and aristocracy to Joyce, Kinsella, and Montague,
respectively, while denying it to Yeats.[27] Nevertheless, in spite of occasional regressions, a more diverse Irish culture seems to be emerging
in which a greater plurality of voices from the past can now be heard.
The very kind of criticism that undermines Yeats's hegemony also provides a limited legitimacy for his undertakings. Meanwhile, a poet who
was a covert unionist, an exalter of a terrible Republican beauty, a creator of a never-existent Ascendancy, and a defender of civil liberties
in the face of a conservative new Irish state, has of necessity become
both his admirers and detractors:

> Now he is scattered among a hundred cities
> And wholly given over to unfamiliar affections;
> To find his happiness in another kind of wood
> And be punished under a foreign code of conscience.
> The words of a dead man
> Are modified in the guts of the living.[28]

## NOTES

1. Quoted in Richard Kearney, "Myth and Motherland," in *Ireland's Field Day*,
ed. Seamus Deane et al. (Notre Dame, Ind.: Univ. of Notre Dame Press, 1986), 71.

2. The other names associated with this group, which was founded in 1980
as the Field Day Theatre Company, are Brian Friel, Stephen Rea, David Hammond,
and Tom Paulin.

3. Tom Flanagan, "Afterword," *Ireland's Field Day*, 114.

4. Denis Donoghue, "Yeats, Ancestral Houses, and Anglo-Ireland," in Des-
mond Guinness and Denis Donoghue, *Ascendancy Ireland* (Los Angeles: Univ. of California, William Andrews Clark Memorial Library, 1986), 48.

5. Stephen Greenblatt, Introduction to *The Forms of Power and the Power of
Forms in the Renaissance*, Genre 15 (1982): 5.

6. Jean E. Howard, "The New Historicism in Renaissance Studies," *English Literary Renaissance* 16 (Winter 1986): 13–43.

7. From a more general perspective, Edward Pechter has recently criticized the
movement for its truncated readings of various Renaissance texts, its overall emphasis
that a will to power is what dictates literary activity, and its rather simplistic use of
Foucault's complex writings. See "The New Historicism and Its Discontents: Politiciz-
ing Renaissance Drama," *PMLA* 102 (May 1987): 292–303.

8. Howard, 15.

9. Declan Kiberd, "Anglo-Irish Attitudes," in *Ireland's Field Day*, 102.

10. Edna Longley, "Viewpoint: Criticism Wanted," *TLS* (Nov. 1, 1985): 1233.

11. Howard, 19.

12. Liam O'Dowd makes this criticism of the Field Day group in "Neglecting the Material Dimension: Irish Intellectuals and the Problem of Identity," *Irish Review* 3 (1988): 8–17. He also questions whether the decolonizing thesis is entirely accurate in its application to an Ireland that, whatever its economic problems, "remains among the thirty wealthiest countries in the world" (17).

13. "Preface," in *Ireland's Field Day*, vii.

14. Seamus Deane, *A Short History of Irish Literature* (Notre Dame, Ind.: Univ. of Notre Dame Press, 1986), 208.

15. Seamus Deane, *Celtic Revivals: Essays in Modern Irish Literature* (London: Faber, 1985), 18.

16. Edward W. Said, *Orientalism* (New York: Vintage, 1979), 26; Seamus Deane, "Heroic Styles: The Tradition of an Idea," in *Ireland's Field Day*, 58. Renan's and Arnold's influence on Yeats and Synge in the matter of what constitutes the Celtic is dealt with briefly in W. J. McCormack, *Ascendancy and Tradition in Anglo-Irish Literary History from 1789 to 1939* (Oxford: Clarendon Press, 1985), 219–38, where the relevance of Said's work is also mentioned.

17. Seamus Heaney, "A Tale of Two Islands: Reflections on the Irish Literary Revival," in *Irish Studies 1*, ed. P. J. Drudy (New York: Cambridge Univ. Press, 1980), 1–20.

18. Daniel Corkery, *Synge and Anglo-Irish Literature* (Cork: Cork Univ. Press, 1931), 13.

19. Patrick Kavanagh, *Collected Prose* (London: MacGibbon and Kee, 1967), 13.

20. Thomas Kinsella, "The Irish Writer," in *Davis, Mangan, Ferguson? Tradition and the Irish Writer* (Dublin: Dolmen Press, 1970), 61–62.

21. Kavanagh, 14.

22. Heaney, "Tale," 12–13.

23. Seamus Heaney, *Preoccupations* (New York: Farrar, 1980), 137.

24. W. B. Yeats, *Essays and Introductions* (New York: Collier, 1961), 518–19.

25. Deane, "Heroic" 50.

26. Conor Cruise O'Brien, "The Nationalist Trend," *TLS* (Nov. 1, 1985): 1231.

27. Denis Donoghue, "A Myth and Its Unmasking," *TLS* (Nov. 1, 1985): 1239.

28. W. H. Auden, "In Memory of W. B. Yeats," *Collected Shorter Poems, 1927–1967* (London: Faber, 1966), 141.

# 5

# TEXTUAL/SEXUAL POLITICS IN YEATS'S "LEDA AND THE SWAN"

WILLIAM JOHNSEN

TEXTUAL/SEXUAL POLITICS, Toril Moi's coinage[1] for the intersection of ideology and form, never had a better example than "Leda and the Swan," a sonnet depicting a rape as a welcome sign of a better future. Yeats clearly foresaw a political reading, for he tells the reader in a note to the poem that it was written at the request of the editor of a new journal recognizable, respectively, as A. E. Russell and *The Irish Statesman* (Sir Horace Plunkett had revived *The Irish Statesman* immediately after the Civil War to support the Pro-Treaty government against De-Valera and the IRA).[2] The note also restates Yeats's preliminary thinking between the request and the poem. "I thought 'After the individualist demagogic movement, founded by Hobbes and popularized by the Encyclopaedists and the French Revolution, we have a soil so exhausted that it cannot grow that crop again for centuries.' Then I thought 'Nothing is now possible but some movement, or birth from above, preceded by some violent annunciation.' My fancy began to play with Leda and the Swan for metaphor and I began this poem: but as I wrote, bird and lady took such possession of the scene that all politics went out of it, and my friend tells me that 'his conservative readers would misunderstand the poem.'"[3] To follow out the dynamic of bird and lady dispossessing all the politics that Yeats knows, across published versions of the poem, gives evidence for the progressive intellectual labor of poetic thinking. The most humble but unarguable threshold of progressive intellectual work is discovering what you do not already know.

80

I will suggest how the successive instances of the poem's published versions indicate a development beyond what Yeats would say, in A Vision for example, that he already knows, toward a systematic understanding of history and the future potentially more comprehensive than A Vision in whatever version. I mean to argue that a hypothesis of poetic thinking as progressive intellectual work can better account for successive versions of this poem, and the "postmodern" reading of the poem that Yeats's revisions make possible, than any political/textual/sexual unconscious (although Jameson and Moi make such a counterargument conceivable).[4] Positive intellectual work has a future beyond its own historical limits, and poetic thinking is an essential part of that work. I will show how Yeats's poem works *for* its own postmodern reading, and what future follows from the work done with Yeats. I have argued elsewhere for René Girard as the most comprehensive theorist of a postmodern future beyond (interminable) deconstruction.[5] Here I will limit myself to aligning the emergent theoretical potential in this poem, superior in its comprehensive power to A Vision, with Girard: "Love" and "War," concord and discord, are the two alternative futures for the mimetic entanglements endemic to all cultural forms, futures that, left up to the gods or the gyres, ensure no future at all.

Although it is difficult to corroborate Yeats's claim that Russell ever requested the poem, the recklessness of "Leda and the Swan" at least is there to see, especially in its earliest versions. The political turbulence of Yeats's imagination at this time was better suited to "a wild paper of the young which will make enemies everywhere and suffer repression, I hope a number of times."[6] Yeats gave Leda to such a paper, To-Morrow, in 1924, and his support for "a first beginning of new political thought" (Letters, 707). Yet the note from The Cat and the Moon quoted above, which accompanied The Dial publication of the poem as well,[7] admits that bird and lady drive all that Yeats recognized as politics out of a poem that had confidently called up the Swan's address to Leda de haute en bas as metaphor for the iron law of a new political order overcoming an older one, a fated rearrangement of history to be explained and maintained by "40 pages of commentary" (Letters, 709) in A Vision (1925).

The key stage in the revising of the poem takes place after the To-Morrow version, in anticipation of its inclusion in A Vision (1925). Here is how the poem first begins:

A rush, a sudden wheel, and hovering still
The bird descends, and her frail thighs are pressed
By the webbed toes, and that all-powerful bill
Has laid her helpless face upon his breast.
How can those terrified vague fingers push
The feathered glory from her loosening thighs!
All the stretched body's laid on the white rush
And feels the strange heart beating where it lies.[8]

The answer of the first version to the question of Leda's consent to this Act of Union (pace Heaney), implied by the poem's phrasing, all but assumes that Leda abandoned thighs and body to the mastering rhythms of Zeus's strange heart and feathered glory. Textual/sexual politics have already taken such possession of the scene that all (nationalist) politics have left the poem.

Yeats's revision of the first four lines of the *To-Morrow* version for *A Vision* (1925) shockingly emphasizes Zeus's forced entry.

A sudden blow: the great wings beating still
Above the staggering girl, her thighs caressed
By the dark webs, her nape caught in his bill,
He holds her helpless breast upon his breast.[9]

Yeats is now more attentive to the violent than to the sacred nature of Zeus's annunciation. For the first time since Yeats began writing this poem,[10] the rape of Leda begins as a violent attack, not as the wonder of an annunciation from above. In the *To-Morrow* version, "still" divides its significance between "quietly" and "yet." Now, the force of "still" emphasizes that Zeus has begun his sexual assault while he is still flying, while Leda is still staggering from the blow.

In the same say, the earlier version for *To-Morrow* shares with the reader Zeus's attraction to Leda's helplessness, locating the instigation of their common desire in the object itself. In revision, a sexist-essentialist view of "frail thighs" no longer precedes to explain the inevitable drawing out of Zeus's manly nature. "Her thighs caressed / By the dark webs" focuses rather on Zeus's chilling attention to the requisite details of amorous conquest, spreading his clawed toes wide enough to caress her thighs "just with the web."

How can those terrified vague fingers push
The feathered glory from her loosening thighs,
And how can body, laid in that white rush,
But feel the strange heart beating where it lies;

The pornographic exclamation mark of the *To-Morrow* version ("thighs!")
is also clearly at Zeus's power and at Leda's expense. How could any
woman's thighs but serve such an apotheosis of manly nature. But the
syntax of questioning, no matter how rhetorical or unquestioning, which
at first seems solely to enlarge upon Zeus's feathered glory, always must
bear a potential resistance to the politics of the poem the more that
Yeats, or any reader, poses it.

The *Tower* (1928) version of "Leda and the Swan," which begins
Yeats's final textual practice of marking these lines as questions, indicates the future of this revisionary labor: it is impossible to ask a question repeatedly without, sooner or later, wondering what other answers
might be possible. Even if the question is answered, it is not always
possible to give the same answer, even to the same question. The history of various prior representations of Leda's rape (which have perhaps preoccupied Yeats scholars as partially hidden sources more than
as public predecessors), in sequence with Yeats's revisions of this poem,
collectively indicate Leda *now*, by virtue of Yeats's late modern version,
as the point of indeterminacy from which Zeus's history can be ques-
tioned more and more comprehensively in future versions.

All questions in this poem derive logically from the first sin of
inquiry, which survived in all versions from the first version: "Did she
put on his knowledge with his power / Before the indifferent beak could
let her drop?" The earlier revision of an exclamation into a question
suggests that the least questionable stage of this question must be, "How
could Leda possibly know what we already know: the history engendered on her by Zeus?" Any answer based on the surviving instances
of Leda in Greek mythology must be "no"; in mythology, as in the poem,
she is nothing—the mere pivot of Zeus's power to make his own history. The only possible "yes" could be that Leda "puts on" in the sense
of "being dressed in" Zeus's power: whenever we see Leda we "see" what
Zeus already had foreseen. Yeats's poem serves only as another link
in the iron chain of association that inevitably calls up the sexual/

textual politics of "the broken wall, the burning roof and tower / And Agamemnon dead" whenever Leda is mentioned.

But Yeats's "40-page commentary" in *A Vision* (1925) is not unrelieved deconstruction, theory rendering natural the text's necessary self-blindness,[11] smugly estimating how far "Leda" must come to reach what we all know. "I imagine the annunciation that founded Greece as made to Leda, remembering that they showed in a Spartan temple, strung up to the roof as a holy relic, an unhatched egg of hers; and that from one of her eggs came Love and from the other War. But all things are from antithesis, and when in my ignorance I try to imagine what older civilization she refuted I can but see bird and woman blotting out some corner of the Babylonian mathematical starlight."[12] Yeats admits that he cannot answer the questions posed by his own poetic thinking. What civilization is "refuted" by Leda? It could be either the civilization that her civilization refuted, 4000–2000 B.C., perhaps even 2000 B.C. to A.D. 1, where Leda already serves as an expression of Zeus's history, a complicit or communicable symbol of Zeus's refutation of her own culture.

Here is the essential difference between the theoretical potential of *A Vision* and poetic thinking: the basic fundamental questions about Leda—who is she, where does she come from, what is she thinking—which Yeats cannot answer, are annulled by the violent symmetry of the dominant formula of *A Vision*: "All things are by antithesis." No problems here. Antithesis can explain and account for Yeats's ignorance. The poem's questions without answers are not permitted by the commentary to propose further thinking. Ignorance merely gives evidence for the symmetry of one gyre refuting another.

The relation between Yeats's theory and Girard's and the poetic labor that connects the limits of the one to the promise of the other, making a postmodern reading of the poem possible, is based on their common emphasis on Heraclitus's fragment on War. (F25. "War is both father and king of all; some he has shown forth as gods and others as men, some he has made slaves and others free.")[13] Yeats follows Heraclitus's formula for violence as the primary differentiating principle, but Girard explains Heraclitus from a more comprehensive hypothesis. "It was this Discord or War that Heraclitus called 'God of all and Father of all, some it has made gods and some men, some bond and some free' and I recall that Love and War came from the eggs of

Leda."[14] For Yeats, Zeus's violence proves his divinity and Leda's mortality; his freedom, her bondage; violence fathers Love and War on her. All things are by antithesis. Girard argues that human violence, legislated by prohibition and ritual to prevent reciprocal rivalry, on the one hand, and to polarize reciprocity on the other, identifies one as the monstrously violent rival of all. One is responsible for everyone's violence and, following his expulsion, for everyone's peace. The difference between peace and strife, the origin of symbolicity itself, is fathered and maintained by violence misunderstood as a divinity.

For Girard, Christ's divinity has been misinterpreted, sacrificed. His divinity is proved not by expulsion, but by his perfect and unique understanding of the necessarily mimetic entanglements of every human society. Christ deconstructs the sacred in the Gospels, offering his listeners the choice between peace fathered by violence, now exposed for the first time, or by positive, nonviolent reciprocity, without exclusions or victims. Christ's alternative of a postsacrificial, nonviolent reciprocal mimesis is temporarily expelled by his Crucifixion, but the apprehension of the Kingdom of God keeps emerging in even the most sacrificial (racist, sexist) texts of western culture, because all exiles are now marked in some way with the sign of Christ's interpretation of every expulsion as victimization: the victims are not uniquely guilty, and the persecutors do not know that they are "scapegoating." *Le Bouc émissaire* (1981) reminds us that we read within this Judeo-Christian hermeneutic every time we interpret medieval narratives that blame Jews for all disorder as "texts of persecution." Even when we have no corroborating historical evidence, we insist that the Jews are scapegoats. This deconstruction of sacrifice as a hypothesis is superior theoretically and morally to all texts of persecution, all mythologies of race and gender. The increasing strength of this truth is demonstrated by the near-universal understanding of the term "scapegoat." Western literature as Judeo-Christian writing is the site of the contest of rival interpretations, violent and nonviolent, the accuser (Satan) gradually losing ground to the defender (Paraclete) of victims. The West's progress is marked by the gradual weakening of matrimonial and culinary taboos, the desymbolization of all differences—even the father as differentiating principle (depaternalization).

The impertinence of arguing that Yeats is working toward the comprehension of (me and) Girard is not what I have in mind. My focus is on what revisionary labor of Yeats makes a postmodern reading of his poem possible. How are we implied, in the work of this poem, toward a future? "Leda" itself is evolving in the context of Judeo-Christian writing from a violent to a nonviolent reciprocity of greater theoretical and moral comprehension. The more Yeats's poem considers the victimization that produces order and difference, the more questionable it all seems. Even if Yeats was a Fascist[15] committed to the sexual/political bond of all-minus-one of sexist/nationalist victimization, fascism cannot account for Leda. Rather, the revisionary textual/sexual practice of this poem is in the service of a comprehension of all dynamics of exclusion.

Whatever Yeats's avowed belief, the revised poem exacts a small but remarkable adjustment from the commentating prose of A Vision, for which the poem was once to serve as metaphor. In the 1938 version of A Vision, we read "what older civilization that annunciation rejected"[16] instead of the earlier "what older civilization she refuted." This prose revision in the face of the poem's revisions admits the civilization blotted out as Leda's, but without her complicity; this civilization was rejected, not refuted, by Zeus's action.

The additional versions of "Leda" already noted further develop the process of revision described in The Cat and the Moon and Certain Other Poems: bird and woman, first called on to function as a single metaphor of annunciation, put out the self-serving political explanation of a new age necessarily replenishing the soil exhausted by the previous one. Here, in A Vision (1938), a rejection rather than a refutation, attributed to Zeus, not Leda, further emphasizes the change from one age to another as an issue of power rather than knowledge. Thus, "Leda" joins company with another great poem of historical transformation, "The Second Coming," quoted a few pages earlier in A Vision.

> Surely some revelation is at hand;
> Surely the Second Coming is at hand.
> The Second Coming! Hardly are those words out
> When a vast image out of Spiritus Mundi
> Troubles my sight: somewhere in sands of the desert
> A shape with lion body and the head of a man,
> A shape blank and pitiless as the sun,
> Is moving its slow thighs, while all about it

Reel shadows of the indignant desert birds.
The darkness drops again; but now I know
That twenty centuries of stony sleep
Were vexed to nightmare by a rocking cradle
And what rough beast, its hour come round at last,
Slouches toward Bethlehem to be born?

"Surely" follows the iron law of antithesis. If mere anarchy is now loose, order surely develops out of disorder, as second comings surely follow first ones. But the "vast image" invoked by the expectations of theory gives Yeats what he did not already know: "Twenty centuries of stony sleep were vexed to nightmare by a rocking cradle." That is, historical Christianity is sacrificial, as Girard freely admits, putting the blame on Jews and every infidel thereafter for the failure of the pax Christi and treating them accordingly. Such cradle rocking orientalized, all other religions as monstrous rivals, others, exiling them to the desert. These religions have been vexed to return as the nightmare of their rejectors. Drawn into violent reciprocity, they pay back one movement of resentment with its monstrous double. There is no way for any postmodern reader to dodge the prescience of Yeats's metaphor for Bethlehem, now.

I am arguing more than the minimalist or formalist line, sometimes encouraged by Yeats himself, that system provided metaphors for poetry, as if any theory could serve this function. Yeats was serious when he put "The Second Coming" and "Leda" to work within the orbit of his system. Yet these metaphors resist Yeats's system, engendering a hypothetical potential equal in seriousness but superior, both intellectually and morally, to the iron law of antithesis and the "poetics of hate."[17]

To recognize the pattern of a new age replacing an older one as a movement of rejection and of resentment is to recognize history as human, not fated, except insofar as humans refuse to understand the history that they have made for themselves by surrendering responsibility to the instincts, the gods, or the gyres. If Zeus's annunciation rejects, rather than refutes, Leda's culture, if the cradle vexes, rather than supercedes, "paganism," these poems of historical change imply movements of power, not knowledge. Following from this, Yeats's ignorance of Leda's culture or the rough beast is likewise an issue of power, repeated, *but not explained,* by "history's" antithetical movements. The poem reenacts Yeats's limits but in the service of posing a question with the hope of a real answer. The question makes the reader as well see his inability to see Leda, or the Semitic double, except as a representation of Zeus's (or historical Christianity's) sacred power.

If Yeats's theory of history and politics cannot explain these poems, perhaps they can explain his theory. If Zeus's history is a rejection of Leda, then this rejection *constitutes* Zeus's knowledge. Patriarchal culture is founded on rejecting a matriarchy it will never know, which perhaps never existed in the form we imagine, except as a patriarchal nightmare.[18] Each revision—each reading of the poem—strengthens the structure of inquisition, of resistance, precisely at the point of indeterminacy, of its own limits. Why can we not see? What does our blindness signify? To repeat, with increasing emphasis, the questions of this poem, is to ask why we have not yet imagined the revolutionary possibility of a modern Leda who brushes this amorous bird aside. This is the real future of "Leda and the Swan." To take in *this* exhilarating image is to feel the whole structure of Zeus's history lose "possession of the scene." The revolutionary possibility of this poem, which Yeats does not realize in his own time, is allocated to a future that, it is to be hoped, will be ours: the imagining of a Leda who can (at the very least) refuse consent to Zeus, the positive equalizing of the sexes in a nonviolent society, where religion, if it is to have a future, means that all are ligated to each other through the imitation of love (not war) without exception.

## NOTES

1. Toril Moi, *Sexual/Textual Politics* (London: Methuen, 1985).

2. Henry Summerfield, *That Myriad-Minded Man* (Gerrards Cross, Bucks.: Colin Smythe, 1975), 215.

3. *The Cat and the Moon and Certain Poems* (Dublin: Cuala Press, 1924), 37.

4. Fredric Jameson, *The Political Unconscious* (Ithaca, N.Y.: Cornell Univ. Press, 1981).

5. "Myth, Ritual and Literature after Girard," in *Futures Present*, ed. Joseph Natoli (Urbana: Univ. of Illinois Press, forthcoming).

6. W. B. Yeats, *The Letters of W. B. Yeats*, ed. Allan Wade (New York: Macmillan, 1955), 706; hereafter cited parenthetically in the text as *Letters*.

7. *The Dial* (June 1924): 493–95.

8. Alt, Peter, and Russell K. Alspach, *The Variorum Edition of the Poems of W. B. Yeats* (New York: Macmillan, 1966), 441.

9. London: T. Werner Laurie, 1925, 179.

10. Richard Ellmann, *The Identity of Yeats* (New York: Oxford Univ. Press, 1964), 176–79.

11. Terry Eagleton, *Criticism and Ideology* (London: Verso, 1978), 18.

12. *A Vision* (London: Macmillan, 1925), 179.

13. Philip Wheelwright, *Heraclitus* (New York: Atheneum, 1971), 140.

14. *A Vision* (New York: Macmillan, 1961), 67.

15. See Bernard G. Krimm, *W. B. Yeats and the Emergence of the Irish Free State* (Troy, N.Y.: Whitston, 1981); Elizabeth Cullingford, *Yeats, Ireland, and Fascism* (London: Macmillan, 1981); Grattan Freyer, *W. B. Yeats and the Anti-Democratic Tradition* (Dublin: Gill and Macmillan, 1981).

16. *A Vision* (1961), 268.

17. Joseph M. Hassett, *Yeats and the Poetics of Hate* (Dublin: Gill and Macmillan, 1986).

18. For feminist skepticism about the matriarchy, see Michelle Rosaldo and Louise Lamphere, eds., *Women, Culture, and Society* (Stanford: Stanford Univ. Press, 1974), especially Joan Bamberger, "The Myth of Matriarchy: Why Men Rule in Primitive Society," 263–80. See also William Blake Tyrell, *The Amazons* (Baltimore: Johns Hopkins Univ. Press, 1984).

6

# THE PERFORMATIVITY OF UTTERANCE IN
# *DEIRDRE* AND *THE PLAYER QUEEN*
### KATHLEEN O'GORMAN

THE PLAYS OF WILLIAM BUTLER YEATS have often been compared to the Japanese No theater, given their bareness of language, stylized gesture, and rituals of chant and dance that often comprise the dramatic substance of his plays. Yet the language of those plays itself can perform action and embody speech as well as gesture, the major components of drama. It does so when it relies on the performative capacity of utterance—that ability of words to do something as well as say something—and it does so in *Deirdre* and *The Player Queen* in a variety of ways.[1] Given that variety, a close study of the speech acts of these plays can suggest ways in which Yeats relies on that capacity of language in his other plays as well; such a study accounts also for much of the dramatic tension of Yeats's drama. While this does not imply that the playwright himself conceived of his work in these particular theoretical terms, it nevertheless validates a number of important assumptions that we all make about language.

In *Deirdre*, the performativity of utterance functions in two important ways. King Conchubar has given his oath to do no harm to Deirdre and Naoise upon their return to his territory—an oath that Fergus and Naoise both accept against the instinctive fears of Deirdre. The giving of a word thus signifies a bond of honor among those who respect it—a bond on which Fergus stakes his friendship with the king and that carries a force sufficient to compel the young lovers to venture into what they would otherwise perceive as a life-threatening trap. When the king breaks that bond and his oath, betraying his plans to

90

take Deirdre from Naoise against their will, Deirdre himself uses language to deliberately deceive King Conchubar. She taunts the king with suggestions of the truth—that she has a knife hidden beneath her garb—while playing on his reluctance to treat her publicly in a demeaning manner. More subtly, Deirdre addresses the musicians as she prepares to kill herself, stating that they know "[w]ithin what bride-bed [she] shall lie this night, / And by what man" (386–87). The lack of specificity of reference deliberately deceives Conchubar into assuming that the referent is himself, when the musicians and the audience know otherwise.

In giving his word to do no harm to Deirdre and Naoise, King Conchubar makes a promise, if an insincere one. Although the audience never hears the words he utters in so doing, they are informed of the king's verbal gesture repeatedly by Fergus and Naoise. When the musicians question the king's intentions, Fergus assures them, "He is my friend; / I have his oath, and I am well content. / I have known his mind as if it were my own" (351). Naoise reiterates the bond established by that oath when he and Fergus discuss the failure of the king to send a messenger. Naoise emphasizes the king's position in guaranteeing fealty to his word: "And being himself, / Being High King, he cannot break his faith. / I have his word and I must take that word, / Or prove myself unworthy of my nurture / Under a great man's roof" (355). Naoise most emphatically validates the binding power of language when Deirdre herself betrays fears of the king's entrapment. Naoise attributes her suspicions to her animal nature and to her upbringing far from the world of men:

> You would have known,
> Had they not bred you in that mountainous place,
> That when we give a word and take a word
> Sorrow is put away, past wrong forgotten.
>
> . . . . . . . . . . . . . .
>
> Listen to this old man.
> He can remember all the promises
> We trusted to.
>
> (364–65)

Conchubar exploits those conditions necessary and sufficient for his word to be considered binding; that Fergus and Naoise both accept it as such demonstrates Conchubar's adherence to those conditions. A closer analysis of his promise in terms of John Searle's formulation of the conditions necessary and sufficient for a promise to be made suggests the rigorousness with which Conchubar sets out to mislead by his utterance of an oath.[2]

In giving his word, Conchubar exploits the assumptions made by Fergus and Naoise about promising that the audience also shares. All assume that Searle's first condition is satisfied: that all of the conditions necessary for linguistic communication to take place have been met, from Conchubar's speaking intelligibly to Fergus's hearing him and understanding the meaning of his words and the commitment implicit in their utterance (with Fergus acting as agent for Naoise and Deirdre).[3] Searle's second condition is one that the audience, as well as Naoise and Deirdre, must accept on Fergus's assurance: that the king established the fact of a promise and delineated its range. They must accept that Conchubar indeed expressed the proposition that he would do no harm to the young lovers upon their return and are compelled to accept this based on Fergus's integrity and upon his own apparent belief in the binding power of the king's words. With those words, Conchubar's refraining from harming Naoise and Deirdre is predicated on the king himself and commits him to that behavior in the future, thus fulfilling the third condition necessary and sufficient for his word to constitute a promise.

With the fourth, fifth, and sixth conditions, Conchubar's exploitation of the illocutionary force of promising manifests itself most cynically. The fourth specifies that whatever is promised "must be something the hearer wants done, or considers to be in his interest . . . and the speaker must be aware of or believe or know, etc., that this is the case" (*Speech Acts*, 59). Naoise and Deirdre clearly want to return to their home in Conchubar's kingdom to live peacefully, and Fergus, as their agent, would like to be instrumental in bringing about such a state of affairs. The king thus multiplies his transgressions by playing on both the lovers' and their agent's desires, both of which he knows well. In fact, he relies on his friendship with Fergus to lend credence to his oath, later violating that friendship as he breaks his word.

As specified by the fifth condition, which indicates that it is not clear to both the speaker and the hearer that the speaker will perform the act promised "in the normal course of events" (*Speech Acts*, 59),

Conchubar, as well as Fergus, Naoise and Deirdre, recognizes the extraordinary nature of his promise to do the lovers no harm. In fact, much of the beginning of the play devotes itself to signalling the skepticism with which such a promise is met, whether by the musicians or by Deirdre herself. This questioning of motives and constant suggestion of possible deception on the part of the king makes explicit the extent to which his promise of no harm deviates from general expectations. Even Naoise and Fergus, who most relentlessly insist on the binding power of the king's word, occasionally betray their own doubts. Naoise finds it worrisome that the king has sent no messenger to welcome them, and Fergus, shortly after Naoise's reference to the fate of Lugaidh Redstripe and his wife, states, "I can remember now, a tale of treachery, / A broken promise and a journey's end— / But it were best forgot" (356). Both suggest in their focus an undercurrent of doubt that further emphasizes the unusual nature of the king's oath.

The sixth condition concerns intention, and here Searle's modification to account for insincere promises is important. Rather than insisting that for a promise to be valid the speaker must intend to perform the act indicated, he instead notes that a promise "involves an expression of intention, whether sincere or insincere" (*Speech Acts*, 62). Searle's conclusion that the speaker intends that his utterance of the promise makes him responsible for intending to perform the act specified neutralizes the question of intent and allows for Conchubar's failure to follow through on his promise. Although he has no intention to be bound by his word while purporting to be so bound, Conchubar does want to be responsible for intending to do no harm to Naoise and Deirdre. Only through the assumption of such responsibility can the king carry out his true intentions. He invokes the illocutionary force of promising with full knowledge that it provides one of the strongest indications of commitment in the language, and his violation of that commitment strengthens rather than diminishes such force. That Conchubar made an insincere promise, then, does not invalidate the illocutionary force of the utterance of that promise: it carries all the force of a sincere promise, with the intention alone distinguishing the insincere from the sincere.

The seventh condition relates closely to that which it follows, emphasizing as it does the notion of obligation implicit in promising. This distinguishes a promise from other kinds of utterances, and in the case of Conchubar's promise in *Deirdre*, it determines the nature of the king's transgression. He does not simply change his mind; he has, through deliberate intent, placed himself under obligation to safeguard the lovers in his kingdom, and he just as deliberately violates that obligation.

The final two conditions that determine the illocutionary force of the utterance of a promise concern semantic rules governing such utterances. The first of these emphasizes the speaker's creating the impression for the hearer that the speaker is indeed undertaking the obligation embodied by the promise. In *Deirdre*, Conchubar creates that impression for the benefit of Fergus, who acts as agent for Naoise and Deirdre, and Fergus, in turn, reassures the wanderers that it is finally safe for them to return home to be reconciled with the king. The final condition, that "the sentence uttered is one which . . . is used to make a promise" (*Speech Acts*, 61), and that insists that the first eight conditions must obtain, stipulates the king's adherence to semantic rules in giving his word to Fergus to do the lovers no harm. The indignation displayed by Fergus when confronted with the musicians' doubts and his insistence on the integrity of the king's word suggest that Fergus is convinced that the king has adhered to all of those conditions necessary and sufficient for his utterance to carry the illocutionary force of a promise; Naoise's willingness to risk his life and that of his beloved on the strength of the bond created by such an utterance indicates his acceptance of Fergus's judgment and suggests that those conditions have been met.

In exploiting the illocutionary force of utterance by making a promise that he had no intention of keeping, Conchubar nevertheless validates the power of language to do something as well as say something. His later breaking of his word emphasizes the assumptions made by all players about its binding power.

Fergus's and Naoise's affirmation of the binding power of Conchubar's word does more than simply ratify agreed-upon social conventions concerning promising. It conditions their response to signs that they would otherwise interpret differently—a difference seen by the audience in Deirdre's reading of the same signs. When the lovers first enter the guest house, Naoise comments on the king's failure to send a messenger to greet them. Fergus interprets the absence as a sign that the king will come himself to greet them. Deirdre suggests the opposite: "An empty house upon the journey's end! / Is that the way a king that means no mischief / Honours a guest?" (357–58).

Fergus insists that the king is readying a feast in honor of their visit. When Fergus invites the two to pass the time playing a game of chess while awaiting the king's arrival, the game board functions as a sign whose meaning Naoise articulates, even as he allows Fergus to diminish its signifying capacity.

> Naoise.   If I had not King Conchubar's word I'd think
>           That chess-board ominous.
>
> Fergus.                           How can a board
>           That has been lying there these many years
>           be lucky or unlucky?
>
> Naoise.                    It is the board
>           Where Lugaidh Redstripe and that wife of his,
>           Who had a seamew's body half the year,
>           Played at the chess upon the night they died.
>
> Fergus.   I can remember now, a tale of treachery,
>           A broken promise and a journey's end—
>           But it were best forgot.
>
>                                        (355–56)

Deirdre follows this exchange with an insistence on the significance of the omens: "The gods turn clouds and casual accidents / Into omens" (356–57). She is rebuked by Naoise, who invokes the fact of the king's promise to dismiss those signs of trouble: "It would but ill become us, / Now that King Conchubar has pledged his word, / Should we be startled by a cloud or a shadow" (357). That Naoise himself earlier acknowledged the threat implicit in such omens while persevering in his refusal to accept what he himself sees testifies to the illocutionary force of the king's promise. It alone compels Fergus and Naoise to ignore or interpret otherwise the signs that would alert them to danger. They interpret the signs in terms of the social convention which gives illocutionary force to promising; Deirdre, raised outside of such society, reads them without that context.

In Conchubar's exploitation of the performative nature of promising, as well as in Naoise's and Fergus's acceptance of the king's word, the social context of promising clearly plays an important role. Fergus and Naoise both draw attention to Deirdre's upbringing away from civilization to dismiss her fears. Fergus states, "It is but natural / That she should doubt him, for her house has been / The hole of the badger and the den of the fox" (355), and later Naoise emphasizes the tacit agreements of society in contravening Deirdre's expressed fears:

> You would have known
> Had they not bred you in that mountainous place,
> That when we give a word and take a word
> Sorrow is put away, past wrong forgotten.
>
> (364)

In the context of socially accepted conventions, then, the promise assumes its illocutionary force. Accordingly, he who holds the highest position in that society, the king, should be bound most absolutely by his word. Naoise insists on this:

> And being himself,
> Being High King, he cannot break his faith.
> I have his word and I must take that word,
> Or prove myself unworthy of my nurture
> Under a great man's roof
>
> (355)

and later "I will not weigh the gossip of the roads / With the King's word" (363-64). In his insistence on the binding power of the king's word, Naoise validates a notion introduced by Emile Benveniste regarding the consideration of performatives. Benveniste asserts that performative utterances are always "acts of authority [which] are first and always utterances made by those to whom the right to utter them belongs."[4] In amending Searle's discussion of performatives in terms of authority, Benveniste isolates a notion that translates into the social sphere and plays a central role in the utterance of performatives in *Deirdre*. Ironically, precisely because he holds the highest social position and embodies the greatest authority, the king feels free to violate the binding power of his own word with impudence and physical force. In breaking his promise, Conchubar invokes the authority of his social position to contravene the authority of his word.

Conchubar is not alone in exploiting the performative capacity of language; Deirdre does the same. Yet while Conchubar's deceptive utterance takes the form of a promise, Deirdre's is assertive. When Conchubar suggests that she might kill herself if left alone with Naoise's body, Deirdre replies, "It may be that I have a knife hid here / Under my dress" (386), and she suggests that he have one of his slaves search her if he really believes that this is true. Once the king bids her make her farewells, Deirdre instructs the musicians to sing, "Knowing that all is happy, and that you know / Within what bride-bed I shall lie this night" (386). Deirdre's statements appear to commit her to Conchubar, yet each contravenes that apparent commitment in a different way.

When Deirdre states that she may have a knife hidden beneath her dress, she uses the conditional tense to make an assertion that in context suggests its own opposite. She invokes the authority vested in the position of queen to demand respect for her word; this means, ironically, that the literal truth of what she utters is negated. By daring the king to have her searched, Deirdre in effect dares him to undermine the integrity of her implied intent. The king's refusal to do so affirms Deirdre's own authority over her word, even as it makes absolute his misreading of her intent. At the same time, in making her assertion, Deirdre commits herself to the truth of the proposition that she expresses. It is precisely the tension between context—compelling Conchubar to interpret her utterance in one way—and the commitment to truth implicit in her utterance that compels the musicians and the audience to interpret her statement in the opposite way, leading dramatic impetus to her words. Deirdre is able to assert one proposition while implying its opposite, a duplicity predicated on the relationship between text and context as it determines intent.

When Deirdre tells the musicians to sing on, knowing "[w]ithin what bride-bed [she] shall lie this night" (386), her lack of specificity creates the duplicity of reference. So, too, does her use of the phrase "bride-bed." Deirdre knows that Conchubar will assume that it refers to his chamber, and she knows with equal certainty that the musicians, one of whom has given her the knife that she has hidden on herself, will realize that the phrase refers to the grave. With such an assertion, then, Deirdre manipulates the reflexive intention of her words: she produces an illocutionary effect that differs for each hearer by getting those who hear her to recognize her intent. Conchubar accepts her earlier assurance that her intent is to bid farewell to Naoise and and return with the king to his chambers; he therefore recognizes Deirdre's intent within that context and misreads it. The musicians, however, have a different context within which to determine the referent of her assertion. They know what Conchubar does not—that Deirdre does indeed hide a knife on her person—and with their words make clear their understanding of her true fate. While Deirdre's assertion commits her to the truth of her proposition, it simultaneously undermines the relationship between utterance and referent, making ambiguous the proposition's referent. In effect, she creates a referential illusion, playing on the self-referential property of such performatives. She can then remain true to her word while contravening Conchubar's expectations of her intent.

The use of performatives in *Deirdre* sets propositional content against context, emphasizing in the process the importance of the latter in any interpretive act. In addition, Conchubar's insincere promise and Deirdre's duplicitous assertions ratify the illocutionary force of utterance by demonstrating the extent to which society confers on language its power to bind. Such power also operates in *The Player Queen*.

Throughout *The Player Queen*, the performative capacity of language is validated repeatedly with regard to different kinds of speech acts. On two occasions, Septimus insists that people stop speaking poorly of the unicorn and of Delphi, suggesting that the translation of their thoughts into words could precipitate some disaster; the townspeople worry that a curse will be brought upon them if they treat Septimus violently; Septimus is accused by Nona of breaking his oath to Decima to play only with her, though he later insists that he would never break a promise; the Old Beggar's braying is said to be the voice of God; and Decima's banishing of the players effects the edict that it decrees. While these last three examples form the principal focus of the performativity of utterance in the play, the earlier suggestions of the power of language lend credence to their force by establishing with lesser intensity the capacity of words to effect change.

With the early mutterings of the townspeople in the first scene of *The Player Queen*, Yeats establishes a context within which the performative capacity of utterance assumes a major role. Septimus's suggestion that some harm will result if he or others speak ill of the unicorn or of the Oracle at Delphi gives preeminence to the spoken word, even as it calls for restraint regarding the content of particular utterances. Septimus emphasizes his respect for the power of language by stating that he would hunt and even kill the unicorn—"shoot it through the head" (725)—but that he would never speak against its character, nor would he allow others to do so in his presence. To grant the spoken word a force greater than that of an instrument of death is to attest dramatically to its potential for effecting change. The mention of the Oracle at Delphi in the same context shortly afterward also draws attention to that source of the spoken word that so dominates ancient mythology. The power of the Oracle was embodied in the spoken word, and any decree uttered by the prophet carried with it the force of an illocutionary act. Such pronouncements differ in an important way from the utterances of the townspeople that Septimus stops: while he fears possible retribution for their speaking against the unicorn or the Oracle, he does not grant the people's utterance *per se* a particular performative capacity. In the case of the Oracle, however, the prophetic function necessarily implies such power. Given the source of utterance, its context, and its propositional content, the words of the Oracle would carry an illocutionary force that the words of the townspeople would not.

In referring to those who would speak against the unicorn and the Oracle, Septimus indicates a significant area of concern for the propositional content of the utterances. With respect to both, he says that he will tolerate no suggestions that they lack chastity. In his insistence, the travelling player intimates that such pronouncements in themselves compromise the purity of both—that words spoken to impugn their honor effect the violation that they describe. Such a perception of the spoken word attributes to it the capacity to do something that goes well beyond its ability to simply say something. While Septimus does not insist on this function of language at this early point of the play, his awareness of it as a possibility and his affirmation of it as a basis for his own behavior tacitly support the performative capacity of the spoken word.

The acknowledgment and fear of the townspeople that violent treatment of Septimus would lead to a curse being put on the town indicate a similar awareness on their part of the power of the spoken word. They believe firmly that a violent act on their part could be reciprocated by an illocutionary act—the cursing of the town. The actual gesture of the curse being pronounced is minimized in this instance, yet its potential is sufficient to condition and restrain the behavior of citizens who otherwise would act against its strictures. By incorporating such tacit acknowledgments of the power of speech acts into the texture of the people's lives, Yeats establishes a context within which the more significant performative utterances of the play gather force.

The taking of an oath and all that such a gesture implies are discussed in *The Player Queen* with reference to Decima, Septimus, and Nona, and all acknowledge the performative capacity of taking an oath, here insisting on such a capacity for the first time in the play. Decima tells Nona of the oath that she made Septimus swear when they were married which specified that he would never perform with an actress other than herself. She taunts Nona with his faithfulness to his word. Nona in return tells Decima that Nona is the only one in the world for whom he will break his oath, and she tells Decima that he will do so because they are lovers. Beyond what this exchange reveals about the relationships among the three and the difficulties that it therefore presents, the conversation draws attention to the extent to which all three respect the binding power of an oath. All of the assumptions made by the three players concerning the illocutionary act of promising are identical to the assumptions that function in *Deirdre* in Conchubar's oath.

One important difference, however, marks Septimus's oath: while Conchubar's promise is an insincere one, Septimus's promise was sincere at the time at which he made it. His expression of intention corresponded with his actual intention, and he fulfilled the additional criteria necessary and sufficient for his words to function as a promise. Decima and Nona both recognize this, intention even in their speculation on whether Septimus would now break that promise. That the promise has bound him this long and that its contravention would mark an important breach of the social order puts the promise itself into a wider context. Most notably, the breaking of the promise seems to assume greater significance than the violation of Decima's and Septimus's marriage. Nona postulates Septimus's anticipated breaking of his promise on the fact that they have been lovers—a fact that Decima resents but one that she minimizes in comparison with his possible breach of promise. Her emphasis on the power of the word to bind Septimus to her in their work as actors draws attention to the illocutionary force of promising *per se*, especially in the context of his marital infidelity. That Septimus would break his promise in no way diminishes that force; on the contrary, his transgression, seen as a very serious violation of all of the social determinants of the binding power of an oath, reinforces those determinants and the performative power of the utterance of the oath.

That power is reasserted when Decima tries to get Septimus to take an oath to banish Nona from the company, never to speak to her or look upon her again. Nona urges Septimus to say whatever Decima wants—to make an insincere promise—but Septimus himself refuses. He acknowledges her ulterior motives in terms of the sincerity condition, saying that she means that an oath can be broken, especially if taken under compulsion. He refuses to make an insincere promise, especially before the eyes of Delphi, and states, "What I promise I perform, therefore, my little darling, I will not promise anything at all" (752). His insistence on the intentional integrity of his word compels Septimus to speak of his oath in terms of its performative capacity. He consciously attributes to it its binding power and refuses to put himself in a position in which he would be so bound by his own word. Septimus considers the oath in terms of its also constraining his own power when he later sees his refusal to make an insincere promise in the following terms: "Because I am an unforsworn man I am strong" (752). That Septimus predicates his strength on his not having taken the oath validates his and society's notions of the capacity of language to do something—in this case, to bind one to a course of action—as well as simply to say something.

One of the most problematic of the illocutionary acts in *The Player Queen* is the Old Beggar's braying. What makes this utterance problematic is its failure to conform to the rule-governed intentional behavior that forms the basic hypothesis of language *per se*.[5] The old man is not, in the most rigorous sense, speaking a language. He is, however, adhering to conditions that regulate his intentional behavior, and in that sense he can be considered to be speaking. The context for his utterance establishes its functioning as language in addition to determining its performative capacity: if he first asks for straw and then has an itchy back, and only if the old man brays, that braying will signal the changing of the crown. The townspeople reveal these conditions early in the play in their discussions of the man's recent presence in town, noting the circumstances surrounding previous changes in the monarchy. As the play progresses and the various conditions are met, there remains only the braying to seal the player queen's position. The prime minister reveals to Septimus what the bishop and others dismiss as the work of an impostor; they assume that the old man is wrong when he does bray because they do not realize that the crown has actually changed hands. The prime minister shakes Septimus and asks, "Do you understand that there has been a miracle, that God or the Fiend has spoken, and that the crown is on her head for good, that fate has brayed on that man's lips?" (759) The utterance of the sound—in this case not even intelligible words—has had the effect of a declaration. The old beggar's braying carries the illocutionary force of an utterance by a supernatural creature—"God or the Fiend"—whose specific identity is not so crucial as its otherworldly power. He serves, then, as the medium through which another speaks and thereby acts, and he does so only by virtue of his adherence to the conditions necessary and sufficient for his utterance to function as a performative. With no other agent and under no other conditions can that sound declare the passing of the crown, points on which the bishop and the townspeople insist.

One of the fundamental ironies of *The Player Queen* is based on this identification of the old beggar as the singular genuine agent of change. When his braying declares the changing of the crown, the bishop is unable to perceive that change and accuses the old man of being an impostor. What the man's utterance has accurately declared, however, is the assumption to the throne of an impostor. While the accusation and identification of the impostor lend the play irony, the role of extralinguistic institutions in establishing a broader ironic base is much greater. Given those institutions, the old man cannot help but issue his declaration; he is compelled by forces beyond himself to signal the change of power in the crown. His pronouncement is irrevocable, and as the prime minister affirms, the braying seals the fate of the crown. Power is ultimately conferred on Decima, although only Septimus, the prime minister, and Decima know that. The old beggar's declaration of the change effects that change and thereby grants power of the crown—another extralinguistic institution—to Decima, the real impostor. In both instances, the extralinguistic institutions determine the illocutionary force of utterance, even though in both instances the issue of the validity of the agent of change is attributed inaccurately. The old man's declaration is binding *because* he is the true agent of the speech act that he performs; Decima's pronouncements as queen will be equally binding *despite* her imposture of the true queen.

Decima's final gesture in the play is to perform two speech acts— a declaration and a promise. Both are compelled in response to Septimus's spoken word: the prime minister informs Decima that Septimus has been speaking against her, "whispering slanders against her Majesty" (759). The statement is accurate in both senses, of course: he has been speaking against Decima, indicating what a difficult wife she has been, and he has been speaking against the fact of her assumption of the throne. Decima's response is to declare, "You are banished" (760), and with her words changes the condition of Septimus and the players. In so doing, her pronouncement satisfies those two special features of declarations not appropriate for other speech acts. Its point is "to bring about some new state of affairs solely in virtue of the utterance,"[6] and it is performed "within some extra-linguistic institution where the speaker is appropriately empowered to bring about new institutional facts solely by the appropriate performance of speech acts" (Searle, *Intentionality*, 171–72). Even though Decima obtains the crown in a deceptive manner, and despite the recognition by Septimus and the prime minister that she is a fraud, the extralinguistic institution of royalty and the beggar's attesting to its veracity grant Decima the power to enact change by virtue of her word. The institution, rather than the individual, empowers the word with its performative capacity. Her promise that the players shall not be any poorer for their banishment relies on the complex illocutionary act of promising as detailed earlier in this study and carries with it the weight of royalty's ability to enact such a promise.

In both plays, the dramatic tension is created by the performative capacity of the language used by the characters. The variety of illocutionary acts embodying that capacity suggests the range and diversity of such acts and defines the importance of context in determining the force of an utterance. For drama in general, and for the plays of W. B. Yeats in particular, the recognition of such potential in the spoken word becomes a recognition also of the ways in which language becomes dramatic, embodies gesture as a part of its definition, and empowers theater with energies for which no previous account has been taken.

## NOTES

1. The plays of William Butler Yeats are quoted from *The Variorum Edition of the Plays of W. B. Yeats*, ed. Russell K. Alspach (New York: Macmillan, 1966). Subsequent quotations are cited in the text by page number in parentheses.

2. Searle sets these forth explicitly in chap. 3 of his *Speech Acts: An Essay in the Philosophy of Language* (London: Cambridge Univ. Press, 1985).

3. That such an assumption operates in this instance is demonstrated by the articulation of its opposite when the musicians note the dark men surrounding the guest house "with murderous and outlandish-looking arms" (349). When Fergus asks them to identify themselves and is met by silence, the musicians state, "They will not answer you" (350), to which Fergus responds, "They do not hear." He needs to invoke fundamental assumptions about communication to try to excuse their behavior.

4. Emile Benveniste, *Problems in General Linguistics*, trans. Mary Elizabeth Meek (Coral Gables: Univ. of Miami Press, 1966), 236.

5. John Searle, *Expression and Meaning: Studies in the Theory of Speech Acts* (London: Cambridge Univ. Press, 1986), 12–30.

6. John Searle, *Intentionality: An Essay in the Philosophy of Mind* (Cambridge: Cambridge Univ. Press, 1983), 171.

# 7

# POETIC RITUAL AND AUDIENCE RESPONSE
## Yeats and the Nō

STEVEN PUTZEL

> It is not the business of a poet to make himself under-
> stood, but it is the business of the people to
> understand him (*E&I*, 207).

WHEN YEATS APPLIED EDWIN ELLIS'S APHORISM delineating the responsibilities of an audience to the actual audiences found seated before
his plays, trouble ensued. A good example of this dichotomy between
the ideal audience and the actual audience is Yeats's description of his
experience as an audience member watching a performance of his own
play, *The King's Threshold*. "In front of me were three people, seemingly
a husband, a wife and a woman friend. The husband was bored; he
yawned and stretched himself and shifted in his seat, and I watched
him with distress" (*VPl*, 415).* The playwright became an audience
viewing his own audience, but rather than spawning a desire to write
a metatheatrical play about play watching and so perhaps engage the
attention of the bored man, the experience spawned a desire to write
into being a new audience that would eliminate forever the offending
yawner.

My task here is to explore, with the help of a few major concepts
from reception theory, Yeats's attempt to draw on his fragmentary knowledge of Japanese drama to forge this new audience. What response did
Yeats expect from spectators? What techniques did he use to evoke this

---

*A list of the abbreviations used in this chapter follows the text.

response? How could he manage to create a novel theatrical experience that would form what we will call a "complicit" response from that hydra-headed beast known as an audience?

When Yeats read translations of a few Japanese Nō plays, he felt that he had found a model for this new audience as well as for new plays. His introduction to *Certain Noble Plays of Japan* by Ezra Pound and Ernest Fenollosa, his many other observations on Nō drama, and his own plays influenced by his conceptions and misconceptions about Nō drama and the Nō stage have provoked thousands of pages of critical and scholarly response. Each noun, verb, and adjective of his claim that he has "invented a form of drama, distinguished, indirect, and symbolic, and having no need of mob or Press to pay its way—an aristocratic form" (*E&I*, 221) has been closely scrutinized; and every assumption, prejudice, social and political implication, and angry jab have been explored and argued over. In keeping with Yeats's own emphasis on language, on the primacy of poetry over action in his drama, and with his insistence that "theatre business"—the day-to-day management of stage space, designs, players, plays, and audience—has "dried the sap out of [his] veins" (*VP*, 260), much of the critical activity has centered around the dramatic text, the plays as literature.

More recently, attention has shifted to Yeats's many comments on performance.[1] Although all of this performance-oriented scholarship and criticism touches on the problems of audience reception and response, I will focus entirely on the dark side of the theater—on the spectator whom Yeats begrudgingly realizes is an integral part of what Patrice Pavis calls the "theatrical relationship." In so doing, I will avoid the temptation to add still one more study of the influence of Nō on Yeats. Instead, I will concentrate on places of intersection between Yeats, the Nō master Zeami, and reception theorists such as Patrice Pavis, Roman Ingarden, Hans Robert Jauss, and Wolfgang Iser, who provide a critical vocabulary that is almost equal to the complexities of Yeats's relationship to his audience. Although I am most concerned here with the actual and the implied spectators of *The Only Jealousy of Emer*, the other *Plays for Dancers: At the Hawk's Well, The Dreaming of the Bones*, and *Calvary* are useful for comparison. The few pages of blank verse lines that confront a reader are, of course, only a fraction of what appears on the stage. Although this is true of all plays, the ritual opening of these plays and the dance sequences at their climaxes are key theatrical moments sketchily outlined by the dramatic text.

From the start, Yeats's relationship with audiences was ambiguous at best and often downright antagonistic. "The mob" suspended disbelief to cheer what they perceived to be *Cathleen Ni Houlihan*'s patriotic call for sacrifice, but at least some of them had given the raspberry to the paganism of *The Countess Cathleen* and *The Land of Heart's Desire*. In what many *aficionados* of Irish theater history consider Yeats's most heroic moment—taking on the rowdy mob disrupting Synge's *Playboy*—Yeats declared a war on the "popular" audience that would rage for twenty-five years, even though he always supported what he called "A People's Theatre."[2] This seeming contradiction, together with Yeats's fascist Blueshirt flirtation and his pointed use of words like "mob" and "aristocratic," have fueled studies such as *Yeats and Fascism* and *Yeats and the Anti-Democratic Tradition* and should compel readers and spectators to scrutinize Yeats's problems with and perceptions of his audience.

Reading Pound and Fenollosa on the Nō, Yeats certainly felt that he had discovered not only a new form of drama but an old form of ideal audience that could be resurrected and placed before his plays. But as Yeats himself realized, the ideal audience, like Stanley Fish's model reader, can never be more than a theoretical construct. "I knew that I was creating something which could only fully succeed in a civilization very unlike ours. I think [the dance plays] should be written for some country where all classes share in a half-mythological, half-philosophical folk-belief which the writer and his small audience lift into a new subtlety" (*VPl*, 566). Nevertheless, Pound's claim that Nō plays "were made only for the few; for the nobles; for those trained to catch [the art of] allusion"[3] reinforced Yeats's conviction that "realism is created for the common people" (*E&I*, 227), and, as he told John O'Leary as early as 1897, it was time for an "esoteric Irish literature for the few" (*L*, 286). Demanding a great deal from an audience is laudable, but the insistence that the dance plays be performed exclusively for "the pleasure of friends and a few score people of good taste" (*E&I*, 222) is antitheatrical and predicated on a misconception of Nō theater. As a result, Yeats's idea of an audience was more limited than the ancient Japanese idea of an audience.

Ezra Pound introduced Yeats to Nō techniques in 1913 while Pound was working on his edition of Fenollosa'a diaries and translations, but Yeats was already aware of and fascinated by the *japonaiserie* craze reflected in the work of James Whistler, Edmund Dulac, Oscar Wilde, Lafcadio Hearn, and others. He mentions having often seen the Japanese prints in the British Museum, he knew of works such as Percival Lowell's *Occult Japan* (1895), and he may have seen early commentaries on Japanese drama such as that by Bishop Hood, or even the translation of a Nō play published in the *Cornhill Magazine* by Basil Hall Chamberlain in 1876. Long before 1913, he was well versed in the same Shinto and Zen-Buddhist traditions that played so important a role in the early development and practice of Nō.[4]

Despite previous knowledge of Nō tradition, Yeats often paraphrases Fenollosa or Pound on Fenollosa in his introduction to *Certain Noble Plays of Japan*, in "A People's Theatre," and in his notes and introductions to collections of his plays. Among the ideas relevant to Yeats's view of audience are: (1) all imaginative art keeps at a distance from reality, forging a "separating strangeness" (*E&I*, 224); (2) realism is the form of "common folk"; (3) common folk are "without the memory of beauty and emotional subtlety" (*E&I*, 227); (4) Nō is exclusively for the "nobility"; (5) the chorus describes the scene and interprets thought but never becomes involved in the action, as does the Greek chorus; and (6) ritual and ceremony are emphasized. Rather than dwelling on the elitist elements here, I am more concerned with the rejection of realism, the meaning of the term "separating strangeness," and the effect of Yeats's chorus and ritualized movement on the audience.

When we go back to Pound's excerpts from Fenollosa, we feel as though we are reading Yeats. Words such as "emotion," "tradition," "inner spirit," and "grace" echo throughout the diary and throughout Yeats's essays on the theater, while Fenollosa's description of Nō's effect on its noble audience sounds very much like what Yeats himself was after. "There is thus a delicate adjustment of half a dozen conventions appealing to eye, ear, or mind, which produces an intensity of feeling such as belongs to no merely realistic drama. The audience sits spellbound before the tragedy, bathed in tears; but the effect is never one of realistic horror, rather of a purified and elevated passion, which sees divine purpose under all violence."[5]

For the most part, Yeats seems to be content with Fenollosa's rather romantic nineteenth-century notions concerning Nō tradition. His own growing interest in preserving the dying culture of the Anglo-Irish ascendancy and in countering the rising democratic, "mass" or "popular" cultural side of the nationalist movement must have found hope in Japan's revival of the Nō form by now impecunious noble families after it had been banned following the 1868 revolution overthrowing the shogunate. As Peter Arnott puts it, "Nō drama became another badge of class, a new ritual among many to set the samurai apart from the despised lower orders. Appreciation was a mark of breeding; it was not the plays that were on trial, but the audience."[6] Yeats's imperfect grasp of Fenollosa's fragmentary understanding of Nō tradition in fact reinforced and perpetuated many of his problems with audience. Behind the nineteenth-century revival of the Nō lies a vast tradition of performances and theory that, when better understood and incorporated into our understanding of theater history and performance theory, enables us to form a paradigm of audience reception that facilitates the hermeneutical task of interpreting Yeats's plays via the assumptions, the conventions, and the codal baggage that audiences bring to these plays.

F. A. C. Wilson and Earl Miner long ago pointed out that *The Dreaming of the Bones* was inspired by the fourteenth-century Nō master Zeami's play *Nishikiqi*, and, more recently, Richard Taylor demonstrated the similarities between *At the Hawk's Well* and another play by Zeami, *Yoro*.[7] Although no more than fragments of Zeami's treatises were available to Yeats via Fenollosa and Pound, Yeats seems to have extracted much of Zeami's aesthetics by imitating many of his dramatic techniques. The concept of aesthetic distance, stylized movement and dance, stasis, the primary of poetry over action, and the function of the chorus are all discussed in the treatises, but Zeami's emphasis on the actor and on the actor's relationship to the audience never filtered down to Yeats. As Yamazaki Masakazu states in "The Aesthetics of Ambiguity," "on the one hand, Zeami was an artist who pursued purity in the theater and gave birth to a highly sophisticated theatrical taste, but on the other hand he set for himself the almost contradictory task of pleasing the popular audience at all times."[8] Zeami was concerned with the reception of his plays by people of all socioeconomic levels, not just by the noble, well-educated elite.

Like postmodern reception theorists, Zeami understood the complex interaction between performance and spectator, or rather, he saw the spectator as an integral and interacting part of the performance. According to Zeami, it is the responsibility of the *shite*, or chief actor, to read and react to the audience's initial emotional, psychological, and educational level and to create a rhythmic, psychological movement that both responds to and molds the audience's reception of the play. One of the final secrets that Zeami wished to pass on to his successors focuses on audience reception. "The level of art that causes a spectator to merely say 'ah!' in expressing his wonderment lies even below the beginnings of the true way of art. This is nothing more than the reaction of a country bumpkin, up to the capital for the first time, who expresses amazement when he sees the great Tōji temple. The highest level of skill may be termed Fascination [omoshiroki]" (Zeami, 192).

Zeami's insights on the interaction between spectator and performance, together with insights of reception theorists, may help us understand how Yeats attempted to bring his audience beyond the naïve "ah!" response to complicit or interactive reception of his performance texts. Zeami, like Yeats, was keenly aware of what audiences bring with them or do not bring with them to a performance—what Jauss, building on the ideas of Gadamer and Husserl, calls the "horizon of expectation." This term is so central to reception theory that it may act as an umbrella under which we can discuss most key aspects of audience response, such as "defamiliarization," "gaps of indeterminacy," "concretization," "complicit reading," "historicity," "aesthetic pleasure," and "aesthetic distance." Although Jauss's theories are only partially applicable to the stage, his three elements constituting horizon of expectation provide a useful framework: (1) "familiar norms" or the "immanent poetics of the genre," in this case the conventions of drama and performance; (2) "implicit relationships to familiar works of the literary-historical surroundings"; and (3) "the opposition between fiction and reality, between the poetic and the practical function of language," or, in this case, the languages of the stage.[9] The aesthetic value of the performances lies not in the fulfillment of these expected elements, but in the systematic undermining and refocusing of audience expectation.

The fourteenth-century Nō audience, noble and commoner alike, and the refined "audience" of the modern revived Nō plays came to a performance with very specific, culturally determined expectations regarding plot, style, ritual, poetic form, costuming, and staging conventions. Each Zeami play (like so many of Yeats's plays) retold hero tales and love stories that had been dramatized many times before. Consequently, the plays fulfilled rather than undermined the audiences' assumptions concerning history, politics, class distinctions, sex roles, and the like. In fact, Zeami stipulates that there are only three basic role types in true Nō drama: the old person, the woman, and the warrior (with the addition in many plays of the demon). The Nō audience also had a fixed idea of the fictional nature of role playing, or *mono-mane* (literally "imitation"), the consciously antinaturalistic poetic form; they expected the gap between the poetic and practical, and this gap was never bridged. The aesthetic value, then, lies not in unexpected twists of plot, unique characters, thought-provoking social views, or the reinterpretation of historical events, but in the unexpected subtle movement, intonation, and varied pitch of the *shite*, the actor/chanter/dancer. Frequently, Zeami records his recognition that audiences with varied levels of experience and knowledge of Nō will have varied levels of expectation. Rather than wishing to limit his audience only to the "few people of good taste," he believes that although "a good player will find it difficult to please an audience that is not discriminating," and that "while it is true that an untutored audience may not grasp the elements that make a performer good, and thereby learn to appreciate him, . . . a truly gifted player, if he really makes use of all his artistic skills, should be able to move even an undiscriminating audience" (Zeami, 39–40). Fully one-third of Zeami's treatises describe ways in which an actor can learn to "read" his audience, to build audience anticipation, to grasp intuitively the "level of tension," and to "absorb the concentration of the audience into his own performance" (Zeami, 82).

In terms of reception theory, here is the essential difference between Yeats's dance plays and his Nō models. His handpicked audience comes to the theater or to the drawing room with a much less specifically defined horizon of expectation. He wants the refined, educated, discriminating side of Zeami's audience without the bother of the less discriminating masses. The norms and conventions familiar to even this artificially created audience are very different from those that an audience experiences in the Yeatsian stage space. Friends of Yeats or not, spectators would be accustomed to the conventions of the nineteenth-century stage and to the modern trend toward realism and naturalism so abominable to Yeats. Presumably, such spectators would be able to determine the "implicit relationships to familiar literary-historical works"; i.e., they would understand the convention of blank verse drama, would draw comparison to Greek drama, would be familiar with Yeats's earlier work, and would recognize allusions to Irish or biblical sources. Yeats himself would have educated such an audience to the differences between the "poetical and the practical" through his many essays outlining his principles of the stage.

Achievement of this level of audience discrimination depends upon two seemingly contradictory elements of response, the process that Yeats called "separating strangeness" and the question of the historicity of a work and its reception. Leading up to what is being called the New Historicism, a long line of theorists, including Schiller, Gadamer, and Brecht, and now Iser, Jauss, and Pavis, have attempted to demonstrate that literary history is formed by the process of reception and that past meanings are part of present readings. Gadamer calls this "effective-history," while Iser is more specific about the interaction between audience and text: each era has its own "configurations of meaning," and it is the reader/audience's task to understand the effect of this "time axis" and to assemble meaning as a process. According to Pavis, the two "historicities" that we must take into account are "that of the work within its literary and social context, and that of the receiver in his own time and within a system of ideological and aesthetic expectations."[10]

Yeats complicates this paradigm by superimposing his own (mis)-reading of Nō texts and audiences onto his dance plays, thus creating an ideal atmosphere for theatrical strangeness. A Japanese audience would have been familiar with the long-standing semiological codes, so that each movement of an arm in billowing sleeve, each nod of the head, and each moment of stasis would have some historical context. The two historicities of fourteenth-century Nō drama could easily meld into a single historicity shared by performers and audience. This, of course, would not be true for a modern Japanese Nō audience for whom the heroic content, as well as the stylized form, harkens back to a different era—to a different historicity with very different values and a very different literary and theatrical tradition. Arnott puts it this way: "The modern Japanese watching *noh* is in the same predicament as Yeats's audience watching his First and Second Musicians sitting crosslegged on the drawing-room floor. It is not his ritual. Understanding is no longer instinctive. It has to be acquired, and must always, with the best will in the world, remain partially foreign."[11]

But Yeats recognized this partial "foreignness" as one of the most successful aspects of his plays. By extension, the chances of creating a sense of the "separating strangeness" or "astonishment" are greater because his dance plays are even more foreign to a late twentieth-century audience, which is for the most part unfamiliar with the Irish heroic tradition and with the drama of the Irish Literary Renaissance, as well as with Nō techniques.

Yeats begins with archetypal themes such as a double love triangle, a wife's self-sacrifice, and a male hero's obliviousness to this sacrifice. But the musicians' songs, the blank verse, the archaic language, and the semantic inversions, together with Edmund Dulac's racially indeterminate masks (part Japanese, part Greek, part Egyptian), gradually draw the audience out of its own historicity, away from familiar themes, and into the "strange" world of the play.

Having stage managed his audience, Yeats's task should be much simpler than Zeami's. Yet it is not. Although Zeami did not have full control of the audience, as author of and chief actor in his own plays, he controlled the performance. Yeats, playing the role of host rather than of Cuchulain, Emer, or Christ, had no such control, and he often voiced his frustration with the limitations of his actors and their inability to translate his vision of a performance text into an actual performance. Even Michico Ito, upon whom Yeats heaps extravagant praise, was not by Zeami's standards or by those of the modern Nō stage a fully trained Nō performer.

If we turn away from the gap between Yeats's theatrical ideals and his actual theatrical experience to the theory of audience reception implicit in the plays themselves, we form a clearer idea of what it means to be complicit spectators/readers of Yeats's dance plays. An examination of a few points of intersection between Zeami's theory, modern reception theory, and Yeats's plays reveals what Yeats expects of his audience and the techniques that he employs to achieve the desired response. Just as Zeami wished to move the audience beyond the simple "ah!" response, so Yeats worked toward provoking what Pavis calls complicit readings from his readers and spectators. That is, he wanted to move members of his audience beyond their initial naïve responses to involve their creative powers. The term "complicit reading" implies that the audience is actively involved as an accomplice, as a partner in something almost duplicitous. This image of writer/audience whispering tête-à-tête conveys the sense that each reading and each interpretation is the product of a personal and private involvement. This is one of Yeats's dilemmas; like Zeami, he hoped that his productions would appeal to spectators' anticipations and emotions and so recreate them as a single entity—an audience—yet he requires the individual's personal creative involvement. Yeats certainly did not want to evoke a naïve emotional or a coldly intellectual response, but he would have embraced the Zenlike response that Zeami articulates so well. "A spectator who understands the heart of the actor as he watches a performance is a gifted spectator. The following might be said concerning making judgments: forget the specifics of a performance and examine the whole. Then forget the performance and examine the actor. Then forget the actor and examine his inner spirit. Then, forget that spirit, and you will grasp the nature of the nō" (Zeami, 102). This desire for complicity that Yeats in his own way shares with his Nō predecessor moves beyond a mere suspension of disbelief; now the spectator is cocreator and coconspirator in the construction of the stage fiction.

Until recently, theories outlining this participatory process have focused on reading, largely ignoring the more complex problems of theater audience reception. For example, when Roman Ingarden identifies the strata and dimensions that form the "schematic structure" confronting any complicit reader, he includes raw semiotic material such as verbal sounds, phonetic formations, semantic units, the "schematized aspects in which objects of various kinds portrayed in the work come to appearance," and the "objectivities . . . projected by the sentences." These strata as perceived simultaneously form one dimension of a literary work, while the ordered sequence of all the parts forms the second, or "temporal," dimension.[12] This paradigm must be expanded to include the language of the stage, the codes or conventions that form the dramatic/theatrical schema confronting an audience. Where Ingarden is most helpful, however, is in his observation that the aesthetic creation presents a schematic system that must be completed by the reader. In the case of theater, the director, the actors, and the designers of set, costume, and lighting must first apply their own creativity to complete what Pavis, applying Ingarden's term to theater, calls the "concretization," the interpretation, and the transformation of dramatic text into performance text. Then a second-level concretization takes place as the spectators recreate in "the eye of the mind" what they see and hear before them. Both dramatic texts and performance texts leave places of indeterminacy produced by necessary and intentional ambiguity.[13] The audience concretizes the production and becomes complicit by bridging these gaps.

A look at the opening stage directions and musicians' songs in the dance plays demonstrates Yeats's own demand for a complicit reading. Ritual action and a few ambiguous lines of poetry leave chasms of indeterminacy in comparison to the mere gaps left by the more fleshed-out schema of realism and naturalism. What is the relationship between the masklike faces of the statuesque musicians and the audience that is seated almost close enough to touch them? In all the dance plays, Yeats subtly provides his audience with directions for and models of complicit responses, first with stage directions, then with the musicians' opening and closing songs, and finally with characters who take on the role of audience in a play-within-a-play.

In the stage directions to *At the Hawk's Well*, *The Only Jealousy of Emer*, *The Dreaming of the Bones*, and *Calvary*, Yeats creates an interdependent, intertextual, and idiolectal paradigm to govern the staging of the plays. Even in *The Collected Plays* (1934), in which the dance plays no longer form a sequence, he assumes that readers or directors will trace the cross-references. In other words, to form a fully complicit reading of *The Only Jealousy of Emer*, we must be familiar with the directions of *At the Hawk's Well*. Yeats imaginatively becomes his own audience for a moment to discuss one of the problems of audience response: "Indeed, I think, so far as my present experience goes, that the most effective lighting is the lighting we are most accustomed to in our rooms. These masked players seem stranger when there is no mechanical means of separating them from us" (*VPl*, 398–99). Conventional modern methods of creating stage illusion, such as stage lights and elaborate sets, give way here to a "patterned screen," a ceremony involving a cloth with a "pattern suggesting a hawk," three musicians with "faces made up to resemble masks," and natural rather than naturalistic lighting. Yeats requires that the audience flesh out the patterns, fill in the gaps, and complete the hermeneutical task of creating stage or fictional space out of "real" space.

Here, then, is our first model of complicity. The masklike faces and the unfamiliar yet obviously sign-laden cloth ceremony, in contrast to the natural setting and lighting, contribute to the process that Viktor Shklovskii calls *ostranenie*, or "making strange," a concept that will develop into Brecht's *Verfremdungseffekt*. For Shklovskii, the unfamiliar, "la différence essentielle," distinguishes a work from its predecessors and from familiar social, linguistic, literary (and, in our case, theatrical) conventions, while at the same time foregrounding the form of the work.[14] For Yeats, the opening devices foreground his stage space, his stage conventions, the rhythmic movement, and his poetic language, thus calling attention to a form with which the audience is not at first familiar. What Yeats calls "separating strangeness" and Shklovskii calls *ostranenie*, Zeami calls "beguiling the audience," or "creating an emotional atmosphere different from that already held by the audience" (Zeami, 187). The same cloth ceremony and similar patterned screens also mark the beginning of *The Only Jealousy of Emer*, *The Dreaming of the Bones*, and *Calvary*. Apart from the pragmatic uses of the cloth (to enable a mask to be changed and players to leave the stage unseen), the folding ceremony creates gaps of indeterminacy requiring audience complicity in ways that traditional nineteenth- and twentieth-century openings and closings of stage curtains cannot. By the time he wrote *Calvary* in 1920, Yeats added one more stipulation—that the audience be seated around three sides of the stage space, increasing the intimacy and at the same time increasing the "strangeness."

*Calvary*, the shortest of the dance plays, also provides the best example of Yeats's attitude toward his gaps of indeterminacy and toward problems of concretization. His note to the play begins with a bitterly ironic assessment of those who will one day attempt to concretize the dramatic text into a performance: "I have written the little songs of the chorus to please myself, confident that singer and composer, when the time came for performance, would certainly make it impossible for the audience to know what the words were" (*VPl*, 789). Despite his impassioned claim in his note to *At the Hawk's Well*, "I need a theatre" (*VPl*, 415), and his earlier vow to "write plays where all would depend upon the player" (*VPl*, 1291), his note seems to condemn his own plays to the closet. With the euphoria of his successful premier of *At the Hawk's Well* before an audience of fifty almost four years behind him, Yeats added an attack on the imperfections of performers to his comments about the "stupidity of an ordinary audience" (*VPl*, 566). To the *Calvary* note he adds that his songs should contain "some mystery or secret," because "a reader can always solve the mystery and learn the secret by turning to a note" (*VPl*, 789). But a spectator cannot or at least should not have to turn to a note to fill the places of indeterminacy.

Perhaps because in 1920 *At the Hawk's Well* was still the only one of the four dance plays that Yeats had seen performed, he sells his own theatricality and potential audiences somewhat short. While Zeami could write, manage, and perform his own plays, Yeats was limited to the writing and managing. While Zeami employed his psychological insight as well as his acting skills to "read" sepctators' intellectual and emotional levels and then to mold their response, Yeats was reduced to playing the role of Club 54 doorman, choosing who would enter, or to imagining his plays performed by ideal actors before ideal audiences. Unlike Pirandello, Yeats never accepted the harsh fact of theatrical life — that the work passes from the control of the author into a life of its own. Even without perfect dancers, singers, and actors, however, the dance plays have often been successfully translated onto the stage, and spectators can enjoy forming a complicit reception, filling in for themselves the many gaps of indeterminacy that mark the aesthetic value of the plays.

The musicians' opening songs direct the level of audience complicity, engaging spectators' active interpretive powers by doing more than merely creating a mood and painting a stage picture, or rather, as Elizabeth Loizeaux points out, sculpting a three-dimensional stage form.[15] In the opening lines of *At the Hawk's Well*, the three musicians sing with one voice, directly engaging the audience with a "call to the eye of the mind," while at the same time acting out the cloth ritual. In a style totally presentational rather than representational, they, like the Nō chorus and unlike the Greek chorus or the musicians in *Deirdre*, dance and sing outside the action that they describe. Far from being a simple prologue or authorial voice, the musicians also become a vulnerable audience, calling spectators' attention to their own vulnerability; the second musician intones, "I am afraid of this place." The song and the rhythmic movement, which are simultaneously mimetic and diegetic, together with the patterned rather than representational set and costume design, let the audience know that they will not be able to relax, sit back, and be transported. Whereas in the more popular theater an audience receives and reacts, here members of the audience must interact, actively transporting themselves.

The picture or sculpture that the song evokes is purposely ambiguous and undetermined. The "choked" and "dry" well is concrete enough, but what specific picture is evoked by "Pallor of an ivory face, / Its lofty dissolute air"? No character is yet on stage, so the audience beings to "see" even before the ivorylike guardian and the masked old man are revealed. As the musicians refold the cloth, which is in itself an unconventional stage convention, they introduce to this picture "a man climbing up" to a bare, windswept place, and before the character appears, they present the audience with an abstract meditation on the questionable value of living to an old age. A reader could see this as an authorial self-indulgence and as a preview of the fifth stanza of his 1927 poem "Among School Children," but what is a theater audience to do with the passage?

> What were his life soon done!
> Would he lose by that or win?
> A mother that saw her son
> Doubled over a speckled shin,
> Cross-grained with ninety years,
> Would cry, "How little worth
> Were all my hopes and fears
> And the hard pain of his birth!"
>
> (VPl, 399)

If the singing does not, in fact, obscure the words, the audience would be reconstructing the lyric through its own interpretation, taking in the chorus's strange movement, the masklike faces, the simple trimeter, and the alternate rhymes and obscure, almost referentless, references. The audience is being fed information that will help to determine its attitude toward Cuchulain's quest for immortality and toward his failure to achieve it. These lines also act as a lyric interlude, painting an image external to the play on the "mind's eye"—a young mother with prescience seeing her child at ninety.

A fully complicit audience response also necessitates previous knowledge of the Cuchulain legend and of the term "speckled shin" (explained in published stage directions). The musicians demand much from the audience; we must listen to their story, form a visual image, and sort out and contemplate obscure allusions and changing historicities, while at the same time we must recognize the patterns and the beauty of language, movement, and design.

The musicians here and in the other dance plays take on the role of chanter, *samisen* (three-stringed instrument) player, and puppeteers of *Bunraku*, present but understood to be invisible to the characters. The words and music of the musicians seem to evoke and give material substance to characters who begin as pure mental constructs. For example, the old man "lifts his head at the sound of a drum-tap" and moves like a "marionette." Who is pulling the strings?—partly Yeats, partly the musicians, partly the old man's own obsession, and partly members of the audience who have also given him life in their mind's eye. As the audience gradually becomes familiar with its own role, the musicians slip into pure diegesis and finally take their places against the wall to play their mood-creating, image-controlling music, until they reassert their power to close the play and dispel the illusion.

In contrast to the beginning of *At the Hawk's Well, The Only Jealousy of Emer* begins with the mood-setting, purposely ambiguous lyric, postponing the verbal setting of the stage ("I call before the eyes"), with the result that audiences form their first images from abstractions rather than from the more concrete diegesis. Again, what can Yeats expect from an audience when he presents them with a multilayered brilliant beginning?:

> A woman's beauty is like a white
> Frail bird, like a white sea-bird alone
> At daybreak after stormy night
> Between dark furrows upon the ploughed land
>
> (*VPl*, 529)

The audience again must respond to these abstractions with only the musicians and their ceremony before its eyes. Scholars and critics, of course, can and have spent as many hours over these lines as they have over all that Yeats has written, but a theater audience does not have this luxury. Here, then, the audience must fill in chasms of indeterminacy. Even an audience trained by *At the Hawk's Well* will find it difficult to respond to the first double simile, to equate "a woman's beauty" to the elaborate fiction describing the frail white bird. After the first sentence, the audience has a vivid mental image of the bird, but the idea of beauty is still just that—an idea. The second sentence introduces still more gaps with an unanswerable question:

> How many centuries spent
> The sedentary soul
> In toils of measurement

> Beyond eagle or mole,
> Beyond hearing or seeing,
> Or Archimedes' guess,
> To raise into being
> That loveliness?

Even an audience hearing these words sung once should be able to respond to the ambiguities and contradictions; the soul (beauty's creator) is both sedentary or static and actively toiling. The "measurement" introduced here is itself a fine model for Ingarden's "indeterminacy." What is "measurement" that is neither up nor down, neither seeable nor touchable, and impervious even to Archimedes' "Eureka!"? The play, we are warned, will be patterned and measured in a poetic sense but will concern unmeasurable ideals. Although the first musician's speech following the song is again straightforward diegesis, describing and introducing, at the end of the play the musicians again take up the question of response and interpretation.

The musicians help to define the role that spectators will play as a complicit audience through both diegetic speeches and mimetic action. Just as the musicians provide background and traditional exposition that enable the audience to place the action in its literary and historical context, so, too, characters such as Emer and the figure of Cuchulain guide the audience through narration as well as through their action. For example, Emer seems to summarize the action recorded in Yeats's earlier *On Baile's Strand* in answer to Eithne's (and perhaps the audience's) question, "How did he come to this?" Bricriu, having assumed the figure of Cuchulain, lapses into a narrative account of how the Sidhe steal and bargain to educate spectators who may not have read *The Celtic Twilight, Fairy and Folk Tales*, or any of Yeats's voluminous studies on the subject. But Yeats also employs diegesis to evoke audience complicity in other ways. Emer describes the signs that will mark her husband's death:

> The very heavens when that day's at hand,
> So that his death may not lack ceremony,
> Will throw out fires, and the earth grow red with blood.
> There shall not be a scullion but foreknows it
> Like the world's end

> (*VPl*, 535)

For most spectators, this passage would call before the mind's eye the *Book of Revelation*, perhaps a passage describing nature's prognosis of the death of Shakespeare's Julius Caesar (1.3.3–32), or most likely Matthew's description of the moment of Christ's "death" (27.51–53); the reception and processing of these allusions raises Cuchulain to a level of respect far exceeding what his actions in the play earn for him.

Far more important to audience reception, however, are the more mimetic sections of the play. Yet, in discussing the "actions" in the play, we would do well to expel the too often misused Aristotelian term "mimesis" in favor of Zeami's *monomane*, or role playing, and *yūgen*, or grace. With these concepts in mind, the *shite* imitates not the external, "realistic" attributes of a character, but the more mystical essence of the character. For example, a Nō actor playing the figure of Cuchulain would never extend an arm made up to look realistically withered, but would instead convey an idea of the withered arm through his own stance and movement, thus again calling on the complicity of the audience to complete the image. Like Zeami, Yeats also experiments with moments of stasis (dating back to his famous threat to rehearse actors in barrels), such as when Eithne "stands a moment in the open door," when the ghost of Cuchulain crouches unmoving by the bed, when Fand enters the stage and stands statuelike before beginning her dance, or when Emer becomes a silent, even temporarily paralyzed, observer. For Zeami, such static moments or *buchi* are moments beyond consciousness that create in the audience "one Intensity of Mind" during which the audience senses that "nothing is happening" yet at the same time is fascinated.

The blending of *yūgen* and *monomane* is most obvious in Fand's climactic dance. She looks and moves like an "idol," and her dance starts slowly in the easy manner of the *jo* section of a Nō performance. It then develops dramatically as in the *ho* section and finally finishes rapidly like the *kyū* at the conclusion of a Nō play or sequence of plays. The near-perfection represented by Fand and her dance could easily be described by Zeami's term for the dance, *yūshufu*, or "mutuality in balance." All aspects of this stylized role playing have a singular effect on audience reception. Yeats would agree with the way in which Zeami puts it: "When it comes to observing the Nō, those who truly understand the art watch it with the spirit, while those who do not merely watch it with their eyes. To see with the spirit is to grasp the Substance;

to see with the eyes is merely to observe the Function" (Zeami, 12, 71).

The role of substance-seeing audience, played by the musicians in the first moments of the play, is subsumed by Emer, who becomes an audience to the Fand-Cuchulain play-within-the-play. Bricriu touches her eyes just as the author has touched the eyes of the audience, and just as Cuchulain is "shut off, a phantom / That can neither touch, nor hear, nor see," so all the characters are shut off from the audience; or, as Ingarden would put it, the performance is "closed." Emer and the audience are so close to the action and to the substance but are held back by Bricriu and by Yeats. Yet Emer has only a few seconds to make the hardest decision of her life: she must interpret the meaning and consequences of the action before her dream-awakened eyes, and she must make her choice immediately and irrevocably. The spectators in their chairs are not personally at risk, but they, too, must respond not to lines that can be read over and over, but to the fleeting stage image before their dream-awakened eyes. Yeats perfects this technique of creating a character who is a judgmental audience/witness in a "closed" performance in *The Dreaming of the Bones*, his next dance play.

As a last experiment, in *The Death of Cuchulain*, Yeats "opens" his stage, dismantling his fourth wall to let the old man address the audience directly, but in the dance plays, the musicians come closest to "opening" the stage. By the end of *The Only Jealousy of Emer*, they reassert their role as complicit audience, perhaps signaling the author's desired level of complicity. As the second and third musicians seem to question the first with, "Why does your heart beat thus?" the audience asks itself the same question. (A few years later, this question is rephrased, "Why does my heart beat so?" as the opening line of *The Dreaming of the Bones*.) Yet not many spectators would share the next response, which Yeats takes directly from translations of Irish sagas, "plain to be understood." In fact, very little is or should be "plain" to the complicit audience. Nevertheless, the assertion that all is "plain" reassures the audience that it is possible to construct a meaning and to complete the hermeneutical task of interpretation.

The musicians' closing song provides commentary that ponders the action that has taken place on stage and speculates on an ongoing "action" off stage: "Although the door be shut / And all seem well enough." Yet it is the last three lines of the last song's refrain that provide a paradigm of audience reception. "And we though astonished are dumb / Or give but a sigh and a word / A passing word." This musician/audience astonishment is something very different from the naive "ah!" response of Zeami's bumpkin or from the bored reaction of the man seated in front of Yeats during the performance of *The King's Threshold*. "Astonished" in this context carries the entire weight of the word's history, conveying the musicians' sense of surprise or wonder, but also the state of paralysis, bewilderment, and stupefaction. Yeats hoped to leave his audience with the sense of "gaiety transfiguring all that dread," what Jauss calls the "aesthetic pleasure" that a complicit audience feels after confronting fascinating indeterminacies. This aesthetic pleasure, Jauss tells us, consists of two moments: "the direct sensuous surrender of the self to an object" (a moment common to all pleasure) and "the taking up of a position that brackets the existence of the object and thereby makes it an aesthetic one."[16] In other words, as Yeats also realized, there must be a distancing of audience from object.

Just as Yeats often voices his conception of the nonexistent ideal audience, so Zeami six centuries earlier described what seems to be a perfect Zen response and what Yeats very possibly would consider the ideal response. "There is a level of skill that will simply make the audience gasp, without reflection, in surprise and pleasure. This level will be termed one of a pure Feeling that Transcends Cognition. The response to such a performance is such that there is no occasion for reflection, no time for the spectator to realize how well the performance is contrived. Such a state might be referred to as 'purity unmixed'" (Zeami, 91). The "astonished" musicians have achieved this level of response, while, as Yeats was painfully aware, most of his audiences have not, and more than a "passing word" has come from and will continue to come from readers and audiences. At least some of these words should address the theoretical and the actual performance texts of Yeats's plays with recognition of the internal guides to reception that Yeats provides. Such studies will dispel the lingering suspicions, fostered by Yeats's own elitist comments, that his plays are not theatrical and will demonstrate that Yeats had assimilated many of Zeami's principles of audience response.

ABBREVIATIONS

A       *The Autobiography of William Butler Yeats* (New York: Macmillan, 1965).

E&I     *Essays and Introductions* (New York: Macmillan, 1961).

E       *Explorations* (New York: Macmillan, 1962).

L       *The Letters of W. B. Yeats*, ed. Allan Wade (New York: Macmillan, 1955).

VP      *The Variorum Edition of the Poems of W. B. Yeats*, eds. Peter Allt and Russell Al-
        spach (New York: Macmillan, 1973).

VPl     *The Variorum Edition of the Plays of W. B. Yeats*, ed. Russell Alspach (New York:
        Macmillan, 1966).


NOTES

   1. Among the most recent or most significant studies of Yeats in performance
are: Gordon Armstrong, "Symbols, Signs, and Language: The Brothers Yeats and Samuel Beckett's Art of the Theater," *Comparative Drama* 20 (Spring 1986): 38–53; Karen
Dorn, "Stage Production and Greek Theatre Movement," *Theatre Review* 1 (1976):
182–204; James Flannery, *W. B. Yeats and the Idea of a Theatre* (New Haven: Yale Univ.
Press, 1976); Warren Leamon, "Yeats: Skeptic on Stage," *Éire-Ireland* 21 (Spring 1986):
129–35; Elizabeth Loizeaux, "Separating Strangeness: From Painting to Sculpture in
Yeats's Theatre," *Yeats: An Annual of Critical and Textual Studies* 1 (1983): 68–91; Liam
Miller, *The Noble Drama of W. B. Yeats* (Dublin: The Dolmen Press, 1977).

   2. Yeats distinguishes between "A Popular Theatre," "A People's Theatre," and
"an unpopular theatre." The first evokes a naïve emotional response; the second – the
form that Yeats claims was inadvertently "created" by himself, Lady Gregory, and John
Synge – accomplishes "the making articulate of all the dumb classes each with its own
knowledge of the world, its own dignity, but all objective with the objectivity of the
office and the workshop, of the newspaper and the street, of mechanism and of politics" (E, 249); the third is the theater that Yeats wanted to create for himself with "an
audience like a secret society where admission is by favour and never to many" (E,
254).

   3. Ezra Pound and Ernest Fenollosa, *The Classic Theatre of Japan* (1917; reprint, New York: New Directions, 1959), 4.

   4. For example, in his *Autobiography*, Yeats mentions "a mediaeval Japanese
painter" (102), a Royal Irish Academy pamphlet on Japanese art that he read as a boy
(126), and "those painted horses that trampled the rice-fields of Japan" (131). Yeats
discusses Lowell's work in his notes to Lady Gregory's *Visions and Beliefs in the West
of Ireland* (1920; reprint, Toronto: Macmillan of Canada, 1976), 360. In *The Japanese
Tradition in British and American Literature* (Princeton: Princeton Univ. Press, 1958),
215, Earl Miner discusses some possible sources for Yeats's pre-1913 knowledge of Nō
traditions.

5. Pound and Fenollosa, 69.

6. Peter Arnott, *The Theatres of Japan* (New York: Macmillan, 1969), 115.

7. F. A. C. Wilson, *W. B. Yeats and Tradition* (New York: Macmillan, 1958), 139; Miner, 261–63; Richard Taylor, *The Drama of W. B. Yeats* (New Haven: Yale Univ. Press, 1976), 118–36.

8. Zeami Motokiyo, *On the Art of the Nō Drama: The Major Treatises of Zeami*, trans. J. Thomas Rimer and Yamazaki Masakazu (Princeton: Princeton Univ. Press, 1984), xxxiii. Henceforth, all references to this work will be included in the text.

9. Hans Robert Jauss, *Toward an Aesthetic of Reception*, trans. Timothy Bahti (Minneapolis: Univ. of Minnesota Press, 1982), 24.

10. Hans-Georg Gadamer, *Truth and Method*, trans. Garrett Barden and John Cumming (New York: Continuum, 1975), 268; Wolfgang Iser, *The Act of Reading: A Theory of Aesthetic Response* (Baltimore: Johns Hopkins Univ. Press, 1978), 78, 149; Patrice Pavis, *Languages of the Stage: Essays in the Semiology of Theatre* (New York: Performing Arts Journal Publications, 1982), 72.

11. Arnott, 114.

12. Roman Ingarden, *The Cognition of the Literary Work of Art*, trans. Ruth Ann Crowley and Kenneth Olson (Evanston, Ill.: Northwestern Univ. Press, 1973), 12.

13. Ibid., 50–51.

14. Viktor Chklovski (also Shklovskii), "L'Art Comme Procédé," in *Théorie de la Littérature*, ed. Tzvetan Todorov (Paris: Éditions du Seuil, 1965), 76–97.

15. Loizeaux, 83.

16. Hans Robert Jauss, *Aesthetic Experience and Literary Hermeneutics*, trans. Michael Shaw (Minneapolis: Univ. of Minnesota Press, 1982), 30–31.

8

# THE DOLL AS ICON
## The Semiotics of the Subject
## in Yeats's Poem "The Dolls"
### KITTI CARRIKER

LITTLE ATTENTION has been given to the problematic role played by
the man-made double, the three-dimensional, physical figures such as
dolls and puppets that fictional characters and craftsmen create in their
own images. In Yeats's poetry, various representations from this group
of literary automata appeal to the reader's fascination with and fear
of images made in human likeness. In this essay, I will center on the
reflexive nature of the doll as icon in poems such as "The Dolls" and
"Upon a Dying Lady," analyzing the way in which, as doubles and imi-
tations in miniature of their human creators, these figures stand in relation to their originals. Viewing the dolls in these poems as manifestations of Freud's notion of the uncanny and Julia Kristeva's concept
of the abject, I will explore the psychological implications of their creation and the extent and the limitations of the power they hold, if indeed any, over the humans who have served as their models and creators. In addition to the uncanny and abject nature of the doll and the
living doll as double, I will explore the iconic value of such figures,
using the semiotics of Umberto Eco.

   In his 1919 essay "The 'Uncanny,'" Freud lists, among those "things,
persons, impressions, events and situations which are able to arouse
in us a feeling of the uncanny in particularly forcible and definite form,
. . . waxwork figures, ingeniously constructed dolls and automata."[1] This
particular group of figures is uncanny in nature precisely because it

contains replicas of a very specific form—the human body. The unique appeal of dolls to the psyche goes beyond the uncanniness of their "ingenious construction" and their resemblance to the human body to include the fact that most dolls are miniatures—miniature idealized bodies.

Freud discusses dolls as a significant element of childhood life, describing how children frequently maintain that their dolls are alive or that they themselves can make the inanimate dolls come to life. He concludes with this observation: "But, curiously enough . . . the idea of a "living doll" excites no fear at all; children have no fear of their dolls coming to life, they may even desire it. The source of uncanny feelings would not, therefore, be an infantile fear in this case, but rather an infantile wish or even merely an infantile belief. There seems to be a contradiction here; but perhaps it is only a complication, which may be helpful to us later on" (Freud, 233). Freud indeed returns again to the issue of infantile fears, wishes, and so forth, but not to the uncanny feelings excited by the idea of a "living doll." It is to these very complications and contradictions that I will turn my attention, using Yeats's poem "The Dolls" to illustrate the contradictions that become apparent when the "living doll," or the created miniaturized double of the subject, stands in juxtaposition with its creator, and to depict the complications that arise owing to its creation, its existence, and its maker's expectations (or, perhaps, its expectations of its maker).

Both Hélène Cixous and Naomi Schor comment on Freud's failure to explicate more thoroughly the uncanny significance of dolls, specifically of the doll Olympia, who figures prominently in Hoffmann's "Sand-Man" (the story used by Freud as being exemplary of the uncanny). Cixous points out that Freud relegates the doll to the background, displacing the *unheimliche* of the doll with the sandman. In *Reading in Detail*, Naomi Schor relies on both Freud's essay "The 'Uncanny'" and Cixous's analysis of it when explaining what she calls "the thrilling terror" of Duane Hanson's life-size sculptures. "One of the reasons why "the theme of the doll" is never dealt with adequately is that Freud consistently occults its specificity, not only its sex (see Cixous, 538), but more importantly its three-dimensional form. . . . Freud does more than displace Olympia in favor of the Sand-Man; he displaces sculpture in favor of literature."[2] Thus, the doll, the three-dimensional figure, and the references to it are all repressed and detail is sublimated.

Schor concludes this chapter on "Truth in Sculpture" by taking the notion of the uncanny one step further and asking a question that Freud does not answer: wherein lies the pleasure of the uncanny? Regarding Hanson's figures, she suggests that it is "the infantile pleasure that comes from taking the doll apart and seeing how it is made, in other words, the pleasure of the critic."[3]

It is, then, the pleasure of the critic not only to "take apart" Yeats's poem but to do so by looking closely at the "living dolls" who inhabit the dollmaker's house and at the role played by the dolls in relation to the human beings who live there as well—the dollmaker, the dollmaker's wife, and their newborn child. Particularly useful in such an analysis are Schor's aesthetics of detail, Susan Stewart's study of the miniature and the gigantic, and Umberto Eco's definition of the material icon. In A Theory of Semiotics, Eco seeks to establish that "the so-called iconic signs are arbitrarily coded . . . and may be subject to a multiple articulation, as are verbal signs," while opposing the assumptions that "the so-called iconic sign has the same properties as . . . is similar to . . . is analogous to . . . is motivated by its object."[4]

Eco deals with the issue of what properties of the denoted object the sign must possess in order to be considered iconic. The dolls in Yeats's poem may be considered iconic in that they possess "optic (visible)," "ontological (supposed)," and "conventionalized properties of the object."[5] Even by this definition, it is important to note, the dolls—the icons—have become the subject and their creator the object. What makes the dolls uncanny, in addition to this reversal of roles, is their property of animation, specifically their ability to speak (shared with the dollmaker and his wife) and their ability to cry (which they share with the child). Concerning such shared properties—and the reader's perception of them—Eco suggests "that in the iconic experience certain perceptual mechanisms function which are of the same type as the one involved in the perception of an actual object." He elaborates upon this proposition, however, by explaining "that iconic signs do not possess the 'same' physical properties as do their objects but they rely on the 'same' perceptual 'structure,' or on the same system of relations (one could say that they possess the same perceptual sense but not the same perceptual physical support)."[6]

"The Dolls," a poem about a dollmaker and the reaction of the dolls in his shop when a child is born to him and his wife, presents an unusual situation—one in which both the original *object* (to use Eco's term) and the icon do indeed require the same perceptual physical support. In fact, the dolls *demand* this similar mode of perception. The conflict of "The Dolls" is centered in the question of whether the dolls are subject or object, and the poem contains what Freud has called "a particularly favorable condition for awakening uncanny feelings." He points out that "in their early games children do not distinguish at all sharply between living and inanimate objects, and that they are especially fond of treating their dolls like live people"; but the adult apparently does not share this perception nor the pleasure derived from it. Quite the opposite, adults look for a clear delineation between the animate and the inanimate and become suspicious "when there is intellectual uncertainty whether an object is alive or not, and when an inanimate object becomes too much like an animate one" (Freud, 233).

The dolls, who speak and who see themselves as rivals to the newborn child, are perceived as uncanny because they are simultaneously inhuman and human, paradoxically striking the reader as inhuman to the very degree that they are animated (or "inhuman"). Stewart describes this eerie sensation of the uncanny thus: "The dream of animation here is equally the terror caused by animation, the terror of the doll, for such movement would only cause the obliteration of the subject—the inhuman spectacle of a dream no longer in need of its dreamer."[7] The obliteration of the subject is clearly at stake in Yeats's poem, for we see dolls no longer in need of a dollmaker. Yet, while the dolls' animation is uncanny to the reader, it is the animation of the child that the dolls find threatening. They see themselves as subject and the child as object because their creation has preceded the child's arrival, and they are the ones who fear displacement.

The opening lines of the poem describe the dolls' outrage at what has come to pass:

> A Doll in the doll-maker's house
> Looks at the cradle and bawls:
> "That is an insult to us."
> But the oldest of all the dolls,
> Who had seen, being kept for show,
> Generations of his sort,

Out-screams the whole shelf: "Although
There's not a man can report
Evil of this place,
The man and the woman bring
Hither, to our disgrace,
A noisy and filthy thing"

(*The Poems*, 126–27)[8]

Their territory has been invaded by a baby or—to invert the concept—a "living" doll. For the dolls, the word "living" is entirely negative in connotation; the baby is "noisy and filthy" because he is alive, crying, eating, drinking, urinating, defecating, requiring the mother's constant attention, distracting the father from his craft, and usurping the privileged position of the dolls.

Although the dolls have acquired the ability to "bawl" and "scream," thus sharing the baby's capacity for noise making, they do not share the bodily needs and functions that make him seem "filthy" to them. Instead, their being is contained and exists within what Susan Stewart calls "the seamless body of the doll" which is not only free from the requisite physiological processes but is also "erased of its sexuality." They do not function, yet they exist as ideal representations of the human body. "What is, in fact, lost in this idealized miniaturization of the body is sexuality and hence the danger of power. The body becomes an image, and all manifestations of will are transferred to the position of the observer, the voyeur. The body exists not in the domain of lived reality but in the domain of commodity relations."[9] The dolls in Yeats's poem are commodities; they are the source of livelihood for the dollmaker, a fact attested to by the oldest doll, who is "kept for show" and who has seen many others sold. And it is true that these dolls live outside the domain of lived reality and outside of sexuality. The sexuality, "the danger of power" that they sense, is the sexuality of the dollmaker and his wife. The dolls proclaim the living, breathing baby to be an "insult" to their "seamless" bodies, and their annoyance is couched in the suspicion that the sexually created child of the man and woman will outrank the dolls themselves—sexless re-creations that the dollmaker has built in his own image. The primary emotion informing their outrage is fear—fear of sexual procreation.

In these self-created miniatures, the body does, as Stewart says, become an image; but the dolls in Yeats's poem maintain, rather than lose, "all manifestations of will." They inadvertently express the very fears from which their seamless bodies should free them—the fears from which the voyeur is freed when he looks upon the sexless body of the doll or upon the miniature or the child dressed as an adult. But these outraged dolls have *become* the voyeurs; they are the observers, spying and eavesdropping on the husband, wife, and child. In another poem, "She Turns the Dolls' Faces to the Wall" (pt. 3 of the sequence "Upon a Dying Lady"), Yeats portrays dolls who are suspected of exercising these same voyeuristic tendencies. Unlike "The Dolls," in which the dolls are granted the primary voice, "She Turns the Dolls' Faces" is narrated from the point of view of a human onlooker who reports the care that is taken to prevent the dolls from spying on "some religious festival" (*The Poems*, 158). Poised in a decorative display, they seem quiet and innocent enough; but any secret intention that they may have of watching the priest say mass or of distracting the audience is thwarted when their faces are turned to the wall by their owner. Significant here is the assumption, the fear perhaps, that the dolls would take any interest in human activity and ceremony. They are treated as objects but are assumed to possess the qualities essential for becoming subjects: sensory perception and the capacity to animate themselves.

In these poems, the dolls are icons—not the body-made-object but the body-made-subject (or, more specifically, the object-made-subject by virtue of animation). Eco describes the significance of such semiotic transference in the designation of a sign as iconic. He says that "transformation seems to be, as yet, the best operational explanation of the impression of iconism." He emphasizes transformation over patterns of "similarity" and "analogy" (although in a passage peculiarly applicable to the conflict expressed in Yeats's poem he calls analogy "a sort of native and mysterious parenthood between things or between images and portrayed things"[10]).

Eco also distinguishes clearly between icons and specular reflections, or mirror images, replicas or doubles, and empathic stimuli. He rules out the reflected mirror image as "pure visual matter" and says that a "double is not the icon of its model-object *except* in a very specific case: i.e., when an object is chosen as an ostensive sign in order to visually describe the character of every object of the same class" (emphasis added).[11] He also makes an exception for what he calls the "absolute icon". "This virtual duplication of stimuli (which sometimes works as if there were a duplication of both my body as an object and my body as a subject, splitting and facing itself), this theft of an image, this unceasing temptation to believe I am someone else, makes man's experience with mirrors an absolutely unique one, on the threshold between perception and signification. And it is precisely from this experience of absolute iconism that the dream of a sign having the same characteristics arises."[12] In fact, these descriptions seem to establish the place of the dolls as both double and icon. In "She Turns the Dolls' Faces," for example, each doll in the collection is a visual description of a group or class of people—a certain social type. First there is a Japanese doll, "Pedant in passion, learned in old courtesies, / Vehement and witty she had seemed"; next, "the Venetian lady / Who had seemed to glide to some intrigue in red shoes"; then "The meditative critic"; and finally, "Even *our Beauty* with her Turkish trousers on" (*The Poems*, 158; emphasis added).

This last doll is more than an icon to exotic beauty, however; she is also the double of the dying lady. The reader ascertains this duality from the opening line of the preceding poem in the sequence. In "Certain Artists bring her Dolls and Drawings" (pt. 2 of "Upon a Dying Lady"), the dying lady, who was in reality Mabel Beardsley (Yeats's friend and the sister of Aubrey Beardsley), is called "our Beauty." The narrator suggests what tokens and gifts her eccentric and talented circle of friends might bring to her beside.

> Bring where our Beauty lies
> A new modelled doll, or drawing,
> With a friend's or an enemy's
> Features, or maybe showing
> Her features when a tress
> Of dull red hair was flowing
> Over some silken dress
> Cut in the Turkish fashion
>
> (*The Poems*, 157–58)

Here, then, the woman herself is the model-object for the suggested doll or drawing; in the following poem, the doll has materialized as a beauty wearing Turkish trousers. Not only has the doll materialized, but it is semiotically indistinguishable from its double, the dying lady.

In "The Dolls," the baby is viewed as representative—an ostensive sign—of what the handcrafted dolls object to in an entire class of beings; thus, the dolls, particularly the one who initially "Looks at the cradle and bawls: / 'That is an insult to us'," and the baby are doubles. On the other hand, the dollmaker has chosen the oldest doll for the iconic purpose of being "kept for show"—to describe visually—every other doll, generation after generation, who passes from his workbench out of the shop. The very word "generations" in the sixth line of the poem articulates the roles played and shared by the dolls and the child: they have all been fathered by the dollmaker; they all are products of his experience.[13]

The oldest doll, then, is both the double and the icon of its model-object, the baby. But it is the doll, not the baby, who possesses the model body. Susan Stewart's explanation of the body as an object of desire illuminates the relationship between the physical generation of the doll-maker's newborn child and the generations of dolls that he has crafted. "In contrast to this model body, the body of lived experience is subject to change, transformation, and, most importantly, death. The idealized body implicitly denies the possibility of death—it attempts to present a realm of transcendence and immortality, a realm of the classic. This is the body-made-object, and thus the body as potential commodity, *taking place* within the abstract and infinite cycle of exchange."[14] In Yeats's poem, the model body and the body of lived experience stand in juxtaposition. The dolls, as idealized commodities of exchange, are also subject to lived experience. This experience—the dolls' memory, their ability to comprehend the continuity of existence, and their sense of passing time—is the source of both their power and their chagrin. They are "insulted" and "disgraced" because they are forced to confront the temporal nature of their animated existence.

They are disturbed not only by the realization that they stand to lose what the baby has to gain, but also by the uncomfortable knowledge that they stand to lose exactly what he has to lose. His wailing presence serves as a reminder that they may not be transcendent, or immortal. As dolls they would be immortal, but not as *living* dolls. Their idealized bodies deny the possibility of death, but their animated psyches reopen the possibility of mortality. Freud discusses the "infantile" motivation of overaccentuating "physical reality in comparison with material reality" and describes the connection between "animism" and the uncanny effect that is "produced when the distinction between imagination and reality is effaced, as when something that we have hitherto regarded as imaginary appears before us in reality, or when a symbol takes over the full function of the thing it symbolizes" (Freud, 244).

Not only does the dolls' ability to express anger efface the boundary between imagination and reality for the reader, but the elimination of this distinction is disconcerting to the dolls as well. They resist taking over the *full* function of the child (the thing that they symbolize); they appropriate the privilege of expressing themselves while eschewing the less appealing physical properties of noise and filth. They choose physical over material reality, even though their value (to the dollmaker and to his customers) resides in their idealized, material bodies.

Stewart says that the "body is culturally delimited"; the value of either the real or the ideal body is determined by social conventions that reflect a scale of measurement and a scale of values.[15] The icon, on the other hand (both Eco and Riffaterre stress this point), is semiotically overdetermined.[16] The doll as icon transcends the limits imposed on its double, the human child. Even the child's mother refers to her baby as a "wretch," accepting the harsh judgment of the dolls that the baby is an insult, a noisy filthy thing, a disgrace, and somehow evil.

> Hearing him groan and stretch
> The doll-maker's wife is aware
> Her husband has heard the wretch,
> And crouched by the arm of his chair,
> She murmurs into his ear,
> Head upon shoulder leant:
> "My dear, my dear, O dear,
> It was an accident."
>
> (The Poems, 126–27)

Implicit in the concluding line is the ultimate distinction between the child and dolls: the dolls are not, and could not possibly be, created by accident. They are crafted painstakingly and deliberately. The icon, the body-made-subject, may be arbitrarily coded and subject to multiple articulation, but it is never an accident. And as this poem aptly illustrates, the icon need not be motivated by its object. The dolls in Yeats's poem, the subjects, not only predate the existence of the child, the object, but maintain that their identities are distinct and separate.

When the critic pauses to take apart the doll as icon to see how it works, what comes to light is the ingenuity and the detail of the miniaturized ideal body. For Naomi Schor, "the modern fascination with the trivial, the playground of fetishism" is the forum for such investigation. Asserting "the detail's claim to aesthetic dignity and epistemological prestige," she says that "to focus on the detail . . . is to become aware . . . of its participation in a larger semantic network, bounded on one side by the *ornamental*, with its traditional connotations of effeminacy and decadence, and on the other by the *everyday* whose 'prosiness' is rooted in the domestic sphere of social life presided over by women."[17] In "The Dolls," Yeats accurately depicts both extremes of this semantic continuum, with the dollmaker and the dolls representing the ornamental and the mother and child representing the everyday. Seeing the doll as icon provides a way to apprehend and understand the contradictions and complications that arise when the representatives of these two ends of the spectrum are granted the uncanny power to confront and be confronted by each other.

The dolls can also be viewed as an embodiment of what Julia Kristeva calls "the abject." This concept stems from the established meaning of "the other" as whatever exists as an opposite of someone or something else, or that which is excluded by something else; yet the abject describes a different entity than the object. Kristeva identifies the abject as having "only one quality of the object—that of being opposed to I"; but in her approach to the concept of abjection, she focuses more on the quality of exclusion than on opposition, recognizing the abject as being more similar to the subject than the object is.[18] In fact, it is the undesired similarity between the subject and the abject that informs the subject's sense of abjection and motivates its forceful separation of itself from the abject.

Kristeva's notion of the abject is derived from an understanding of the other, which is similar to the views held by Lacan. For example, Lacan has expanded his assertion that the unconscious is like a language by equating the unconscious of the subject with the discourse of the other. For both Lacan and Kristeva, the other, like language, "is always anterior to us and will always escape us, that which brought us into being as subjects in the first place but which always outruns our grasp"; unconscious desire is both directed toward and received from the other.[19] The abject, on the other hand, while it is related to and does proceed from the subject, is antithetical to desire. Not "an otherness ceaselessly fleeing in a systematic quest of desire," it is at once more deeply rooted in the subject and is rejected by the subject. Rather than involving a ceaseless chase, it involves a ceaseless confrontation: "discourse will seem tenable only if it ceaselessly confronts that otherness, a burden both repellent and repelled, a deep well of memory that is unapproachable and intimate: the abject" (*Horror*, 1, 6).

Kristeva describes the abject as a kind of "jettisoned object," standing apart from the subject yet distinct from the object. The abject is "radically excluded," the ego and the superego having combined forces to drive it away (*Horror*, 1, 2). Seen in this light, the dollmaker of Yeats's poem is both ego (in relation to the child) and superego (in relation to the dolls). His role as dollmaker has merged temporarily with his role as father; and, much to the dolls' dismay (and perhaps to the dollmaker's dismay as well), it is this second calling or responsibility that is given his immediate priority. Consequently, the dolls have been jettisoned – radically excluded.

The conflict between the dolls and their master parallels the conflict between the abject and its master: the abject "lies outside, beyond the set, and does not seem to agree to the latter's [the superego's] rules of the game. And yet from its place of banishment, the abject does not cease challenging its master. . . . it beseeches a discharge, a convulsion, a crying out." In the poem, one doll "bawls" while another "out-screams the whole shelf" in an angry and concerted effort to challenge the master and regain his undivided attention. Kristeva's analogy, "to each ego its object, to each superego its abject," is metaphorically drawn by Yeats – to each father his child, to each dollmaker his doll (*Horror*, 2).

Intrinsic to the concept of the abject is a well-defined sense of the improper/unclean, the loathing of "filth, waste, or dung," or the turning away from "defilement, sewage, and muck." This is the loathing of the dolls for the child, whom they perceive as filthy and disgraceful. They experience what Kristeva calls "the shame of compromise, of being in the middle of treachery. The fascinated start that leads me toward and separates me from them" (*Horror*, 2). These ambivalent feelings and this ambiguous position mark vividly the uncomfortable situation in which the dolls feel bound and trapped. It is this very repugnance that inspires their clamor of disgust. Like Kristeva, who describes her repulsion as a child for "that skin on the surface of milk" that her parents urged her to drink, and the assertion of self that her refusal required, the dolls are in the "process of becoming an other at the expense of [their] own death." They "give birth to [themselves] amid the violence of sobs. . . . without either wanting or being able to become integrated" into the "symbolic system" of the family unit; the "I"–the child of Kristeva's narrative, the outraged doll of the poem–"reacts . . . abreacts . . . abjects" (*Horror*, 3).

For Kristeva, symbolic systems are normative positions and standardized value judgments, providing the means by which the subject learns to identify itself as distinct from other objects, such as the mother, within a sign system. The dictates of the symbolic order are always present, waiting to be encountered and recognized, a fact realized only gradually by the subject, whose earliest existence is rooted in another order–the semiotic. In contrast to the symbolic system, constantly challenging and being challenged by it, the semiotic order "refers to the actual organization, or disposition, within the body, of instinctual drives . . . as they affect language and its practice.[20] The dolls of Yeats's poem are similar to the resistant child of Kristeva's anecdote in their attempts to challenge the existing symbolic order, but, paradoxically, they also represent the order with which they are in conflict. The child's birth awakens them to a recognition of their own domain; their semiotic challenge to the symbolic is a confrontation not only with the dollmaker but, more significantly, with themselves. Each doll, desiring to partake of both orders simultaneously, is in conflict with itself, just as the two orders are in dialectical conflict with each other: "The semiotic is the 'other' of language which is nonetheless intimately entwined with it. . . . it is bound up with the child's contact with the mother's body, whereas the symbolic . . . is associated with the Law of the father."[21] The child is the product of the mother, created by her (and by the father's) instinctual drives, whereas the dolls are the product of the law and order and judgment of the father as craftsman.

Kristeva shares with Lacan the idea that the father embodies the law and the belief that language and experience can be ordered into two primary categories. For Lacan, these categories are the symbolic and the imaginary. The imaginary state, like Kristeva's semiotic order, is a condition in which the subject lacks any clear center of self; as the subject comes to perceive its own identity, determined by its relations of difference and similarity to the other subjects around it, the subject moves from the imaginary into the symbolic register, accepting the preexisting social codes and sexual roles that make up the various symbolic units (e.g., society, religion, the family).

In "She Turns the Dolls' Faces," the dolls, as configurations of the imaginary, are placed in opposition to the symbolic law of the church: "Because to-day is some religious festival / They had a priest say Mass, and . . . [all the dolls] must face the wall" (*The Poems*, 158). The word of the priest is law, so the dolls and the worldliness connoted by their presence are temporarily vanquished to accommodate his wish: "Because the priest must have like every dog his day / Or keep us all awake with baying at the moon / We and our dolls being but the world were best away" (*The Poems*, 158). Imaginative creations, the dolls are in many ways more symbolic than imaginary. The wise Japanese courtesan and the fashionable Venetian lady possess a certain self-consciousness and refinement unknown in the imaginary realm; in fact, the dollmaker's craft is usually one of overrefinement. At odds with the priest's law is the symbolic system of decadence and artificiality, ascribed to by the poem's narrator (whose doll is "The meditative critic") and the dying lady ("our Beauty with her Turkish trousers").

Even though Yeats's dolls are the product of the craftsman's symbolic world, their existence—because of their ideal, material bodies—is one of the imaginary: "the "imaginary," where loss and difference are unthinkable, where it seemed that the world was made for us and we for the world. There is no death in the imaginary, since the world's continuing existence depends upon my life just as much as my life depends upon it; it is only by entering the symbolic order that we confront the truth that we can die, since the world's existence does not in fact depend upon us. As long as we remain in an imaginary realm of being we misrecognize our own identities, seeing them as fixed and rounded, and misrecognize reality as something immutable."[22] This summary of the imaginary realm accurately describes the life led by "The Dolls" until the child's birth, when they suddenly comprehend that there are two modes of existence. Because they are not human (and thus not capable of ever being fully integrated into the symbolic system of the dollmaker's family), their self-perception has been accurate: their seamless bodies *are* fixed and rounded, and reality for them *is* immutable. However, when they venture to the border of the imaginary and question its juxtaposition to the symbolic, when the child's cry suggests that the world was made for more than them and that its continuing existence may not depend upon them, then their immutability is called into question and their death becomes a possibility.

The properties—"These body fluids, this defilement, this shit," to borrow Kristeva's list—that the dolls reject as signifiers of the baby's life (and his eventual death) are for the human child not symbols but indeed the requisite facts of existence: "Such wastes drop so that I might live" (*Horror*, 3).[23] Kristeva refines her discussion of the improper/unclean with the observation that "It is not lack of cleanliness or health that causes abjection but what disturbs identity, system, order. What does not respect borders, positions, rules." The newborn in Yeats's poem hovers at such a border; it is like the dolls in some ways but like their master, the dollmaker, in others. The dolls see the baby as "the in-between, the ambiguous, the composite" (*Horror*, 4). They confront the child at a border between living and nonliving, a border that contains life and signification, a border of such mammoth symbolic and physically real proportions that it "has become an object." Kristeva examines the dilemmas of existence at this metaphorical border in terms of both birth and death. She describes the act of giving birth as a "strange form of split symbolization (threshold of language and instinctual drive, of the 'symbolic' and the 'semiotic')."[24] And she describes the nonliving corpse for which all borders have been erased as "death infecting life. Abject. It is something rejected from which one does not part, from which one does not protect oneself as from an object. Imaginary *uncanniness* and real threat" (*Horror*, 4; emphasis added).

In the seven sections of "Upon a Dying Lady," Yeats captures various aspects of the dissolution of borders brought about by death. For example, in "Certain Artists Bring Her Dolls and Drawings," the dying lady's "new modelled doll, or drawing" may feature the characteristics of self or other, friend or enemy, female or male, adult or child. The passionate animation of her life has been reduced to a collection of inanimate dolls and drawings that may—or may not—resemble her. In a reversal of Freud's proposition, the animate being is becoming too much like an inanimate object: "We have given the world our passion, /

We have naught for death but toys." In "The End of Day" (pt. 4 of the sequence), the woman's preparations for death, the "great enemy," are portrayed as child's play: "She is playing like a child . . . Fantastical and wild." The child in this scenario is wise enough to know that "some one soon / Will come . . . and say— / Though play is but half done— / 'Come in and leave the play'" (*The Poems*, 157–60). The erasure of boundaries that determine identity, the transition from animate to inanimate, and the return to motifs of childhood all suggest the uncanniness of and the threat of death.

Kristeva's definition of "abject" and the extent to which the subject is affected by abjection is related to Freud's notion of the uncanny. Freud, too, focuses on the corpse as a source that can generate in the living uncanny feelings "in the highest degree." He attributes fear of the dead to "the old belief that the dead man becomes the enemy of his survivor" (Freud, 241). Kristeva's denomination of the corpse as abject updates this "old belief" and offers a detailed explanation of why the corpse, the nonliving, must become the enemy of the living; it has crossed that all-important border and become a "thing that no longer matches and therefore no longer signifies anything." Having now become "the utmost of abjection," it remains an "other." Yet—the question remains—an "other" in relation to what subject? (*Horror*, 4).

Central to both theories is the confrontation of self and other. Such encounters are sometimes unexpected, sometimes unwilling; but at other times the "I" wills the meeting or involvement—or at least it willingly embraces the confrontation with the other in one of its forms: object or abject. Kristeva writes from the ego's point of view: "I endure it [brutish suffering], for I imagine that such is the desire of the other. A massive and sudden emergence of uncanniness, which, familiar as it might have been in an opaque and forgotten life, now harries me as radically separate, loathsome" (*Horror*, 2). Despite certain similarities, the uncanny and the abject are distinct sensations. As Kristeva points out, the state of abjection is characterized not by involuntary repetition and recognition, but by a *lack* of repetition and a decided absence of familiarity. It is permeated by unfamiliarity: "Essentially different from 'uncanniness,' more violent, too, abjection is elaborated through a failure to recognize its kin; nothing is familiar, not even the shadow of a memory" (*Horror*, 5).

Freud, however, insists on the significance of familiarity, recognition, and involuntary repetition in the subject's perception of the uncanny: "for this uncanny is in reality nothing new or alien, but something which is familiar and old-established in the mind and which has become alienated from it only through the process of repression." The factor of involuntary repetition lends an uncanny atmosphere to events that would otherwise be perceived as mere chance or coincidence. Events that would otherwise be considered "innocent enough" are instead interpreted as "fateful and inescapable." In addition, involuntary repetition can recall "the sense of helplessness experienced in some dreamstates," the opaque, forgotten life described by Kristeva. Freud elaborates on these ideas, tracing them back to infantile psychology (he refers the reader to *Beyond the Pleasure Principle*) and to the "dominance in the unconscious mind of a 'compulsion to repeat' proceeding from the instinctual impulses." He draws the conclusion "that whatever reminds us of this inner 'compulsion to repeat' is perceived as uncanny."

The dollmaker's creations are the product of this inner compulsion to repeat, which motivates human beings to fashion objects in their own image. The dolls are uncanny as reminders of this compulsion and as inanimate bodies that have become too much like their animate originals. They are both uncannily like their creator and abjectly removed from his consciousness, artificial replicants who have somehow acquired the ability to express emotion. As uncanny doubles of the child, as icons, or as embodiments of the abject, their outcry is both captivating and distressing. In "The Dolls," they are the "me miserable treasure of the signifying act," as well as the subject or ego.[25] Their voices provide the "operating consciousness" of the poem, a role that is primary to the linguistic or semiotic conception of the subject. This operating consciousness simultaneously constitutes "the (transcendental) real object, and the ego (as far as it is transcendent)."[26]

The dolls, designed by Yeats as the speaking subjects of the poem, perceive and express what the child is too young to know. They voice the parents' conflict, the anguish of the mother, the father's emotional distance from the event, and the distress that the child's birth has caused the family—the disruption of the symbolic order. The child exists as yet entirely in the semiotic realm, in relation to the mother; but the dolls, uncanny in their animation and iconic in their ideal form, traverse the semiotic/symbolic border, asserting their position as subject from a perspective of perfect outrage.[27]

The semiotic subject, when contained within the body of a doll, can be abject, iconic, or uncanny; and the theories of Eco, Freud, and Kristeva suggest means by which to apprehend the problems of identity and idealization that are manifested in images of the doll. Rescuing the three-dimensional figure from displacement, Yeats displays the doll as icon, celebrating its detail and, in poems such as "She turns the Dolls' Faces," its exotic beauty. Representing and then imitating its maker, threatening and then displacing its model-object (the human body), the dolls in Yeats's poetry provide an unsettling vision or reflection of the self. They make their appearance at the thresholds of birth and death, where they unhesitatingly disturb identity and order. In "The Dolls," they herald the birth of a child with envy and horror. In "Certain Artists Bring Her Dolls and Drawings," they are hollow tokens of tribute, brought to the sickbed of a dying friend. Yet, to this courageous dying lady who "lived in joy and laughed into the face of Death," they are still "pretty things that may / Please a fantastic head" (pt. 6, "Her Courage," *The Poems*, 159).

Intricate and decorative, "ingeniously constructed" by imaginary craftsmen, the doll represents a utopian world of perfection and self-enclosure. Although they are creatures of the symbolic system, their seamless bodies are not bound by borders and rules. These miniature, idealized figures of the human form remain fantastic, pleasing, and uncanny to their fictional beholders and to the intrigued reader who is ever lured by detail and fascinated by the clockwork of the doll and the poem.

NOTES

1. Sigmund, Freud, "The 'Uncanny,'" in *The Standard Edition of the Complete Psychological Works*, trans. and ed. James Strachey (London: Hogarth Press, 1953–74), 17:226. All further references to this essay will appear in the text, marked as "Freud."

2. Naomi Schor, *Reading in Detail: Aesthetics and the Feminine* (New York: Methuen, 1987) 138. See also Hélène Cixous, "Fiction and Its Phantoms: A Reading of Freud's 'Das Unheimlich,'" *NLH* 7 (1976): 524–48 (a translation of an article originally published in *Poétique* 10 (1972): 199–216).

3. Schor, 140. Susan Stewart also comments on Hanson's life-size figures. In *On Longing: Narratives of the Miniature, the Gigantic, the Souvenir, the Collection* (Baltimore: Johns Hopkins Univ. Press, 1984), 27, she says that "in the sculptures of Duane Hanson we search for clues of the subjective in the midst of an objective surface; hence

our delight when we uncover the artist's signature . . . or, amid the Hanson's when the tourist turns out to be a real tourist after all."

4. Umberto Eco, *A Theory of Semiotics* (Bloomington: Indiana Univ. Press, 1976), 191–92.

5. Ibid., 207.

6. Ibid., 193.

7. Stewart, 172.

8. Quotations from W. B. Yeats's work are cited in the text. All page references are from Richard J. Finneran, ed. *The Poems: A New Edition* (New York: Macmillan, 1983).

9. Stewart, 124.

10. Eco, *Theory of Semiotics*, 200, 201.

11. Ibid., 202.

12. Umberto Eco, *Semiotics and the Philosophy of Language* (Bloomington: Indiana Univ. Press, 1984), 210.

13. See David Lynch Simpson, *Yeats: The Poetics of the Self* (Chicago: Chicago Univ. Press, 1979), 101. In chapters entitled "Sons and Mothers," "Fathers and Sons," and "Fathers and Mothers," Simpson analyzes the impact of various familial relationships in Yeats's poetry. But he mentions "The Dolls" only in passing, commenting on tone rather than on the role of the father.

14. Stewart, 133. For more on the model body, the body as commodity, the body as object, etc., see Susan Suleiman, ed., *The Female Body in Western Culture: Contemporary Perspectives* (Cambridge: Harvard Univ. Press, 1986). The essays in this collection present "both a new poetics and a new politics" of the body. A number of the issues central to Yeats's "Dolls" are similar to the issues dealt with in the various essays of this text: "Having power [particularly in the form of control over one's own body] versus lacking it, speaking [particularly finding a voice with which to speak about the experiences of the body] versus keeping silent, acting versus supporting action, existing for oneself, as subject, versus existing for the other as object" (Suleiman, 7, 3). See esp. Christine Brooke-Rose, "Woman as a Semiotic Object," 305–16; and Nancy K. Miller, "ReReading as a Woman: The Body in Practice," 354–62.

15. Stewart, xiii.

16. See Michael Riffaterre, *Text Production*, trans. Terese Lyons (New York: Columbia Univ. Press, 1983), particularly chaps. 14 and 15 ("Overdetermination in the Prose Poem" pts. 1 and 2). Writing of the pun as an independent genre, Riffaterre says that "the genre's characteristic artifice becomes in his [Ponge's] work a marker of overdetermination and the icon of its mechanicalness" (272). He also explains the overcoding and overdetermination used by Chateaubriand in a description of "silence." He explains how the climactic development of the passage in question is accomplished through the use of various figures of speech; e.g., analogous reversal, hyperbole, metonymy, oxymoronic generation, paradox, and, finally, neologism and iconism: "The neologism in a case like this is nothing more than the ultimate point of the development. An iconic value is added to its semantic content: it seems to reach beyond the

realm of possible signifiers and is a kind of image of limits surmounted. Language—quite literally—outdoes itself" (68).

Eco, in a discussion of "Iconism and Convention," attributes such overdetermination of the conflict between cultural habits and iconic representation. Portraying semantic knowledge rather than visual experience, the icon, "however stylized it may be, appears to be more true than the real experience, and people begin to look at things through the glasses of iconic convention" (*Theory of Semiotics*, 205). Stewart says that, unlike the world of the body, "the miniature world may always be seen as being overcoded as the cultural" (68).

17. Schor, 6, 7, 4.

18. Julia Kristeva, *Powers of Horror: An Essay on Abjection*, trans. Leon S. Roudiez (New York: Columbia Univ. Press, 1982), 1. Subsequent references to this work are cited in the text as *Horror*.

19. Terry Eagleton, *Literary Theory: An Introduction* (Minneapolis: Univ. of Minnesota Press, 1983), 174.

20. Julia Kristeva, *Desire in Language: A Semiotic Approach to Literature and Art*, ed. Leon S. Roudiez; trans. Thomas Gora, Alice Jardine, and Leon S. Roudiez (New York: Columbia Univ. Press, 1980), 18.

21. Eagleton, 188.

22. Ibid., 186.

23. Kristeva, when relating abjection to the sacred, explains how art and religion deal with these essential elements of defilement, uncleanliness, impropriety, etc. It is a process of purification that makes the abject a source for both religion and art: "The various means of *purifying* the abject—the various catharses—make up the history of religions, and end up with that catharsis par excellence called art, both on the far and near side of religion. Seen from that standpoint, the artistic experience, which is rooted in the abject it utters and by the same token purifies, appears as the essential component of religiosity. That is perhaps why it is destined to survive the collapse of the historical forms of religion" (*Horror*, 17).

See also Lacan, who says that "up until the advent of psycho-analysis, the path of knowledge was always traced in that of a purification of the subject, of the *percipiens*. Well! We would now say that we base the assurance of the subject in his encounter with the filth that may support him, with the *petit a* of which it would not be untrue to say that its presence is necessary." Jacques Lacan, *The Four Fundamental Concepts of Psycho-Analysis*, ed. Jacques-Alain Miller; trans. Alan Sheridan (New York: Norton, 1978), 258.

24. Kristeva, *Desire*, 240.

25. Kristeva says that "it is possible to detect in Husserl the basis of linguistic reasoning (structural or generative) . . . Husserl masterfully understood and posited that any signifying act, insofar as it remains capable of elucidation by knowledge, does not maintain itself by a 'me, miserable treasure' but by the '*transcendental ego*'" (*Desire*, 128).

26. Kristeva, *Desire*, 132.

27. Kristeva writes that "as long as there is language-symbolism-paternity, there will never be any other way to represent, to objectify, and to explain this unsettling of the symbolic stratum, this nature/culture threshold, this instilling the subjectless biological program into the very body of a symbolizing subject, this event called motherhood" (*Desire*, 242).

9

# "THE STRANGE REWARD
# OF ALL THAT DISCIPLINE"
Yeats and Foucault
CHERYL HERR

## THE LIMITS OF VISION

To make the leap from Michel Foucault's historical genealogies and ar-
chaeologies to the interpretation of a poem or play poses enormous
logistical problems. And yet a writer like Yeats—who wrestled all his
life with epistemological issues—teases us, after the fact, with echoes
between his own poetic vocabulary and Foucault's central concepts of
discipline, power/knowledge, sexuality, authority, subjection, prohibition, and humanity. The reader of Foucault may well pause over Yeatsian conundra such as "Did she put on his knowledge with his power?"
But working through the connections between poetic significance and
Foucauldian theory cannot begin by deciphering such superficial echoes.
Rather, matters of deeper structure in both writers first demand comparison. For this reason, I center in this essay principally on Foucault's
much-debated work, *The Order of Things* (1966), which, for all of its
flaws and challenges, presents a structural model that helps us to understand the historical significance of Yeats's work *A Vision*. In the mystical tract over which he labored from 1917 until close to his death, Yeats
attempts to put his own torque on apparent messages from a suddenly
communicative eternity; Foucault's depth-probe of the Western world's
epistemological strata constitutes an attempt to decipher the dense and
partly obscured messages of the past. Linking the underlying frame-
146

works of these endeavors are cultural cables fashioned by Nietzsche and variously assimilated by Yeats and Foucault, whom I regard as dual exponents of modernism on the cusp.

It is useful to consider, at the outset of this inquiry, the similarities in the writers' feelings about their own theories. For instance, despite all of his formidable work, then years after publishing *The Order of Things*, Foucault looked back over his efforts in some distress. In lecture form, he confesses that much of it has "failed to develop into any continuous or coherent whole." "Diffused and at the same time repetitive," his researches "have continually re-trod the same ground." Again he laments of the work, "repetitive and disconnected, it advances nowhere."[1] Foucault's wry humility over the recycled aspects of his writing sounds very much like Yeats's own confession at the end of *A Vision*. In his strictly autobiographical pieces, Yeats is not reluctant to display his private worries and their somatic equivalents, but in *A Vision*, the defeat feels global, unequivocal, highly frustrating, and defensively rationalized. Yeats avers that although he has spent his life waiting for "this moment," "nothing comes." Referring to his system, he wonders how to "work out upon the phases the gradual coming and increase of the counter movement, the *antithetical* multiform influx." The writer has gone to the limits, again and again, of his ability to make sense of his exceedingly diverse psychic experience and insights, and he has failed. He suggests, "Perhaps I am too old."[2] Here, age becomes Yeats's image for his perception of limits that cannot be reversed, for his position in a cycle so vast that its curves appear to be linear and irreversible. Caught up in the crumbling of some moon or other, he frequently glimpses an order at once coexistent with and beyond his own time and experience; but, like Foucault, Yeats cannot achieve to his satisfaction an overriding organization of these insights.[3] Neither writer makes prophecy the stated aim of his investigations, but the desire to tell the future in the present resonates throughout their work, providing impassioned rhetorical moments that register both hope and failure. On the margins of history, carrying well-worn volumes of *The Will to Knowledge*, Yeats and Foucault walk side by side, shouldering against oddly familiar rough beasts that do not acknowledge them and that they cannot name.

In addition to these feelings of frustration, Yeats and Foucault express symmetrical conceptions of temporal order. Foucault's theory of *epistemei* provides a framework against which to pose the etiology and meaning of *A Vision*, a fact that I find important because for all of the critical attention lavished on *A Vision*, the work has few actual readers. Because Nietzshe's influence on both writers prepared the ground for their similar interpretations of empirical history, of History-as-system, and of the speculative historian's task, comparison of *Vision* and *Order* makes both works more readable, more explicable as documents of historical modernism. Not only did the Nietzschean impact create in Yeats's thought the same reluctant sense of failure that Foucault expresses, it also produced in Yeats complex misreadings of his poetic precursors. These misreadings, eloquently explored by Harold Bloom, occur not just for psychodynamic reasons but also, as Foucault helps us to see, as a function of epistemic changes – cultural shifts that Nietzsche celebrates in his own work and through his virtual presence in the writing of Yeats and Foucault. Below, in order to isolate the deep structural significance for twentieth-century thought of the implicit conversation among three of its major exemplars, I consider the historical theory of *A Vision*, Foucault's notion of the *episteme*, Bloom's explorations of Yeats's poetic precursors, and the linking function of Nietzsche's "Eternal Recurrence."

## TIME AND *A VISION*

In the 1937 version of *A Vision*, Yeats calls his work "an elaborate classification" of humanity, a symbolic system with prophetic possibilities.[4] The "great wheel" that he produces from his Instructors' hints and dictations "is every completed movement of thought or life, twenty-eight incarnations, a single incarnation, a single judgment or act of thought."[5] All of history – past, present, and future – finds representation in Yeats's basically simple (though often and variously summarized) system of cycles and gyres.

The failure of vision experienced by Yeats[6] intimately relates to his obsession with history – with the passing and ordering of time. His pre-*Vision* conception of time addresses two issues relevant to my argument. First, Yeats's anti-progressive stance is well-known. He heaps abuse on the "happy counter-myths of progress" that structured much of the historical thought in his era. At one point in *A Vision*, he tellingly discusses temporal progression in terms of the tolling of Big Ben,[7] and it is an aggressively Anglo-specific notion of historical progress that Yeats both lives within and intuitively rejects. As important as this point of view is the nostalgic cycling back into the Irish past of Yeats's early poems. Northrop Frye notes Yeats's references to Tir na nOg, where "time is arrested," a fact noted abruptly when a wanderer like Oisin forgets to keep his feet above earthly flux.[8] From merely rendering, in the poetry, different imaginative realms, in *A Vision*, Yeats organizes such difference under the aegis of comprehensive cycles. The individual, born in one of twenty-eight lunar phases, completes a life span that, overdetermined by the attributes of the lunar phase and by the relations between the lunar phase and both adjacent and opposing sectors, itself cycles through a replication of the total lunar movement.

At the microlevel from which Yeats himself struggled toward structure, in a movement expressed most fully in book I, parts 1 and 2 (preceding the twenty-eight horoscopes), we discover the "examination of the wheel" congealing into rules for "finding the true and false creative mind" and for "finding the body of fate"–tips on how to read history. Within this great wheeling (considered from the level of individuality), there are complex relations among the "four faculties" that, spinning through time, pulsate in an ordered but finally mysterious fashion to produce relations, differences, personality itself. Yeats provides a table cryptically aligning with each of the twenty-eight sectors the faculties of will, mask, creative mind, and body of fate. On the historical scale, the same cycles and pulses find expression as civilizations phase through time. At the farthest edge of this system, we are promised a great return in all aspects of human life and history, but a recurrence with a difference–a return not *of* formerly known personality types and historical characteristics as much as *to* a point in the cycle marked "rebeginning."

## IRELAND AND *A VISION*

It is obvious that this kind of summary, from the external angle of vision implied in the work of Yeatsian masters like Adams and Frye, poses many problems. For one thing, in such commentaries on Yeats's operations manual for history, time takes on an archetypal and supernatural quality that may be more imposed by the non-Irish eye than inherent in the system. In fact, Yeats has shaped the information provided by the presumably unaffiliated or international Instructors into a design with quite specific Irish content. Yeats embeds in his system, so incongruously that critics have virtually ignored this information, several details about his native land. The "Stories of Michael Robartes and His Friends" contains many local allusions. At Robartes's house, where Yeats meets Daniel O'Leary, Robartes talks of having started an abortive cabalistic society on Howth Pier before leaving the country for a standard Irish exile to the continent ("finding time and place were against" his enterprise). In addition, the curious saga of the Irish residents John Bond and Mary Bell is recited. Bond specializes in "the subject of Irish migratory birds"; not himself a "wild goose," he becomes involved with Bell's attempt to fulfill the life goal of her husband, who has sought to teach cuckoos to make nests, only to find that "even the cleverest birds make no attempt to weave . . . into a structure" the materials at their disposal.[9]

Yeats's comedy here relates to his own systematizing at home, of course, against the pressures of time, place, and conservatism; there is much multipointed irony, appropriate to Ireland's long-term colonial situation, in the fact that cuckoos lay their eggs in others' nests, adopting others' systems. His 1920 letter to Lady Gregory specifically presents *A Vision* as "a political and literary testament intended to give a philosophy to the [Irish] movement. Every analysis of character, of Wilde, Henley, Shaw & so on builds up my philosophic nationalism—it is nationalism against internationalism, the rooted against the rootless people."[10] This context of national self-definition finds emphasis in John Aherne's letter to Yeats, in which Aherne mentions that Robartes and Owen Aherne hiked through Ireland in 1919, 1922, and 1923—times of civil strife when they met "Free State soldiers, irregulars, country gentlemen, tramps and robbers." Finally, Yeats showily closes "The Great Wheel" with the inscription, "Finished at Thoor Ballylee, 1922, in a time of Civil War."[11]

My point is that for all of his efforts to generate a universal system of history, Yeats retains his commitment to some version of the "Irish Ireland" sought during the cultural Renaissance in which he played an instrumental role. What complicated that movement of coming-to-nationhood was, among other things, the contradictory quality of the vehicles supporting such definition. In the various Irish renascences, we find the return to traditions as a gesture of self-authorization and cultural authenticity. But in addition to being a sign of unity and integrity, such circling back has acquired, over the past two hundred years, the secondary codings of conflict, invasion, disaccumulation, violence, and fragmentation[12] that Yeat's local allusions adumbrate. For my purposes, it is important that in aesthetic and social contexts, Irishness identified itself with conflict and further associated the cyclic, repeated process of coming to national self-awareness with precisely the strife that might in other countries have been viewed as merely a transient stage in the manufacture of self-representation.

It is in accessing this double coding of the circle that A Vision presents itself not merely as a transhistorical piece of prose, but also as a work that demonstrates in abstract terms the evolving pattern of self-representation in modern Irish culture. In this context, Yeats's work is not so much a contribution to mystical writing as it is a reaching out from such spheres into the traditions of speculative history. It is, if you like, an Irish mystical system, the orchestration and design of which are political decisions. About speculative history itself Yeats explains, "When the automatic script began, neither I nor my wife knew, or knew that we knew, that any man had tried to explain history philosophically."[13] Having become so aware, Yeats explored Gerald Heard, Henry Adams, Petrie, Spengler, Vico, Marx, and Sorel; he came to associate their correlations with his ideas as confirmation of the unstoppable universal truth of his system. At the same time, A Vision communicates from its interior poise a response to the local civil conflicts of his day. Despite the poet's often stated concern over the cooptation of art by propaganda and despite his acquaintance with generalized speculative history, Yeats could not unask the political and social questions that he poses in his drama and poetry, and his thoughts on historical design extend those probings. So it is that Yeats assumes order and proceeds to discover it from an Irish angle of vision that introduces its own complicating lens and that desperately seeks a mediating faculty—some powerful force that, like magic, can materialize whole, living roses out of shredded paper. In very specific terms, Yeats's seemingly ethereal system, apparently derived from incorporeal sources, actively engages with local history of a peculiarly complicated and apocalyptic variety. Yeats's role in the dialogue with eternity seems, in fact, to have been the contextualizing of abstractions. To this highly historical end, Yeats, like Robartes, sings the "strange reward of all that discipline."[14]


## POWER AND DISCIPLINE

At this moment a turn to Foucault's positioning of his own historical inquiries becomes fruitful. One of the most nuanced concepts to emerge from those studies, however unsatisfactorily fragmentary they were to Foucault himself, is his notion of power. As is well known, in the "Two Lectures" of 1976, Foucault calls for a study, not to determine who dominates and for what purposes, but to explore the "real effects" of power. "Let us ask," he counsels, "how things work at the level of ongoing subjugation, at the level of those continuous and uninterrupted processes which subject our bodies, govern our gestures, dictate our behaviours etc."[15] Creating networks, power à la Foucault distributes itself throughout the system, reticulating differences and producing subjectivity in complex but more or less predictable ways. For Foucault, disciplinary mechanisms, such as prisons, hospitals, insane asylums, and schools, produce codified, socially usable subjects. Power and discipline inhere in the system as a whole; they are not limited to some single part that can be cut loose, toppled, or replaced; they are dispersed throughout the matrix, joining oppressor and oppressed. This vision of an integrated disciplinary mechanism of culture echoes eerily in Yeats's system, one that uses local allusion to tap the underground pool of colonial discontent over insistent English power machines. At the same time, a horoscope, especially one as totalizing as that evolved by Yeats and his Instructors, suggests, at a reductive level, related concepts of order and power. It suggests that history systematically disciplines individual behavior at points that appear to be empowering, as well as at points that locate suffering and disfranchisement. A horoscope like that of Yeats rests on the existence of some unthought pure order of being that cannot be known except in its effects.

In *The Order of Things*, Foucault isolates (some readers have said manufactures) a principle—the *episteme*—that he finds organizing what Yeats sees as historical phases. What Foucault describes are not only the continuities of but also the ruptures among historical periods: the moment in the seventeenth century when the Renaissance gave way to the classical (Foucault's term) era; the nineteenth-century shift into the modern period; and the 1960s, when Foucault saw the coming of a new era shorn of the historical construct, "Man," and its attendant human sciences. These discontinuities remain abrupt and inexplicable but also incontestable, or so Foucault represents them. For the purposes of literary study, before a period shift, words have fixed arcs of significance; after a shift, their placement within a subtly altered cultural lexicon fractures the old meanings. As Michel de Certeau comments about Foucault's epistemic breaks, following Foucault's lead brings the reader to recognize that "we can no longer *think* a thought from the past."[16] Radical differences in meaning grow from differences in what is considered to be knowledge, in how knowledge organizes itself into "disciplines," in the relationship of human beings to those disciplines, and in the role, reflexive or representational, played by language in the communication of such bodies of knowledge—all of which Foucault discusses painstakingly.

Foucault clearly identifies a change, occurring at the end of the eighteenth century, in the conditions of possibility for the organization of thought and for the ordering of experience. Around 1790, the classical *episteme* gave way to the structures of modernity. In contrast to the similitude- and resemblance-based Renaissance *episteme*, the classical order of things "analyzed . . . in terms of identity, difference, measurement, and order."[17] Relatedness, enumeration, the primacy of the entity over the always arbitrary word—these things marked the classical era; and the "sign system" of that thought "gave rise simultaneously to the search for origins and to calculability; to the constitution of tables that would fix the possible compositions." Modernity, in contrast, insists that "the general area of knowledge is no longer that of identities and differences, that of non-quantitative orders, that of a universal characterization, of a general *taxonomia*, of a non-measurable mathesis, but an area made up of organic structures, that is, of internal relations between elements whose totality performs a function."[18] Such distinctions have value in interpreting the epistemological foci of life during a given century, as well as in unravelling the period's own conception of the order represented by history itself. For example, in the modern *episteme*, Foucault traces the split between History as "an empirical science of events" and "that radical mode of being that prescribes their destiny to all empirical beings."[19] Enter Comte, Marx, Collingwood, Spengler, Toynbee, Yeats, and Foucault himself through the door of history-as-speculation, history-as-order, history-as-horoscope.

## CULTURAL SHIFTS

Once inside this time zone, Yeats directly addresses the modern *episteme*'s putative history versus History division in the bifurcation of his own career. In some very loose sense, much of his poetry may be considered the rendering of "historical" moments, empirical events. But in his visionary activities, Yeats assimilates events into the big principles underlying the birth, development, and fall of civilizations. The mediating design, predictably enough for someone reared in the assumptions of Irish culture and even for someone not especially turned in to supernatural communicators, was the cycle or gyre. In book 5 of *A Vision*, the most Foucauldian of the chapters, Yeats attends to the "historical cones" that organize time up to May 1925. He assumes knowledge of the vast body of established empirical data as ballast for his at once rigid and speculative ordering of History. Like Foucault, Yeats becomes aware that each era, like each phase of the moon in its impact on individual personality type, imposes limitations on thought and action. Certain ideas are prevented, while others are aired by the turns and shiftings of spiraling time.

By this line of reasoning, *A Vision*, based as it is on Yeats's speculations about history, should align with other philosophical systems of his time, as well as display limitations in relation to alien concepts from the epistemically remote past. There are a number of problems with demonstrating this thesis, however. On the one hand, we fall into a trap of circular logic when we try to demonstrate a principle based on the informing system's program. Similarly, if our own thoughts are limited by the *episteme* in which we live and that we may or may not share with Yeats, how can we say anything useful about what we cannot re-

trieve or, at present, think beyond? On the other hand, if Yeats's Instructors were not of his *episteme* (a notion requiring a certain willing
suspension of disbelief but one that I think should be entertained)—
and we have no certainty about their identities and origins—there could
easily be material in *A Vision* that will not yield adequately to interpretation in our day and age. These objections, specific to *A Vision*,
mirror the criticisms that readers have had of Foucault's whole epistemic enterprise.

Aware of such difficulties, rather than revise the conclusions of
*Order*, Foucault later turned to tropes other than that of the *episteme*
in an effort to produce a more empirically subtle and less totalizing
vision of history. But even in *Order*, Foucault provides an escape hatch
from dead ends like those cited above. As Certeau comments,

> After having ensured the "positivity" of a historical period, the
> "foundation" suddenly crumbles to make way for another ground, a new
> "system of possibility" which reorganizes the floating world of words and
> concepts and implies, with its mix of vestiges and invention, an entirely
> different "epistemological field" (*episteme*). Over time, and in the den-
> sity of its own time, each *episteme* is made up of the heterogeneous: what
> it does not know about itself (its own grounding); what it can no longer
> know about other *epistemei* (after the disappearance of the "foundations"
> they imply); what will be lost forever of its own objects of knowledge
> (which are constituted by a "structure of perception").[20]

Yeats's Communicators do not, even from their eternal angle of
vision, know everything. Far short of being omniscient, they tell Yeats
that they need the living in order to refine their own understanding
of gyric workings. Quasi-Bakhtinian beings, they operate best through
dialogic modalities and display truth as metaphoric responses to questions, not as solemn pronouncement. But even if Yeats's Communicators occupied different epistemic environments during their earthly
tenure, their various senses of the order of things might be *detected*
within the system, either as ambiguity or as seemingly superficial noetic
contradiction. And Yeats's own insistence on allowing his poetic precursors to speak in his work, as well as his celebration of literary tradition, both Irish and international, speaks to a considered cultivation
of cross-epistemic nuance. Finally, if we take seriously Foucault's suggestion that his own time was possibly seeing "the end of Man"[21] and

a correlative epistemic adjustment, then we must be aware that Yeats, the self-styled "last romantic," might also have been one of the first postmodernists. Consider the posture of Georgie Yeats, the poet's wife, who, passive in the face of History and eternity, becomes an automatic writing machine producing fragmentary responses to questions that may or may not have been the questions posed. Surely her mediating role—the subjection to discipline that has a disconcertingly contemporary cast—demands attention in any future exploration of this topic.

In any case, when Foucault speaks of sudden epochal transformation, he certainly implies that the event may take one or more decades. Yeats, struggling to read the future, poised on the verge of visionary apocalypse, and writing through the chaos of Irish civil war and its aftermath, might be said to have lived through an epistemic shift that *A Vision* attempts to organize and express. Put another way, *A Vision* projects itself rhetorically into a "timeless" site (Yeats insists on the timeless and spaceless quality of ultimate reality[22]) in which the contradictions among *epistemei*, rather than the putative simple uniformity or discontinuity of *epistemei*, are made visible. Renaissance and classical vestiges continue to emit content; futuristic insights begin to glow with significance. This is not to deny Foucault's argument for discontinuity, only to reemphasize the presence, in the dominant paradigm, of other semiotically active ordering principles. The premise itself suggests that creative genius may flourish not merely in times of social upheaval but also when such upheaval coordinates with epistemic shift. In times of slippage, words do not fit experience, and what is lost in authorial feelings of precision is gained in evocativeness. It is this point in (Irish) history/History that Yeats occupies.

Cultural heterogeneity of the sort charted by *Order* looks, in practice, like a heightened form of uneven development—not surprising given Foucault's practical task of reacting to and against powerful Marxist theories of history. Looked at from this perspective, Yeats's system is a mechanism for processing or accounting for uneven development in human beings—for relative nonsynchronicities of individual typology and the spirit of the age. Along the way, the cosmic machinery disciplines humanity into organic expression of the order of things, even in Yeats's historical juncture of epistemic shift, even in Ireland in the midst of civil war. Two provisional conclusions seem important here. First, reading Yeats against Foucault helps us to go beyond many simplistic contemporary theories of ideological inscription at the levels of individuality and of historical periodicity; we can appreciate the anti-reductive impulses moving Yeats, that great poet of bipolarity. Second, time itself is the register that may reveal most about Yeats's own inscription into history by History.

## HISTORY AND THE ANXIETY OF INFLUENCE

Yeatsian critics have long been exercised by the poet's indebtedness to the past. Such scholars have both asserted the influence of earlier writers on Yeats and immediately, sometimes defensively, moved into charting the many ways in which Yeats deviates from replicating, say, Blake's mythology and assumptions. Hazard Adams's early work on this topic still rewards study; Bloom's return to that terrain tells us why that is so, for in *Yeats* (1970), Bloom first presented his theory of the anxiety of influence. In thinking about what made Yeats the figure stimulating Bloom's important conception of creativity, Bloom's reader discovers that the latter poet's "swerve" from some of his poetic mentors is remarkably clear, rich, complex, and challenging—and that it is all of these things, because cutting across the chains of poetic influence is the "Great Culture Shift"[23] of epistemic change. Bloom's approach, for all of its immense complexity, does rest on a conviction that time is linear and that progress is a meandering halt-step into the poetic future. Poets become more anxious, more burdened, and thus more subtle in their use of words; the passage of time and their place in that passage forces them into these reactions. From their suffering comes immense cultural benefit, the rich and strange rewards of this alternative discipline of anxiety. To me, locating all of these effects psychodynamically seems restrictive, seems unduly to take history into consideration. I am not arguing that each of the instances charted by Bloom in his post-1970 work on the anxiety of influence relies on an epistemic shift occurring consonantly with a major poet's revisionism. But I do find significant the coalescence of "swerve" and shift in Yeats, both of which measure the distance between him and the romantics, both of which come to a focus when we think of Nietzsche's place in Yeats's work.

Before getting to Nietzsche, however, I want to linger on Bloom's strategy in *Yeats*. There, he painstakingly and wonderfully discriminates among the meanings ascribed by Blake and Yeats to concepts that they appear to share and that Yeats apparently believed that he had adopted from Blake's mythos. Hence, we find many passages such as the following: "For Yeats's Phase 15 is not Blake's Eden, any more than his Byzantium is Blake's Golgonooza or City of Art. The phase of the Full Moon belongs to Blake's Beulah with its dream of indefinitely prolonged forms of love and beauty, a dream that Yeats of course, like Blake, knows to be illusive. But Yeats, as a poet of Phase 17, accepts the tragedy of loss as his Last Judgment, where Blake does not."[24] Again, "Yeats evidently confuses Blake's idea of Innocence with more primitive notions . . . and the curious result is that Blake's true Mask turns out to be "Illusion," his false one "Delusion," which does not seem at all adequate to the actual Blake, but shows us a great deal about what Yeats wanted Blake to have been."[25] Such instances can be multiplied indefinitely. For me, in addition to the sometimes willful, sometimes unintentional misreadings of Blake by Yeats that are abundantly evident in the latter's work, Bloom's passionately specific charting of difference yields the conviction that deep structural, temporally determined ruptures separate the two poets. And Foucault's image of the *episteme* works as well as any for representing that culture shift. Although it is possible to find vestigial agreements between the two poets, these residues serve as much to obfuscate meaning as to clarify it.

There are other ways, however, to address the Blake-Yeats relationship. For instance, a reader might position Yeats along the lines of Daniel Stempel's "Blake, Foucault, and the Classical Episteme." Opposing the usual designation of Blake as arch-romantic, Stempel argues Blake's classicism on the basis of the naming and categorizing functions that he sees operating in the poetry. He finds in Blake verification of Foucault's idea that the structures of a classical text conform to the "four divisions of general grammar"—designation, derivation, articulation, and attribution."[26] Focusing for a moment on classification, a reader notes that in *A Vision* there is a decided tension between various conic/cyclic designs and Yeats's impulse to tabulate, categorize, and codify. Yeats works very hard at these tabular functions (which mark the classical vision), pondering terms, debating positions, questioning his Instructors when he cannot bring himself to accept their designations without hesitation. His thought resonates with Foucault's discussion of the underlying unity of classical discourse, in which "to know clearly and distinctly is to place the name in its proper location in the space of analysis. . . . everything is open to observation, and everything has a proper place in the order of things."[27]

As Foucault apprises us, "The fundamental task of Classical 'discourse' is *to ascribe a name to things, and in that name to name their being.*"[28] Yeats's laboring over the terms of his investigation and over how to organize them, a task that strikes us as naïvely anachronistic, was not by any means taken lightly.[29] The disciplinary force of each moment depends on some such vision of the possibility of the tabular, of getting things right. By this light, Yeats's great wheel and cones look like tables produced by centering linear hierarchies and then putting a spin on them. Concerning their astrological significance, the designations of personality might just as well, phase by phase, be represented in spreadsheet form. Sharing Blake's penchant for unusual terminology, Yeats also adheres to a classical precision standing apart from the mystifications of Madame Blavatsky in works like *The Secret Doctrine* or *Isis Unveiled,* in which the whole point is *not* to communicate empowering words.[30] It is against theosophical mysticism that we must measure Yeats's place in speculative history. And it is against Foucault's sense of the modern *episteme* that we must come to terms with the reaching into Yeats's work of classical impulses drawn from Blake and other writers of his period.

But Yeats also withdraws from Blake in a way that is essential to his system and that involves a question seen by Foucault as central to our era—the problem of history and time. One way to demonstrate the contrast with Blake is to consider two moments in the brief epic called *Milton.* In that poem (II, 69–70), at the sound of the lark, the sun stands still, an event derived from *Joshua,* chapter ten, in which the prophet calls on God to prolong the day in order to provide time for an Israeli victory. Although in Blake's hands the sun stands still seemingly of its own accord, the solar imagery of the poem radically identifies the sun with Milton, Los, and the prophetic speaker, as well as with Christ. The sun, which measures time by its movement, becomes a portent of eternity and an emblem of Christ when it stops during Ololon's descent into Beulah, an event that is ambiguous in that the sun takes on an uninspired passivity in this situation. In fact, it is a positive sign for the sun to move again, for time to carry on.

The prolongation of time that Joshua sought from God signified divine control of earthly existence, but the full six thousand years of Blakean history, intricately divided into twenty-seven churches, must not be shortened even by divine intervention.

Yeats's system rests on an alternative typology from Blake's. In Blake's mythos, Beulah is a state of passivity, a static space that contains no possibility for progression;[31] yet as George Harper makes clear, in *Milton* time is merciful because in time God's goals are accomplished and humanity is redeemed.[32] In Yeats's hands such distinctions are lost, and a grimmer cycle is embraced as though it had the mandate of History itself from both classical and modern *epistemes*. Blake created his own prophetic books as adjuncts to the Bible so that Joshua's stopping of the sun and Blake's use of that event are two distinct manifestations of the final apocalyptic reality in which Christ will end time, in which the prophetic power and inspiration that stop time will be general. For Yeats, cycle, time, prophecy, and apocalypse constitute themselves at odds with their systematizing in Blake, resonating as they do against the seeds of postmodern *différance* and postapocalyptic, Nietzschean gaiety.

Renouncing linearity and having withdrawn from the ideology of progress, Yeats sets up the circular spins mentioned above, both expressing his alignment with Nietzschean modernism and masking the vestigial classicism that speaks itself in *A Vision* (where the agency for that voicing resides with Instructors, as well as with Blake's and with Yeats's own Bloomian "misprision" of him). Yeats, in fact, has it both ways. Evoking the tabularity of classicism, he also insists on the complex, organic relations of the modern *episteme*. Time here has less to do with linear movement or stasis and the cultural graphs that they chart than it does with the totalizing power of History. It is in the interpenetration of gyres, in their constant organic movement, that the system has its most powerful connections with modernity. Foucault's tracing of the split between history as a study of events and History as a machine for prescribing destinies helps us to see that History is memory constituted as a "metaphysic": "In the nineteenth century, philosophy was to reside in the gap between history and History, between events and the Origin, between evolution and the first rending open of the source, between oblivion and the Return."[33] In this temporal zone, Yeats's speculations take on enhanced usefulness. Quite apart from the many rhetorical absurdities that surface in the horoscopes of book 1 ("The Hunchback is his own *Body of Fate*"; "At Phase 22 stupidity is obvious, one finds it in the correspondence of Karl Marx, in his banal abusiveness"; "None of those phases where the *tinctures* open into the Whole, except Phase 27, produces character of sufficient distinctiveness to become historical"[34]), Yeats both clinically and lyrically works the terrain "between oblivion and the Return."

At the same time, the cycles conceived by Yeats are not the ones that he thinks he appropriates. They are so much a function of his epoch that they cannot align with what he imagines he sees in Blake, particularly in "The Mental Traveller," a poem that he places at the heart of *A Vision*. It is instructive to compare the treatments by Adams and by Bloom of the relationship between Blake and Yeats on this issue of the cyclic. Adams specifically addresses the question of pattern in "The Mental Traveller." He cites with approval S. Foster Damon's assessment that the poem relies on "the analogy of organism not only to growth of ideas but also to all movement in time, the central form of which is called history." He goes on to say that "strangely enough," the poem shows us only the Orc-Urizen relationship, without either "linear teleology" or "spiraling progress." And he notes that Yeats called the underlying pattern "the perpetual return of the same thing."[35] Bloom adds, "What Blake presents as disaster Yeats accepts as revelation." According to Blake, "Imagination can reverse the Fall," but for Yeats there is only "a cyclic necessity, which he implies the imagination must accept."[36]

## THE NIETZSCHEAN INTERVENTION AND THE FAILURE OF DESIRE

Acceptance stands somewhere on the horizon "between oblivion and Return," a phrase in which Foucault notates his debt to Nietzsche in identifying the elements of modernity. Yeats, too, finds Blakean ideas of return intercepted by his reading of the German philosopher. Frances Nesbitt Oppel makes clear in her *Mask and Tragedy* that between 1902 and 1909, Yeats read or came to own several volumes of Nietzsche in translation, including *The Will to Power*, volume 1.[37] As Oppel notes, the "doctrine of Eternal Return, which Nietzsche . . . calls the 'highest formula of affirmation that is at all attainable,'" demands "the acceptance of life *exactly* as it is, with no hope of escape from circularity."[38] Nietzsche's version of return seems utterly unmitigated; as he says in *The Will to Power*, "Let us think this thought in its most terrible form: existence as it is, without meaning or aim, yet recurring inevitably without any finale of nothingness: '*The eternal recurrence.*'" Far from crediting any notion of progress, Nietzsche proclaims, Foucauldianly, "'Mankind' does not advance, it does not even exist."[39] And so, armed with the conviction that cultural decay cannot be reversed by imposing a "new *center,*" Nietzsche states, "To the paralyzing sense of general disintegration and incompleteness I opposed the *eternal recurrence.*" And he heroically adds, "That *everything recurs* is the closest *approximation of a world of becoming to a world of being:*—high point of the mediation."[40]

Such rhetoric empowered Yeats's vision in surprising ways. He energetically affirmed recurrence rather than lamenting its grim reality. Into this affirmation, he erroneously swept up Blake, for whom return was less a matter of deep structure than a function of clouded vision and faulty assumptions. Writing as he did in the decades of epistemic shift or slide, and having primary affiliations to a cultural tradition for which the cycle had assumed highly contradictory meanings, Yeats composed a system that reached into the past as well as into the future, that spoke the structures of classicism while turning back upon the projected, more or less finished modern era in order to name, visionarily, its shape and read it for signs of a futurity already embedded in the past. It is this sense of the cycle that stays with the reader of Yeats and with Yeats's shuttling back and forth between the past in the past and the future in the past.

Because of this highly conscious and futuristic elaboration of the concept of return, Yeats's thought wonderfully aligns with many of the conclusions reached by Jean Baudrillard in "Forgetting Foucault." Baudrillard assesses Foucault's work and, like the author himself, finds it evocative but deficient. That is, Baudrillard argues that Foucault can speak only of those issues that are already dead—that Foucault can no longer even imagine; for instance, the register of desire. From Baudrillard's angle of vision, we might argue that the homology between Foucault and Yeats locates itself not only in historical terms but also in terms of tropes like desire, sites hidden for both of them under the rubrics of truth-seeking, of knowledge, and of power. Yeats predicts, simply by considering simultaneously the disjunctions between *epistemei* and Nietzsche's pronouncements on the postapocalyptic order of things, the failure in Foucault of lived desire, of "'libidinal' economy."[41] So it is that, in *A Vision*, we find, not passion itself, but the effects on history – past, present, and future – of irretrievably finished desire. Connecting the disparate moments of gestation and incarnation calatogued by Yeats, many shudders in the loins mark the emptying of desire in a gesture that at once completes a pattern, renews itself as historical potentiality, and ratifies its emergent status as simulacrum. We discern Yeats's nostalgia for a time before the complex relations of modernity placed between the individual and fulfillment the necessity for a Nietzschean (and Yeatsian) mask of difference. Nostalgia, *nostos*, return – these provide much of the torque for the gyric system that Yeats constructs on the cusp between modernism and postmodernism.

A final contrast with Blake may help to sharpen the epistemic location of *A Vision*. In the famous words from *Milton*, Blake asserts:

> There is a Moment in each Day that Satan cannot find,
> Nor can his Watch Fiends find it; but the Industrious find
> This Moment & it multiply, & when it once is found
> It renovates every Moment of the Day if rightly placed.[42]

For Blake, the movement out of time and into eternity was a vision-clearing blink of discovery. For Yeats, who could only embed classical order within modern recycling, there was also such a "moment"–or a reasonable equivalent. I am thinking of the "thirteenth sphere," itself a cycle "which is in every man" and that constitutes a chance for "freedom" within the individual's experience of the (Irish) cycle of conflict and authenticity. In the midst of his concern over the failure of vision, Yeats claims of the sphere, "Doubtless . . . it knows what it will do with its own freedom but it has kept the secret."[43] Earlier, when Yeats introduced the thirteenth sphere, he associated it with "ultimate reality."[44] It is in relation to this ultimate reality that Yeats's dictum takes on value: "the limit itself has become a new dimension."[45] But in these moments of self-revelation, where he stands stymied before the limitations that he shares with Foucault, Yeats deludes himself into thinking that because he has "already said all that can be said,"[46] there is therefore some stated but as yet unrecognized escape from the round, a hope for the future that Nietzsche did not intuit but that Blake adumbrates. Yeats thus wills himself into an antinomian, conceptual blindness; he stands amid the systemic contradictions that, primed by his historical situation, he has made graphically visible. Caught in epistemic shift and in a country bound to cycles of violence, the poet nostalgically voices the discontinuities and uneven developments of his time, before cutting them free to find their own places in the disciplines of history.

## NOTES

1. Michel Foucault, Two Lectures," trans. Kate Soper, in *Power/Knowledge: Selected Interviews and Other Writings, 1972-1977,* ed. Colin Gordon (New York: Pantheon Books, 1980), 78.

2. William Butler Yeats, *A Vision* (New York: Macmillan, 1965), 301, 302.

3. Hazard Adams points out that despite the determinism of Yeats's view of history, and despite the lack of progress in human civilization, in Yeats's view the occasional presence of "mystery" becomes apparent to "time-borne" man, whose "flashes of insight" point the way to "spirituality and eternity." *Blake and Yeats: The Contrary Vision* (New York: Russell and Russell, 1968), 245. Foucault helps us to talk about such moments in language that is more historically precise.

4. Yeats, *Vision,* 9.

5. Ibid., 81.

6. The failures stated in *A Vision* reinforce others in Yeats's work. Cf. Adams, who believes that Yeats's engagement with "violent exertion and striving" against insurmountable odds "restates an archetypical tragic theme which is also Yeats's major theme" (268-69).

7. Yeats, *Vision,* 262, 248.

8. Northrop Frye, "The Top of the Tower: A Study of the Imagery of Yeats," in *The Stubborn Structure: Essays on Criticism and Society* (Ithaca: Cornell Univ. Press, 1970), 263.

9. Yeats, *Vision,* 37, 45, 49. Cf. Colin McDowell, who finds the Michael Robartes information merely "a covering device, a way to protect Yeats from the scorn of critics who find him endorsing outlandish things in the book proper." "To 'Beat Upon the Wall': Reading *A Vision,*" *Yeats Annual No. 4,* ed. Warwick Gould (1984): 222. This approach is widespread.

10. Richard Eilmann, *Yeats: The Man and the Masks* (New York: Norton, 1979), 242.

11. Yeats, *Vision,* 53, 184.

12. Although lack of room in this essay precludes development of this notion of double coding, evidence for the position may be found throughout Seamus Deane, *Celtic Revivals: Essays in Modern Irish Literature, 1880–1980* (Winston-Salem: Wake Forest Univ. Press, 1985).

13. Yeats, *Vision*, 261.

14. Yeats, "The Phases of the Moon," *Vision*, 61.

15. Michel Foucault, *The Order of Things: An Archaeology of the Human Sciences* (New York: Random, 1970), 97.

16. Michel de Certeau, *Heterologies: Discourse on the Other*, trans. Brian Massumi (Minneapolis: Univ. of Minnesota Press, 1986), 177.

17. Foucault, *Order*, 52.

18. Ibid., 63, 218.

19. Ibid., 219.

20. de Certeau, 173.

21. Foucault, *Order*, 386–87.

22. Adams, *Blake and Yeats*, 287.

23. Daniel Stempel claims, "What Foucault views as the disintegration of classical discourse is the effect of a shift as simple and as pervasive as the Great Vowel Shift between Middle and Modern English." See "Blake, Foucault, and the Classical Episteme," *PMLA* 96 (1981): 404.

24. Harold Bloom, *Yeats* (New York: Oxford Univ. Press, 1970), 237.

25. Ibid., 247.

26. Stempel, "Blake, Foucault," 394–401.

27. Ibid., 389.

28. Foucault, *Order*, 120.

29. See "Editorial Introduction," in *A Critical Edition of Yeats's "A Vision"* (1925), ed. George Mills Harper and Walter Kelly Hood (New York: Macmillan, 1978), for discussion of the concordance cards that Yeats used to organize the headings of his inquiry. According to Harper, "Beginning on 24 October 1917 and continuing as late as 4 June 1921, the Automatic Script itself required or was the result of some 450 sessions, in which the answers to at least 8672 recorded (and many unrecorded) questions were answered on 3627 pages." "'Unbelievers in the House': Yeats's Automatic Script," *Studies in the Literary Imagination* 14 (1981): 15.

30. Cf. my discussion of Blavatsky in "Theosophy, Guilt, and 'That Word Known to All Man' in Joyce's *Ulysses*," *James Joyce Quarterly* 18 (1980): 49.

31. Harold Bloom, "Commentary," in *The Poetry and Prose of William Blake*, ed. David V. Erdman (Garden City, N.Y.: Doubleday, 1965), 837.

32. George Mills Harper, "The Neo-Platonic Concept of Time in Blake's Prophetic Books," *PMLA* 69 (1954): 148.

33. Foucault, *Order*, 219.

34. Yeats, *Vision*, 178, 162, 105.

35. Adams, *Blake and Yeats*, 242, 243.

36. Bloom, *Yeats*, 261.

37. Frances Nesbitt Oppel, *Mask and Tragedy: Yeats and Nietzsche, 1902–10* (Charlottesville: Univ. Press of Virginia, 1987), 1, 203.

38. Ibid., 230. One fascinating piece of information, which Oppel cites from Harper and Hood, is that the Instructors' first designation of people to phases was of Nietzsche to phase 12 and of Zarathustra to phase 18 (230).

39. Friedrich Nietzsche, *The Will to Power*, trans. Walter Kaufmann and R. J. Hollingdale, ed. Walter Kaufmann (New York: Random, 1967), bk. 1, 35, 55.

40. Ibid., bk 2, 224; bk. 3, 330.

41. Jean Baudrillard, "Forgetting Foucault," *Humanities in Society* 3 (1980): 92.

42. William Blake, "Milton" in *English Romantic Writers*, ed. David Perkins (New York: Harcourt, Brace & World, 1967), "Book the Second," 260–63.

43. Yeats, *Vision*, 302.

44. Ibid., 193.

45. Ibid., 300.

46. Ibid., 302.

# 10

# YEATS/BAKHTIN/ORALITY/DYSLEXIA

R. B. KERSHNER

AT FIRST GLANCE, the notion of approaching a lyric poet by way of the critical thought of Bakhtin may seem oxymoronic, or at least perverse. After all, in Bakhtin's morality play of literary genres, poetry is generally the villain; it is characterized as monologic, deaf to the rich interplay of social languages, which for Bakhtin is basic to the artistic importance of the novel. In "Discourse in the Novel," Bakhtin is most explicit on the subject: "In genres that are poetic in the narrow sense, the natural dialogization of the word is not put to artistic use, the word is sufficient unto itself and does not presume alien utterances beyond its own boundaries. Poetic style is by convention suspended from any mutual interaction with alien discourse, any allusion to alien discourse. . . . [A] critical qualified relationship to one's own language (as merely one of many languages in a heteroglot world) is alien to poetic style."[1] Elsewhere, Bakhtin makes much the same point with regard to the drama.

Clearly, Bakhtin here is primarily concerned with inverting the traditional hierarchy of genres. In championing the upstart genre of the novel over poetry and drama, he constructs an aesthetic intended to denigrate those modes of writing almost by definition. But there are several loopholes in his hyperbolic argument. For one thing, he is admittedly describing a tendency of what he sees as "pure" lyric poetry; actual poetry, as words in the world, is necessarily in dialogical relationship to the surrounding language. Bakhtin allows, "Of course this relationship and the relationship of his own language (in greater or lesser degree) could never be foreign to a historically existent poet,

167

as a human being surrounded by living hetero- and polyglossia," although he insists that "this relationship could not find a place in the *poetic style* of his work."[2] For another, Bakhtin admits that poetry, like other genres, is susceptible to *novelization*, which can also render the poetic word dialogical: once the genre of the novel was established, a "lengthy battle for the novelization of the other genres began, a battle to drag them into a zone of contact with reality."[3] For example, a romantic poem—and here Bakhtin probably has in mind narratives like *Lara*—is really a "novelized poem."[4]

Still, in Bakhtin's eyes, even the romantic novel proper cannot approach the dialogical richness of Dostoevsky's novels because the varied speech of characters within it is "objectified," consciously used for illustration or atmosphere, instead of being allowed to enter into serious, dialogical relationship with the authorial language. Dostoevsky's greatness lies in his ability to stand outside his own language, to oppose it with a variety of strong languages attached to characters in his works. By contrast, the poet "is not able to oppose his own poetic consciousness, his own intentions to the languages he uses, for he is completely within it." The intervention of other languages in the novel is encouraged by the fact that it is an explicitly *social* genre, whereas "poetic language" evolves by "sealing itself off from the influence of extraliterary social dialects."[5]

Behind these invidious comparisons are several unstated presumptions. One is the belief, foregrounded in *Rabelais and His World*, that literature reaches its greatest potential when it is infused with popular speech and thus with the heterological, disruptive carnival spirit of "the people" or "the folk." Another even more fundamental axiom is that language is primarily an *oral* phenomenon. Bakhtin sees poetry as tending toward the *written*—toward expression rather than toward interchange—and therefore as frustrating the dialogical potential of language itself. In *Marxism and the Philosophy of Language*, Bakhtin/Volosinov attacks the "*dead, written, alien language*" with which linguistics is traditionally concerned.[6] In this regard, he is diametrically opposed to Derrida, who attacks the traditional Western metaphysics of presence by ("strategically" but still influentially) elevating the written over the spoken, *graphie* over *phonè*. Bakhtin accomplishes his own demolition of the authorizing *self* by his vision of language as always already a battlefield of conflicting speech genres and of consciousness as being dependent upon language. Because language is social and ideological from the beginning, so is selfhood: "Consciousness becomes consciousness only once it has been filled with ideological (semiotic) content, consequently, only in the process of social interaction."[7] But the fact that Bakhtin's "decentering" of the self resembles in many regards that of Derrida and other postmodernist critics should not blind us to the implicit stress the Russian critic places upon language as that which is spoken, and upon literature as a sophisticated form of conversation.[8]

Anyone familiar with Yeats's work will immediately see several important parallels with Bakhtin's thought. First is the poet's stress upon poetry as an oral form. Throughout Yeats's writing on poetry, the idea of good writing as a peculiarly direct sort of speech, unmediated by the artificial devices of rhetoric, recurs. In 1913, Yeats wrote to his father of his desire to use "a speech so natural and dramatic that the hearer would feel the presence of a man thinking and feeling." In 1932, writing to Olivia Shakespear, Yeats announced his proud discovery while correcting proof: "I have just finished the first volume, all my lyric poetry and am greatly astonished at myself, as it is all speech rather than writing."[9] Most explicitly, in his 1937 essay "A General Introduction for My Work," Yeats claimed, "I tried to make the language of poetry coincide with that of passionate, normal speech. I wanted to write in whatever language comes most naturally when we soliloquise, as I do all day long, upon the events of our own lives or of any life where we can see ourselves for the moment."[10] For Yeats, the natural movement of the mind, which is the movement of direct, interpersonal speech, is inherently poetic and opposed to the artificial language of the novelist, which is in a pejorative sense "literary." "'If I can be sincere and make my language natural, and without becoming discursive, like a novelist, and so indiscreet and prosaic,' I said to myself, 'I shall . . . be a great poet; for it will no longer be a matter of literature at all.'" What Yeats somewhat paradoxically calls "personal utterance"—for in a sense it is not personal at all—might provide "as fine an escape from rhetoric and abstraction as drama itself."[11]

Another parallel with Bakhtin's thought is Yeats's conviction that the roots of art are in the people—the "folk"—and that serious art must draw upon that source. The poet's rationale for this belief is, of course, very different from Bakhtin's Marxist presuppositions, and it is therefore all the more striking that both thinkers should find the same tragic gaiety, the same life-affirming, irreverent obscenity to be the most power-ful message of the people. This was not Yeats's initial position, of course; it is only in the last books that his verse becomes to a degree "carnival-ized." But in the "Chambermaid's Songs" and the "Crazy Jane" poems, rude sexuality rears its butting head in carnivalesque response to the life-denying spirituality represented by the Bishop in a process that precisely parallels the dialogics Bakhtin finds in Rabelais. That "Love has pitched his mansion in / The place of excrement" captures neatly Rabelais's paradoxical overturning of ideal concepts by means of "bod-ily lower stratum."[12]

But even early in his career, during his more idealist phase, Yeats informed George Moore that it was only from the peasants that "one could learn to write, their speech being living speech, flowing out of the habits of their lives, struck out of life itself."[13] Indeed, at times Yeats presents himself simply as the transcriber of peasant narrative and wis-dom. Speaking of his uncle's illiterate servant Mary Battle, Yeats ob-serves, "much of my *Celtic Twilight* is but her daily speech."[14] For Yeats, the speech of the peasantry provided access to genuine Irish folk cul-ture, which was of value both in itself and also as a poetic buttress for the Nationalist movement; but in addition, it enabled him to tap the timeless sources of mystical wisdom that were available to the un-lettered people of all countries, uncorrupted as they were by modern materialism. Still, as the work of a poet like Rolleston testifies, an in-terest in folk materials by no means guarantees that a poet will enter into genuine dialogue with the "folk voice." In Yeats, it is precisely this dialogue that gives much of the strength to his lyrics. In such lyrics as "Down by the Salley Gardens," Yeats himself found it impossible to distinguish the folk source from his own contribution.

A third parallel in the thought of the Russian critic and the Irish poet is the idea that conflict or opposition is the central principle of selfhood, as it is of history. The principle, of course, takes different particular shapes in the work of the two men. Bakhtin imagines the formation of consciousness as a battle between an undefined self, which must define itself through language, and the surrounding languages, which are already "owned": "when a member of a speaking collective comes upon a word, it is not as a neutral word of language, not as a word free from the aspirations and evaluations of others. . . . His own thought finds the word already inhabited."[15] Inner speech or outer speech for Bakhtin is a continuous confrontation with the words of others, a confrontation usually imaged as a form of conflict. Within cultures as a whole, the same process operates. Rabelais's work, by assimilating the carnivalesque voice of the people, launches an attack on the dominant monological culture of the church—an attack that defines the Renaissance spirit.

On the level of the individual, the central conflict for Yeats is articulated through his famous doctrine of the Mask, in which the self erects an oppositional "anti-self" against which it stands in tension. In an insightful essay, Robert Langbaum traces the idea of conflict in Yeats's thought from the psychological level through the historical; he observes that Yeats reverses the nineteenth-century idea that a man finds his identity through self-realization. Instead, "after some years came the thought that a man always tried to become his opposite, to become what he would abhor if he did not desire it."[16] By the time he had elaborated the system of A Vision, with its opposing gyres and primary and antithetical ages, Yeats had concluded that the world at large was governed by the principle of conflict. "I had never read Hegel, but my mind had been full of Blake from boyhood up and I saw the world as a conflict . . . and could distinguish between a contrary and a negation."[17] Both Bakhtin and Yeats assert—rather against the evidence—that their systems of conflict issue in a governing unity. Although for Bakhtin the self is never finalized or totalized—is never "equal to itself"—he cannot resist asserting that in truly dialogical novels such as Dostoevsky's, the apparent chaos of interacting genres and languages is somehow held together by an aesthetic unity on some other level.[18] Similarly, Yeats sometimes imagines that out of the quarrel with one's fractured self comes the movement toward what he mystically terms "Unity of Being."[19] At other times, he seems to despair of unity for his poetic self: "I commit my emotion to shepherds, herdsmen, cameldrivers, learned men. . . . Talk to me of originality and I will turn on you with rage. I am a crowd, I am a lonely man, I am nothing."[20]

The relationship of these three principles—the primacy of speech, the authority of the folk, and the fundamental nature of conflict—is far from clear in the thought of either man. From a philosophical perspective, it is tempting to take the idea of conflict as a starting point; and, indeed, conflict as power is the dominant theme of Denis Donoghue's excellent short study of Yeats.[21] More contemporary critical approaches, however, tend to take language as a point of departure, as does Bakhtin explicitly and, it may be argued, as does Yeats implicitly. From a writer's initial relationship to language, much may be deduced; and in the case of Yeats, this relationship is especially intriguing. Because of Yeats's stature, it is less evident to us now that some of his presuppositions run directly counter to the general poetic current of his time, but his commitment to poetry as an oral form is certainly unexpected in a period otherwise dominated by Mallarmé and Eliot, perhaps the two most "literary" poets ever to have written. Certainly, he had the good fortune to be born in a country where the powerful remnants of an oral culture still existed—a culture to which, for ideological reasons, he might have been drawn. But he was also born into the Anglo-Irish aristocracy and into a home filled with books, where the "high" cultural tradition was ever-present. Given his familial and cultural inheritance, Yeats might easily have regarded poetry—as did most of his contemporaries in the Decadent movement—as a proudly artificial, unnatural, fundamentally *written* mode of art.

That Yeats did not do so, indeed *could* not do so, may be greatly owing to an accident of neurology: it is quite possible that the young Yeats was dyslexic. The idea of a dyslexic writer may seem self-contradictory; but, in fact, it is asserted by the highly accomplished postmodernist writer of science fiction, Samuel R. Delany, who was himself profoundly dyslexic. Delany suggests that not only Yeats, but Flaubert and perhaps Virginia Woolf were dyslexic: "There's an easy and natural relation to written language that the dyslexic just doesn't have. You think of Yeats with his 'fascination for what's difficult.' Well, part of the difficulty was that he didn't really learn to read until he was sixteen."[22] In a broad, general sense, of course, there is no doubt that Yeats was dyslexic in his youth; that is, he had inordinate difficulty in learning to read and write, spell and punctuate. As he recounts in "Reveries over Childhood and Youth," "I was difficult to teach. Several of my aunts and uncles had tried to teach me to read, and because they could not, and because I was much older than children who read easily, had come to think, as I have learned since, that I had not all my faculties. . . . My father said if I would not go to church he would teach me to read. . . . He was an angry and impatient teacher and flung the reading-book at my head, and next Sunday I decided to go to church. My father had, however, got interested in teaching me, and only shifted the lesson to a weekday till he had conquered my wandering mind."[23] According to Joseph Hone, John Yeats's lessons began in 1873, when the poet was eight. His father took to berating him with his "moral degradation," and at some point thereafter, as Richard Ellmann observes, "in a state of terror, he learned to read," although certainly "he never learned to study successfully."[24] There is no way of determining at what point Yeats's wandering mind was satisfactorily conquered, but a time-table of lessons in his hand from the Godolphin School, which he attended from about 1875 to 1880, describes his subjects as "Scripter," "Riting," "Reading," "Inglish," "Gramar," and "Arithmithick." Like many dyslexics, the schoolboy Yeats excelled in mathematics, was quite poor at languages, and was worst of all at literature, being under the impression that "Shakespeare was being read for the grammar only."[25]

The question of interest here, however, is whether Yeats suffered from what is sometimes called specific developmental dyslexia, a syndrome whose very existence is still open to discussion. Few authorities would dispute the fact that an unexpectedly large number of children of normal or above-average intelligence have abnormal difficulty learning to read, but educational psychologists often claim that no single cause can explain the bulk of these cases. Eleanor Gibson and Harry Levin, for example, group the causes into four categories: communicative emotional deprivation, in which the proper stimulation for language acquisition in the family or in the larger social environment is lacking; cultural or emotional deprivation, often the result of poverty; minimal brain dysfunction, in which, because of illness or lack of normal physical development, subtle deviations occur in the functioning of the central nervous system (as are found in hyperactive children); and a rather general category of genetic makeup, indicating a hereditary inability to learn to read normally despite the absence of the other three causes. A child, they argue, may be dyslexic because of any combination of these four broad categories.[26] Clinical neurologists, on the other hand, are likely to assert that a single neurological syndrome is responsible for many of the examples of dyslexia that are conventionally treated as a result of emotional disturbance or cultural deprivation. Dyslexia in this sense was independently hypothesized in the 1890s by two British doctors, James Kerr and Pringle Morgan, and was originally termed "congenital word-blindness." Specialists in the field conservatively estimate that of the roughly 10 percent of all schoolchildren in England and America who have reading difficulties, perhaps one-fifth of the boys and one-twentieth of the girls are technically dyslexic.[27]

Because of the work of the American Samuel Orton, who published books and papers on dyslexia from the 1920s through the 1960s, the hypothesis that dyslexia is a result of incomplete brain asymmetry, and that it is usually evidenced by letter reversals and left-right reversals in writing, gained a great deal of popular currency. More current research suggests that such reversals and lateral confusions are common among all children and that they do not particularly characterize dyslexics.[28] Macdonald Critchley has written a general description of the difficulties experienced by dyslexics surrounding the problem of reading:

> The dyslexic cannot readily associate the sound of a word with its appearance on paper, and even when he has achieved some ability to read and write, he often has lingering doubts as to the correct orientation of certain letters. He may experience hesitation in serial thinking, and his ability to spell usually lags behind his modest skill at reading. Furthermore, a dyslexic almost always finds it anything but easy to express his thoughts fluently and rapidly on paper. Creative and imaginative, full of ideas perhaps, he is hindered when setting them down. He is also slow in copying to dictation; and at a later age he finds it difficult to take adequate notes at a lecture or meeting. Even well into adult life he may continue to be a reluctant reader, finding it simpler to absorb information by word of mouth, and also to impart it orally rather than by writing.[29]

Critchley has observed a number of additional symptoms of dyslexic children that are particularly suggestive for Yeats. Dyslexic children seldom read aloud at a normal rate; rather, they read quite slowly. In some, reading aloud is accompanied by "an excessive prosody or sing-song type of elocution." One highly intelligent dyslexic found his attention riveted by the white spaces between the print rather than by the words themselves and also reported having hallucinations when dropping off to sleep and a tendency to see faces and forms in the folds of curtains or in the marks on walls.[30] Dyslexics tend to write slowly, with heavy pressure. They may fuse or malform letters, frequently cross out or erase, make copious mistakes in spelling and punctuation (or may omit punctuation altogether), have little sense of paragraphing, and in rapid writing sometimes run horizontal lines together or at wild angles to one another. Surprisingly, Critchley finds that many dyslexic boys and girls greatly enjoy listening to poetry and, indeed, sometimes show far greater skill in writing poems than in writing normal prose. That there may be an organic correlation to this phenomenon is shown by the fact that some adults who became aphasic as a result of brain damage have successfully written verse, and even marketed it, while being unable to compose a simple letter to a friend.[31]

Yeats's odd characteristic style of declamation—for prose or for poetry—is, of course, well-known, and he elaborated an aesthetic about it, influencing a generation of Irish actors to adopt an artificial, slow, and cadenced delivery. But even as a schoolboy he "declaimed his essays just as he did those of Demosthenes."[32] From childhood he occasionally saw visions, as he testifies in the *Autobiographies*. Yeats's manuscripts are notoriously unreadable, complete with the ambiguous symbols that Critchley finds frequently in dyslexic writing. John Stallworthy notes that a single curved line may stand for a capital *I* or *O* or even an ampersand. Further, "'not' and 'but' are sometimes undistinguishable, as are also: 'then,' 'there,' 'their,' 'the,' 'this,' 'these,' 'those'; likewise: 'in,' 'on,' 'or,' 'an.'"[33]

But these are fairly minor habitual problems, found in more or less finished drafts. At earlier stages of composition, sometimes entire manuscript pages are unreadable, as in many of the drafts that David R. Clark examines in *Yeats at Songs and Choruses*.[34] Stallworthy comments, "Latterly, Mrs. Yeats told me, he frequently could not himself read what he had written: there is much that she has never been able to read, even with a strong magnifying glass. As he grew older he wrote, I believe, often with no intention of reading what was before him on the page: his fingers were simply turning the dials."[35] Certainly, the mature Yeats, like many former dyslexics, was able to write a legible hand when he set his mind to it; but in the throes of composition his lines, of which a remarkable number were crossed out, often wandered illegibly all over the page. Relatively few of the published early drafts of poems have any punctuation whatsoever. Yeats wrote to Robert Bridges, "I do not understand stops. I write my work so completely for the ear that I feel helpless when I have to measure pauses by stops and commas." As late as 1932, he assured his publisher, "I have never been able to punctuate properly. I do not think I have ever differed from a correction of yours in punctuation. I suggest that in the remaining volumes you do not query your corrections."[36] In point of fact, it was often Mrs. Yeats or the publisher who was the first to punctuate an unpunctuated manuscript.

Whether he would today qualify as a victim of specific developmental dyslexia, there can be no doubt that Yeats was from the first committed to, even mesmerized by, the spoken word, with consequences that have not been fully explored. From a psychological perspective, his father's practice of reading poetry and novels aloud to him from Yeats's early childhood well into his teens was undoubtedly an important factor, especially considering the passionate, violent passages which John Yeats favored, and in which he had an obvious emotional and aesthetic investment. Poetry, John Yeats insisted, must be "an idealisation of speech."[37] Once he had painfully mastered reading, Yeats took pleasure in everything from boys' papers through Andersen and Grimm, but there was a strange insubstantiality to that experience. Reminiscing about that time afterward, he observes, "I have remembered nothing that I read, but only those things that I heard or saw."[38] He was struck primarily by the stories of peasant neighbors of the Middletons, sailors in Galway Harbor, or even the tales of other boys. While his father had treasured the voice as the testament of character, Yeats from the first valued a certain anonymity in it. Even his own voice, or the voices in his head, seemed to come from elsewhere. Once he began writing, he composed aloud, sometimes—to his embarrassment—unconsciously and in public. One of the more bizarre manifestations of his obsession with the spoken word is that, from childhood onward, he quite literally heard "the voice of conscience." "From that day the voice has come to me at moments of crisis, but now it is a voice in my head that is sudden and startling. It does not tell me what to do, but often reproves me."[39]

Clearly, for Yeats, the spoken word is real, *present*; the written word is insubstantial, an abstraction. So far, this is no more than the common Western orientation that Derrida finds in Rousseau, descending from Plato. But for Yeats, the spoken word is not simply the testimony of a speaking subject that lends authority to the word, as God lends authority to *logos*; instead, speech bifurcates, multiplies, and reveals itself as subjectless. It leads beyond itself, often backward in time, to a series of other voices in constant dialogue. In one of the "tales" from

*The Celtic Twilight,* "By the Roadside," Yeats recounts going to "a wide place on the Kiltartan road to listen to some Irish songs." "The voices melted into the twilight, and were mixed into the trees, and when I thought of the words they too melted away, and were mixed with the generations of men. Now it was a phrase, now it was an attitude of mind, an emotional form, that had carried my memory to older verses, or even to forgotten mythologies. I was carried so far that it was as though I came to one of the four rivers, and followed it under the wall of Paradise to the roots of the Trees of Knowledge and of Life. There is no song or story handed down among the cottages that has not words and thoughts to carry one as far."[40] Other critics have noted the tendency of the speaking voice in Yeats's writing to dissolve. Hillis Miller, for instance, argues that the voice of his poetry is "not personal at all but another voice, universal, anonymous, depersonalizing, a voice speaking through the poet. It is the voice of human experience generally, of literary and philosophical tradition. It is the voice ultimately of 'nothing,' of that no one and no place from which the desolate winds blow in 'Nineteen Hundred and Nineteen.'"[41] But a voice that becomes a decentered plurality is not, after all, the voice of "nothing"; Miller, who wishes to demonstrate that a vacancy exists at the center of the topography of Yeats's poems, does not distinguish here between voice and text. Where a Derridean reading finds the self-questioning and splintering of Yeats's voice(s) an aspect of the poem's impetus to interrogate the arbitrary nature of signs in a text, a Bakhtinian reading lingers on the interplay of voices.

A single voice, for Yeats as for Bakhtin, finally has neither authority nor autonomy; voices are brought forth by other voices, confront them, contest them, respond to them in the conflictual process that Bakhtin calls "dialogism." Yeats's writing, far more clearly than in the case of most other poets, is radically dialogical, a representation of intertwined and conflicting voices. The dialogical dimension of the work is both "internal" and "external" from the beginning. That is, Yeats works through conscious collaboration with others—either individuals or unspecified representatives of the "folk"—while his "own" voice in poem after poem bifurcates, represents itself to itself through a dialogue between competing elements. Internal dialogization tends to be based on opposing ideological positions between which the writer is torn, while external dialogization is often more a matter of syntax and vocabulary. Yet each of these aspects of voice is involved in and helps to generate the other.

Because for later poets Yeats has sounded such a dominant individual voice, it is difficult to realize to what extent that voice was a collaborative effort. In the tales of *The Celtic Twilight*, Yeats consciously attempts to efface his own presence—to put it at the service of the rural people in whose mingled speech he hopes to discern a single note. At times, he quotes at several removes, such as when he records his version of an Ulster friend's version of an old woman's version of what a faery woman once said.[42] More directly, friends like Lady Gregory reworked his prose—such as the *Stories of Red Hanrahan*, "Rewritten in 1907 with Lady Gregory's Help"—so that Yeats's style progressively reflects the influence of writers with whom he worked or collaborated, such as George Moore and Pound or even, in *A Vision*, the voice speaking through his wife. It is only one of the many paradoxes of this literary echo chamber that Georgie Yeats's automatic writing should resemble the voice of Yeats's own mystical speculations, and that he should then choose to collaborate with it.

The internal dialogization of Yeats's voice is equally apparent. From his earliest juvenilia onward, Yeats was drawn to verse drama, where two or more strong voices could contend for dominance. In *The Countess Cathleen*, for example, Oona's pragmatic voice balances Aleel's romantic one, while Cathleen's self-sacrificial Christian rhetoric is opposed both by Oona's earthbound conservatism and by Aleel's pagan, almost epicurean, urge to escape. Although it could be argued that Oona's voice is still "objectified," that hers is not a genuine contributor to the dialogics of the play, clearly Yeats has a strong investment in both Cathleen and Aleel. Their dispute is one instance of Yeats's argument with himself. That argument exfoliates throughout the poetry as well, most obviously in the semidramatic poems in which two voices explicitly contend—Hic and Ille, Aherne and Robartes, Saint and Hunchback, Soul and Self, Man and Echo, He and She—but equally strongly in the poems like "When You Are Old" (a collaboration with Ronsard) or "No Second Troy," in which every word of the poet's persona is addressed to, anticipates, conciliates, or contests the language of a figure like Maud Gonne, whose ideology Yeats respects but must battle against. Often, the refrain lines of a poem constitute a second voice that mocks or transforms the voice of the stanzas proper: "'What then?' sang Plato's ghost. 'What then?'"

The terms of the argument and the positions change, but contestation remains. Yeats's habit, ploy, and necessity was to give voice to each of the mutually exclusive positions that he wished to embrace – to each side of the binary oppositions that structured his psyche: engagement and escape, responsibility and self-indulgence, credulity and cynicism, aspiration and lethargy, hope and despair, "spontaneous joy" and "the fascination of what's difficult," and so on in endless sequence. Even the doctrine of the Mask itself, which is at one level responsible for generating these oppositions, is expressed through the argument of two lovers in a poem once entitled "A Lyric from an Unpublished Play" – a title that captures perfectly the feeling given by most of Yeats's lyrics. And it is in a reading of the poems and plays as a whole that fragmentation succeeds the bifurcation of voice, as what had appeared to be a single, coherent speech in one work is revealed in another to be compounded of its own internal contentions. Aleel, in *Countess Cathleen*, speaks as lover, poet, pagan priest, and escape artist; while in separate poems, lover must vie with poet, mystic with lover, and the urge to escape with the urge to possess mystical knowledge, as each of these positions generates its own powerful rhetoric.

From *Responsibilities* (1914) onward, positions are increasingly articulated by beggars, hunchbacks, and fools, as if Yeats had abandoned the possibility of finding an affirmation that he could speak with his own unmediated voice. His voice is never simply given or accepted by him: "I even do my writing by self-distrusting reasons," he confided to a private diary.[43] Unless we ourselves are mystically inclined, we can find the most bizarre manifestation of Yeats's internal dialogization in the poet's exchange of letters with his oppositional daimon, Leo Africanus. Once Leo Africanus has "spoken through" Yeats in a letter, the poet adds in his own suspicious postscript that "I am not convinced that in this letter there is one sentence that has come from beyond my imagination. . . . I have been conscious of no sudden illumination." Even the poor daimon cannot speak with the free, unmediated voice of full presence and authority because, as Leo Africanus writes, "I am aware of a constraint upon my thoughts or my passion deepens because of one who is remote & silent & whom I wile [sic] I lived in Rome

I was forbidden to call Mahomet."[44] The further Yeats penetrated into hermetic studies, the more clearly he realized that behind each voice of authority were more masters whose message was only approximated by the available voices, none of whom could speak without interference, or what Georgie Yeats's spirit informant termed "frustration." On the other side of the veil, beyond the cacophony of earthly babble, the initiate could expect to be greeted with transcendent babble.

Aside from dialogism, what might be the consequences of Yeats's orientation toward orality in language, assuming that this is one major consequence of his dyslexia? The answers to such a question must be highly speculative because the problem itself falls between any number of disciplines—neurology, psychology, literary theory, speech, anthropology—all of which are tangentially illuminating but none of which makes a specific study of the problem. Experimental psychologists with a neurological orientation have studied the mechanics of the reading process with some attention to dyslexia; this might be characterized as a "microscopic" approach. Meanwhile, several cultural anthropologists and literary theorists have explored some of the differences between oral cultures and literate cultures and the transition between the two; this could be termed the "macroscopic" approach. Neither, of course, addresses directly the question of individual psychology, especially as it relates to the written production of an orally oriented writer of genius.

Some consequences of Yeats's orientation toward language, given his early experience, seem fairly straightforward. He should be reluctant to embark on courses of formal study, although he might well be drawn to arcane, unsystematic, "impressionistic" researches. He should be attracted to those—like the Irish peasants of his time—whose culture is itself greatly oral and in which his own investigations must be oral. He should be at home in debating societies and discussion groups and, among the literary arts, drawn to drama. If he is not simply to think of himself as unintelligent, he should develop a personal ideology that will denigrate conventional formal instruction and that will allow him to develop a self-image as an independent, intuitive thinker whose self-absorption and access to sublimer sorts of knowledge prevent his success in school. Indeed, even Yeats's intransigent opposition to Locke's mechanism—whatever its philosophical and social validity—can also be seen as an elaborate rationalization of his difficulty with "book-learning."

Such explanations, however pragmatically tempting, are also obviously reductive. Reading research reveals, for instance, that in the reading process some kind of "speech processing" takes place: we ordinarily subvocalize as we read and as a result find some kinds of reading comprehension improved. On the other hand, when subvocalization is artificially eliminated, readers are still perfectly capable of reading, although their scores on the comprehension of difficult material are lower. Robert Crowder suggests that "people have two strategies available for word processing tasks — one using speech and the other bypassing it" — and that at least unconsciously they have considerable choice regarding which strategy to use.[45] Use of the "speech mode" in reading may be linked with short-term memory, which allows an entire line of text to be stored for a short while. It is tempting to suppose that dyslexics have some sort of genetic difficulty in using the "non-speech" mode of lexical access, with possible consequences for their thought and writing processes; but for now, no evidence is available to support such a hypothesis. On this "microscopic" level, the situation is simply too complex, with too many unknowns.

Anthropologists and linguists studying the effects of literacy have similarly been faced with extremely basic questions. The strongest hypothesis with respect to the oral-written distinction was put forth by L. S. Vygotsky, who claimed that, in learning to read, a person's mental processes are changed fundamentally through the external symbolic system that comes to mediate the organization of all of his or her basic intellectual operations. As Jack Goody has noted, however, Vygotsky ignored the mediation of a literate culture on the oral environment of such a person; probably no one in the civilized world learns to read within a culturally pure oral environment.[46] For practical reasons, it is very difficult to compare meaningfully the thought processes of individuals in pure oral societies with those of readers — the difference in cultures alone is a huge barrier to comparison. Work has been done, however, on the difference between the spoken and written "registers" of several languages, and Goody summarizes the results. Lexical features of the written register include: a tendency to use longer words; increased nominalization as against a preference for verbalization in speech; a greater variety of vocabulary; more attributive adjectives; fewer personal pronouns; and, in English, a more Latinate vocabulary. Syntactic features include: a preferential use of elaborate syntactic and semantic structures; a preference for subordinate rather than coordinate construction; the use of declaratives and subjunctives rather than imperatives, interrogatives, and exclamations; the use of passive rather than active voice; the use of definite articles rather than demonstrative modifiers; the making explicit of all assumptions; the reliance on a more deliberate or rationalized method of organizing ideas; and elimination of the many redundancies that characterize ordinary speech.[47]

Most of these differences are fairly obvious, and the question remains in regard to which of them are accidents of the typical genres of writing in Western cultures (predominantly prose genres, one would suppose) and which are essentially linked to the act of writing itself. It is also unclear, of course, to what degree each feature represents a difference in thought process, whatever that may mean. Eric Havelock, a classicist who specializes in the interface between oral and literate cultures with particular reference to the ancient Greeks, has pointed out that we derive from the character of written language the very terms of our analysis of oral communication. "A communication system of this sort is an echo system, light as air and as fleeting. Yet we are given to describing its character and effects as though they were some sort of material existing in some kind of space. They become 'patterns' and 'codes' and 'themes' and 'monumental representations.' They have 'content' and 'substance.' Their behavior becomes, linguistically speaking, a matter of 'grammar,' a term which by its very definition betrays the source of its invention in the behavior of words as written, not spoken."[48] To this we might add Bakhtin's powerful critique of conventional linguistics as opposed to dialogics: that an analysis of the written record of spoken words denudes those words of the very interpersonal, cultural, and ideological context that gave them meaning. Havelock suggests that special features of spoken language must be emphasized in order for an oral culture to capitalize upon language's repeatability and thus produce "oral documents" that can ensure the survival of cultural tradition. Ritualized utterance must be memorized, and thus acoustic rhythm is exploited; in turn, this leads to the secondary effect of what Havelock calls "semantic rhythm," the balancing of terms and notions, or the balancing of narrative episodes. When new material is added, it must be as a partial echo of what has come before, a "difference within the same." Finally, Havelock notes that oral poets rely upon narrative, a sequence of actions with actors, rather than upon exposition. That narratives are additive sequences, he argues, is respon-sible for the paratactic syntax of oral poetry.[49]

Naturally, much of Havelock's description applies to Yeats, sim-ply because Yeats is a poet who writes as one even in his prose; generi-cally, poetry has not forgotten its oral base, and features like rhythm, semantic balance, parataxis, and narrative organization are character-istic of the writings of most poets, whatever their personal orientation toward language. Similarly, many of the features of the spoken register identified by Goody still echo in the written work of poets. But if Yeats is a special case, specific features of his writing may retain the trace of the oral, even in comparison to more obviously "conversational" poets such as Robert Frost or even James Whitcomb Riley. Nor can we nec-essarily find this trace in the purportedly "simple" and "realistic" dic-tion and syntax of Yeats's mature style. As Paul de Man has pointed out, "Yeats's mature diction is anything but mimetic." Indeed, it "in-troduces again many of the more 'literary' forms of style which the early revisions had been eager to eliminate," forms that, he claims, "accen-tuate the distinction between spoken and written language."[50] But here de Man makes the same implicit equivalence between the spoken lan-guage and the "natural," the "simple," and the "realistic" that many postmodernist critics invoke in order to oppose to it a Derridean im-age highlighting the complex artifice of the network of written lan-guage. In fact, both written and spoken registers are arbitrary and complex webs of artifice, although for ideological reasons we find this easier to see in text than in speech. And in the culture of Yeats's Ire-land, as in our own, the two registers interpenetrate; no speech is to-tally devoid of the logic of writing, any more than writing is totally independent of the structures of speech.

The primary sign of Yeats's oral commitment, as seen earlier, is the overwhelmingly dialogical character of his writing. Another sign may be found in an analysis of his characteristic syntax. In a recent book, Joseph Adams has subjected the verse to a minute syntactic scrutiny, identifying instances of what he terms "syntactic masks." These are patterns of syntactic ambiguity that, Adams feels, exemplify both a shift in the notion of subjectivity toward the idea of the self as a textual construct and the role of "difference" in language. Although Adams does not put it this way, he implies that at the furthest exten-sion, each syntactic mask might be seen as a miniature Derridean *aporia.*[51] There is some irony, then, in the fact that a great number of the specific syntactic structures studied by Adams are specifically oral formulations that Yeats adapted from the Anglo-Irish repertoire. For example, Adams points out that Yeats's use of relative clauses is uniquely ambiguous. In general prose usage, a restrictive clause is not set off by commas and is signalled by an introductory "that," while a nonrestrictive clause typically is set off by commas and is introduced by "who" or "which." Yeats tends to introduce both sorts of clauses with "that" and often fails to include the commas that mark nonrestrictiveness, so that the reader simply cannot determine which type of clause is intended.[52] This is the effect of lines like, "Love is all / Unsatisfied / That cannot take the whole," or "The unavailing outcries and the old bitterness / That empty the heart."[53]

Another syntactic example—actually, a more generalized form of a supersyntactic pattern of which ambiguous relative clauses are a subset—is what Adams calls "additive structuring." Additive structuring refers to Yeats's way of "concatenating the segments of language" in his poems so that the grammatical function of each segment possesses a hanging ambiguity. Because line breaks have a pseudogrammatical function, especially for Yeats, each line tends to assert a certain independence from the putative syntax of the sentence in which it is embedded. As Adams remarks, "each line partly becomes a separate and equal block with no necessary connection with the preceding or following blocks."[54] The first quatrain from "Another Song of a Fool" is a good example:

> This great purple butterfly,
> In the prison of my hands,
> Has a learning in his eye
> Not a poor fool understands.

Although the general thrust of the syntax is clear enough on quick reading, each line raises anew the question of its relationship to the other units of meaning. The second line, although enclosed in commas, is probably a restrictive phrase further identifying the butterfly; the fourth line, with its archaic and Irish-colloquial form of the negative statement, is misleading in several directions. The initial "not" momentarily appears to modify "in his eye," as if it were going to tell where the learning is *not*; "not" is also ambiguously related to "poor fool," in that there seems a momentary possibility that some *other* sort of fool might understand. The line as a whole initially seems to mean that "not a single poor fool understands" the butterfly's learning. In connection with the title, however, the line is more likely to be read as "this poor fool does not understand" it.

One other example of additive structure is Yeats's characteristic use of conjunctions to string together units of meaning as conjoined structures, rather than to array them in logical hierarchy. A sentence from "Adam's Curse," in which the conjunctions are italicized, displays the effect:

> We saw the last embers of daylight die,
> *And* in the trembling blue-green of the sky
> A moon, worn *as if* it had been a shell
> Washed by time's waters *as* they rose *and* fell
> About the stars *and* broke in days *and* years.

Here, the syntactic slippages run rampant. To begin with, we are unsure whether to read the second through fifth lines as a further predicate of "saw" or as a second independent clause. Each phrase gives the effect of modifying a noun in the previous phrase, regardless of its importance, so that one has the feeling of descending ever more deeply into a syntactic chain from which there is no exit. The "and" of which Yeats is so fond is a major culprit because it can be followed by many different kinds of syntactic structure; often, the reader must keep several provisory syntaxes balanced for the length of several phrases—or, as in the passage above, for the length of the entire sentence.

The interesting point about Adams's syntactic masks from our perspective is that the majority of them depend either upon oral usage or upon the interface of oral usage with a written text (as in the case of line endings). Reading Yeats is like listening to an oral informant in that information must be processed additively and linearly, rather than in the hierarchical way in which we can read sentences of ordinary prose. More precisely, it is like listening to a speaker who uses the artifices of rhetoric—those tricks of balance and parallelism to which Havelock points—in ways that continually frustrate a reader's desire for syntactic logic. Surely it is no coincidence that both Havelock and

Goody, in different ways, emphasize the linear, sequential, additive nature of oral communication, while Adams finds additive structure to be Yeats's primary syntactic signature. Adams is within his rights in finding in the syntactic masks evidence of the role of difference in language, but this structuralist perception is perhaps more generalized than necessary. The oral dimension of Yeats's writing points more directly to the untotalized, unfinalizable nature of speech, which always proceeds by modifying, defining, and interrupting itself in a linear chain without beginning or end. As Bakhtin reminds us, "there is neither a first nor a last word and there are no limits to the dialogic context (it extends into the boundless past and the boundless future). . . . Nothing is absolutely dead: every meaning will have its homecoming festival."[55]

## NOTES

1. Mikhail Bakhtin, *The Dialogic Imagination: Four Essays*, ed. Michael Holquist (Austin: Univ. of Texas Press, 1981), 285.

2. Ibid.

3. Ibid., 39.

4. Ibid., 7.

5. Ibid., 286–87.

6. V. N. Volosinov [/Bakhtin], *Marxism and the Philosophy of Language* (Cambridge, Mass.: Harvard Univ. Press, 1986), 73.

7. Ibid., 11.

8. Juliet Flower MacCannell, in "The Temporality of Textuality: Bakhtin and Derrida," *MLN* 100 (Dec. 1985): 968–86, makes some similar distinctions and parallels between these two figures.

9. Both quoted in Richard Ellmann, *Yeats: The Man and the Masks* (New York: Dutton, 1958), 211, 272.

10. W. B. Yeats, *Essays and Introductions* (New York: Macmillan, 1961), 521.

11. W. B. Yeats, *The Autobiography of William Butler Yeats* (New York: Macmillan, 1965), 68, 69.

12. See chap. 6, "Images of the Material Bodily Lower Stratum," in M. M. Bakhtin, *Rabelais and His World* (Bloomington: Indiana Univ. Press, 1984).

13. Ellmann, 147–48.

14. Yeats, *Autobiography*, 46.

15. M. M. Bakhtin, *Principles of Dostoevsky's Poetics* (Minneapolis: Univ. of Minnesota Press, 1984), 202.

16. Quoted in Robert Langbaum, "The Exteriority of Self in Yeats's Poetry and Thought," *New Literary History* 7 (1976): 579–80.

17. W. B. Yeats, *A Vision* (New York: Macmillan, 1956), 72.

18. Bakhtin, *Principles*, 204.

19. Yeats, *A Vision*, 214.

20. Yeats, *Essays*, 522.

21. Denis Donoghue, *William Butler Yeats* (New York: Viking Press, 1971).

22. Larry McCaffrey and Sinda Gregory, eds. *Alive and Writing: Interviews with American Authors of the 1980s* (Urbana: Univ. of Illinois Press, 1987), 98–99.

23. Yeats, *Autobiography*, 14.

24. Ellmann, 25.

25. Joseph Hone, *W. B. Yeats, 1865–1939* (London: Macmillan, 1965), 18, 27–28, 32.

26. Eleanor J. Gibson and Harry Levin, *The Psychology of Reading* (Cambridge, Mass.: MIT Press, 1975), 486–92.

27. Macdonald Critchley, "Developmental Dyslexia: History, Nature, and Prospects," in *Reading, Perception and Language: Papers from the World Congress on Dyslexia*, ed. Drake D. Duane and Margaret B. Rawson (Baltimore: York Press, 1974), 9–11.

28. See Robert G. Crowder, *The Psychology of Reading: An Introduction* (New York: Oxford Univ. Press, 1982), 242–43.

29. Macdonald Critchley and Eileen A. Critchley, *Dyslexia Defined* (Chicester, Sussex: Charles C. Thomas, 1978), 7–8.

30. Ibid., 27, 29, 30.

31. Ibid., 48, 63.

32. Hone, 40–41.

33. John Stallworthy, *Between the Lines: Yeats's Poetry in the Making* (New York: Oxford Univ. Press, 1963), 11.

34. David R. Clark, *Yeats at Songs and Choruses* (Amherst: Univ. of Massachusetts Press, 1983).

35. Stallworthy, 9.

36. Quoted in Stallworthy, 12.

37. Yeats, *Autobiography*, 42–43.

38. Ibid., 30.

39. Ibid., 6.

40. W. B. Yeats, *Mythologies* (New York: Macmillan, 1959), 138–39.

41. J. Hillis Miller, "Yeats: The Linguistic Moment," in *William Butler Yeats*, ed. Harold Bloom (New York: Chelsea House, 1986), 195. Reprint. "Yeats," in *The Linguistic Moment: From Wordsworth to Stevens*, ed. J. Hillis Miller (Princeton: Princeton Univ. Press, 1985), 316–48.

42. "The Friends of the People of Faery."

43. Quoted in Ellmann, 138.

44. Quoted in Ellmann, 200–1, 197.

45. Crowder, 187. See this entire chapter, "The Role of Speech in Reading."

46. Jack Goody, *The Interface Between the Written and the Oral* (New York: Cambridge Univ. Press, 1987), 216.

47. Ibid., 263–64.

48. Eric Havelock, *The Muse Learns to Write* (New Haven: Yale Univ. Press, 1986), 66.

49. Ibid., 70–77.

50. Paul de Man, "Imagery in Yeats," in Bloom, 183. Reprint. "Image and Emblem in Yeats," in *The Rhetoric of Romanticism*, ed. Paul de Man (New York: Columbia Univ. Press, 1984), 145–238.

51. Joseph Adams, *Yeats and the Masks of Syntax* (New York: Columbia Univ. Press, 1984), 1.

52. Ibid., 42–52.

53. Peter Allt and Russell K. Alspach, eds. *The Variorum Edition of the Poems of W. B. Yeats* (New York: Macmillan, 1957), 510, 198.

54. Adams, 56, 59.

55. M. M. Bakhtin, *Speech Genres and Other Late Essays* (Austin: Univ. of Texas Press, 1986), 170.

SELECTIVE BIBLIOGRAPHY
NOTES ON CONTRIBUTORS
INDEX

# SELECTIVE BIBLIOGRAPHY

## POSTMODERNISM

Arac, Jonathan. *Critical Genealogies: Historical Situations for Postmodern Literary Studies.* New York: Columbia Univ. Press, 1987.

Blau, Herbert. *The Eye of Prey: Subversions of the Postmodern.* Bloomington: Indiana Univ. Press, 1987.

Calinescu, Matei. *Five Faces of Modernity: Modernism, Avant-Garde, Decadence, Kitsch, Postmodernism.* Durham, N.C.: Duke Univ. Press, 1987.

Fekete, John, ed. *Life After Postmodernism: Essays on Value and Culture.* New York: St. Martin's Press, 1987.

Fokkema, Douwe. *Literary History, Modernism, and Postmodernism.* Amsterdam and Philadelphia: John Benjamins, 1984.

―――, and Hans Bertens, eds. *Approaching Postmodernism.* Amsterdam and Philadelphia: John Benjamins, 1986.

Foster, Hal, ed. *The Anti-Aesthetic: Essays on Postmodern Culture.* Port Townsend, Wash.: Bay Press, 1983.

Hassan, Ihab. *The Postmodern Turn: Essays in Postmodern Theory and Culture.* Columbus: Ohio State Univ. Press, 1987.

Hutcheon, Linda. *A Poetics of Postmodernism: History, Theory, Fiction.* New York and London: Routledge, 1988.

Huyssen, Andreas. *After the Great Divide: Modernism, Mass Culture, Postmodernism.* Bloomington: Indiana Univ. Press, 1986.

Lyotard, Jean-François. *The Postmodern Condition: A Report on Knowledge.* Translated by Geoffrey Bennington and Brian Massumi. Minneapolis: Univ. of Minnesota Press, 1984.

―――. *Le postmoderne expliqué aux enfants: correspondence, 1982–1985.* Paris: Galilée, 1986.

191

McCaffrey, Lawrence F., ed. *Postmodern Fiction: A Bio-Bibliographical Guide.* Westport, Conn.: Greenwood Press, 1986.

McHale, Brian. *Postmodernist Fiction.* New York: Methuen, 1987.

Owens, Craig. "The Allegorical Impulse: Toward a Theory of Postmodernism. Part I." *October* 12 (1980): 67–86.

————. "The Allegorical Impulse: Toward a Theory of Postmodernism. Part II." *October* 13 (1980): 59–80.

Trachtenberg, Stanley, ed. *The Postmodern Moment: A Handbook of Contemporary Innovation in the Arts.* Westport, Conn.: Greenwood Press, 1985.

Wallis, Brian, ed. *Art after Modernism: Rethinking Representation.* New York: New Museum of Contemporary Art, 1984.

Wilde, Alan. *Horizons of Assent: Modernism, Postmodernism, and the Ironic Imagination.* Baltimore: Johns Hopkins Univ. Press, 1981.

## POSTSTRUCTURALIST CRITICISM AND THEORY

Adams, Hazard, and Leroy Searle, eds. *Critical Theory Since 1965.* Tallahassee: Univ. Presses of Florida/Florida State Univ. Press, 1986.

Davis, Robert Con, and Ronald Schleifer, eds. *Contemporary Literary Criticism: Literary and Cultural Studies.* 2d ed. New York and London: Longman, 1989.

Easthope, Antony. *British Post-Structuralism: Since 1968.* London and New York: Routledge, 1988.

Harari, Josué V., ed. *Textual Strategies: Perspectives in Post-Structuralist Criticism.* Ithaca, N.Y.: Cornell Univ. Press, 1979.

Harland, Richard. *Superstructuralism: The Philosophy of Structuralism and Post-Structuralism.* London and New York: Methuen, 1987.

Hosek, Chaviva, and Patricia Parker, eds. *Lyric Poetry: Beyond New Criticism.* Ithaca, N.Y.: Cornell Univ. Press, 1985.

Lewis, Philip. "The Post-Structuralist Condition." *Diacritics* 12, no. 1 (1982): 2–24.

Machin, Richard, and Christopher Norris, eds. *Post-Structuralist Readings of English Poetry.* Cambridge: Cambridge Univ. Press, 1987.

Natoli, Joseph, ed. *Tracing Literary Theory.* Urbana: Univ. of Illinois Press, 1987.

Orr, Leonard. *Research in Critical Theory Since 1965: A Classified Bibliography.* Westport, Conn.: Greenwood Press, 1989 [lists and indexes more than 5,000 items].

Young, Robert, ed. *Untying the Text: A Post-Structuralist Reader.* Boston and London: Routledge, 1981.


## YEATS CRITICISM

Adams, Joseph. *Yeats and the Masks of Syntax.* New York: Columbia Univ. Press, 1984.

Archibald, Douglas. *Yeats.* Syracuse, N.Y.: Syracuse Univ. Press, 1983.

Bornstein, George. *Poetic Remaking: The Art of Browning, Yeats, and Pound.* University Park: Pennsylvania State Univ. Press, 1988.

Butler, Christopher. *Interpretation, Deconstruction, and Ideology: An Introduction to Some Current Issues in Literary Theory,* 8–18, 36–45. Oxford: Clarendon, 1984.

de Man, Paul. *The Rhetoric of Romanticism.* New York: Columbia Univ. Press, 1984.

Finneran, Richard. "W. B. Yeats." In *Anglo-Irish Literature: A Review of Research,* edited by Richard Finneran, 216–314. New York: Modern Language Association, 1976.

———. "W. B. Yeats." In *Recent Research on Anglo-Irish Writers,* edited by Richard Finneran, 85–153. New York: Modern Language Association, 1983.

———. *Editing Yeats's Poems.* New York: St. Martin's Press, 1983.

———, ed. *Critical Essays on W. B. Yeats.* Boston: G. K. Hall, 1986.

Fletcher, Ian. *W. B. Yeats and His Contemporaries.* New York: St. Martin's Press, 1987.

Good, Maeve. *W. B. Yeats and the Creation of a Tragic Universe.* Totowa, N.J.: Barnes & Noble, 1987.

Harper, George Mills. *The Making of Yeats's A Vision: A Study of the Automatic Script.* 2 vols. Carbondale: Southern Illinois Univ. Press, 1987.

Hassett, Joseph M. *Yeats and the Poetics of Hate.* Dublin: Gill and Macmillan; New York: St. Martin's Press, 1986.

Helmling, Steven. *The Esoteric Comedies of Carlyle, Newman, and Yeats.* Cambridge and New York: Cambridge Univ. Press, 1988.

Jakobson, Roman. *Verbal Art, Verbal Sign, Verbal Time.* Oxford: Blackwell, 1985.

Jochum, K. P. S. *W. B. Yeats: A Classified Bibliography.* Urbana: Univ. of Illinois Press, 1978.

Johnson, Anthony L. "Sign, Structure, and Self-Reference in W. B. Yeats's 'Sailing to Byzantium.'" In *Literary Theories in Praxis,* edited by Shirley F. Staton, 135–54. Philadelphia: Univ. of Pennsylvania Press, 1987.

Johnston, Dillon. *Irish Poetry after Joyce*. Notre Dame, Ind.: Univ. of Notre Dame Press, 1985.

Keane, Patrick J. *Yeats's Interactions with Tradition*. Columbia: Univ. of Missouri Press, 1987.

————. *Terrible Beauty: Yeats, Joyce, Ireland, and the Myth of the Devouring Female*. Columbia: Univ. of Missouri Press, 1988.

Kiberd, Declan. *Men and Feminism in Modern Literature*, 103–35. London: Macmillan, 1985.

Kinahan, Frank. *Yeats, Folklore, and Occultism: Contexts of the Early Work and Thought*. Boston: Unwin Hyman, 1988.

Loizeaux, Elizabeth Bergmann. *Yeats and the Visual Arts*. New Brunswick, N.J.: Rutgers Univ. Press, 1986.

Longenbach, James. *Stone Cottage: Pound, Yeats, and Modernism*. New York: Oxford Univ. Press, 1988.

Martin, Heather C. *W. B. Yeats: Metaphysician as Dramatist*. Waterloo, Ont.: Wilfrid Laurier Univ. Press, 1986.

McCormack, W. J. *Ascendancy and Tradition in Anglo-Irish Literary History from 1789–1939*. Oxford: Clarendon, 1985.

McDiarmid, Lucy. *Saving Civilization: Yeats, Eliot, and Auden Between the Wars*. Cambridge and New York: Cambridge Univ. Press, 1984.

McGowan, John P. *Representation and Revelation: Victorian Realism from Carlyle to Yeats*. Columbia: Univ. of Missouri Press, 1986.

O'Hara, Daniel. *Tragic Knowledge: Yeats's Autobiography and Hermeneutics*. New York: Columbia Univ. Press, 1981.

Putzel, Steven D. *Reconstructing Yeats:* The Secret Rose *and* The Wind Among the Reeds. Totowa, N.J.: Barnes and Noble, 1986.

Richardson, James. *Vanishing Lives: Style and Self in Tennyson, D. G. Rossetti, Swinburne, and Yeats*. Charlottesville: Univ. Press of Virginia, 1988.

Schricker, Gale C. *A New Species of Man: The Poetic Personae of W. B. Yeats*. Lewisburg, Penn.: Bucknell Univ. Press, 1982.

Spivak, Gayatry Chakravorty. "Finding Feminist Readings: Dante–Yeats." In *American Criticism in the Poststructuralist Age*, edited by Ira Konigsberg, 42–65. Ann Arbor: Univ. of Michigan Press, 1981.

Stanfield, Paul Scott. *Yeats and Politics in the 1930s*. New York: St. Martin's Press, 1988.

Wright, David G. *Yeats' Myth of Self: The Autobiographical Prose*. Totowa, N.J.: Barnes and Noble, 1987.

York, R. A. *A Poem as Utterance*, 109–27. London: Methuen, 1986.

# NOTES ON CONTRIBUTORS

WILLIAM BONNEY teaches at Mississippi State University. He is the author of *Thorns and Arabesques: Contexts for Conrad's Fiction* (1980) and of numerous articles in *Victorian Poetry, ELH, Conradiana, Nineteenth-Century Fiction,* the *Journal of Narrative Technique, Victorian Institute Journal,* and elsewhere.

KITTI CARRIKER recently completed her dissertation on "Literary Automata: Lacanian and Figurative Approaches to the Self-Created Miniature" at the University of Notre Dame.

CHERYL HERR teaches at the University of Iowa. She has published *Joyce's Anatomy of Culture* (1986) and *For the Land They Loved: Irish Political Melodramas, 1890–1925* (1991). She has also published articles in journals such as *Journal of Modern Literature, James Joyce Quarterly, Essays in Literature, Theatre Quarterly,* and *Midwest Quarterly.* She has held an NEH fellowship and a Howard Foundation Fellowship.

WILLIAM JOHNSEN teaches at Michigan State University. He is the editor of *The Poet and the Language* and the author of many essays in such journals as *Boundary 2, MLN,* and *Society for Critical Exchange Reports.*

R. B. KERSHNER, who teaches at the University of Florida, has published a book on Dylan Thomas and numerous essays on Joyce. He has also written on Iris Murdoch and Elizabeth Bowen and frequently reviews for *Georgia Review.* His poems have appeared in *Poetry, APR,* and other magazines and collections. His book *Joyce, Bakhtin, and Popular Literature* was published in 1989.

KATHLEEN O'GORMAN teaches at Illinois Wesleyan University. She has edited *Charles Tomlinson: Man and Artist* (1988) and coedits the annual *Studies in 20th-*

*Century British Literature*. She has published essays on Beckett, Tomlinson, Geoffrey Hill, and David Jones. She is currently writing a book applying feminist theory to Beckett's plays.

LEONARD ORR teaches at the University of Notre Dame. He is the editor of *De-Structing the Novel: Essays in Applied Postmodern Hermeneutics* and the author of *Semiotic and Structuralist Analyses of Fiction, Research in Critical Theory since 1965: A Classified Bibliography*, and, forthcoming, *Problems and Poetics of the Nonaristotelian Novel*. He has published essays on Joyce, Conrad, Arnold, narrative theory, and critical theory. He recently completed *A Dictionary of Critical Theory*.

STEVEN PUTZEL teaches at Penn State University (Wilkes-Barre). He is the author of *Reconstructing Yeats: "The Secret Rose" and "The Wind Among the Reeds"* (1986) and articles on Eugene O'Neill, Sam Shepard, Joyce, James Stephens, and Yeats. He is currently writing a study of Yeats and ritual.

KIERAN QUINLAN teaches at the University of Alabama at Birmingham. His *Defining a Secular Faith: The Pursuit of John Crowe Ransom* is forthcoming from Louisiana State University Press. He is the author of articles on Seamus Heaney, Walker Percy, Donald Davie, and Laura Riding, and is currently completing *Walker Percy and the Silence of God*.

RONALD SCHLEIFER teaches English at the University of Oklahoma. He is editor of *Genre* and coeditor of *The Oklahoma Project for Discourse & Theory*, a series of scholarly books published by the University of Oklahoma Press. He has published widely on modern literature and literary theory. His most recent books are *A. J. Greimas and the Nature of Meaning* and, coedited with Robert Con Davis, *Contemporary Literary Criticism*. He is currently working on a book entitled *The Rhetoric of Criticism: The Modernist Language of Contemporary Literary Discourses*.

# INDEX

197

YEATS AND POSTMODERNISM

was composed in 11 on 13 Goudy Old Style on Digital Compugraphic equipment
by Metricomp,
with display type in Goudy Handtooled by Dix;
printed by sheet-fed offset on 50-pound, acid-free Glatfelter Natural Hi Bulk,
Smyth-sewn and bound over binder's boards in Holliston Roxite B,
and with dust jackets printed in one color
by Braun-Brumfield, Inc.;
designed by Sara L. Eddy;
and published by

SYRACUSE UNIVERSITY PRESS
SYRACUSE, NEW YORK 13244-5160

RICHARD FALLIS
*Series Editor*

Irish Studies presents a wide range of books interpreting aspects of Irish life and culture to scholarly and general audiences. Irish literature is a special concern in the series, but works from the perspectives of the fine arts, history, and the social sciences are also welcome, as are studies that take multidisciplinary approaches.

**Other titles in the series are:**